LAND USE,

ENVIRONMENT,

AND SOCIAL CHANGE

The Shaping of Island County, Washington

LAND USE,
ENVIRONMENT,
AND SOCIAL CHANGE

The Shaping of Island County, Washington

RICHARD WHITE

Foreword by William Cronon

UNIVERSITY OF WASHINGTON PRESS
Seattle and London

Copyright © 1980 by the University of Washington Press
Foreword to the 1992 edition copyright © 1992 by the
    University of Washington Press
Preface to the 1992 edition copyright © 1992 by the
    University of Washington Press
First paperback edition, 1992
Second printing, 1995
Printed in the United States of America

Library of Congress Cataloging-in-Publication Data
White, Richard, 1947–
    Land use, environment, and social change : the shaping of Island
County, Washington / Richard White ; Foreword by William Cronon. —
1st paperback ed.
        p.   cm.
    Includes bibliographical references and index.
    ISBN 0–295–97143–6 (pbk.)
    1. Land use—Environmental aspects—Washington (State)—Island
County—History. 2. Island County (Wash.)—Economic conditions.
I. Title
[HD211.W3W47   1992]   91–33199
304.2'09797'75—dc20   CIP

The paper used in this publication meets the minimum requirements of American
National Standard for Information Sciences—Permanence of Paper for Printed Library
Materials, ANSI Z39.48–1984. ∞

For my mother, and to the memory of my father

CONTENTS

ILLUSTRATIONS

FOREWORD

When it was first published in 1980, *Land Use, Environment, and Social Change: The Shaping of Island County, Washington,* introduced readers to a young scholar who has since emerged as a major American historian. More than a decade later, Richard White is widely recognized as one of the most productive, rigorous, and creative scholars of his generation, a historian who has made path-breaking contributions to environmental history, to the history of the American West, to Indian history, and to American history generally.

Land Use, Environment, and Social Change earned enthusiastic critical notices when it came out in 1980, a typical review calling it "important and provocative . . . a major and compelling study." It eventually won the Forest History Society's prize for the best book of environmental history published that year, and many historians now regard it as one of a small group of books that helped chart a course for the new field. Despite all the enthusiastic acclaim, however, the book's sales never measured up to its obvious merit. More than ten years had to pass before it finally appeared in this first paperback edition. It is a textbook case of an underappreciated classic.

Why has such an important book had trouble finding its proper audience? One reason is surely the title, which could hardly be called inviting. *Land Use, Environment, and Social Change* sounds more like a doctoral dissertation than a book, and is austere enough to put off all but the most fearless readers. I've often thought that the book might have had a more positive reception had title and subtitle simply been reversed. *The Shaping of Island County, Washington,* in fact gives a much more concrete sense of what the book is all about.

But the subtitle suggests another, less legitimate reason why readers may have stayed away. Island County hardly looms large on the mental maps of most Americans. Aside from those who live in the vicinity of Puget Sound, most have never heard of Whidbey and Camano islands. Even Seattleites are not likely to think of Island County as an "important" place. And so the would-be reader's natural impulse is probably to pass up this little book as antiquarian, a purely local history of no interest to anyone who doesn't already own a vacation home on the two islands whose stories it tells in such painstaking detail. Why should anyone care about the shaping of Island County, Washington?

It's an obvious question, but could hardly be more wrong-headed. The historian Sam Bass Warner once published a famous article entitled, "If All the World Were Philadelphia: A Scaffolding for Urban History," in which he argued that a close reading of that city's past would reveal not just Philadelphia's story, but the broad historical patterns that have shaped *all* American cities. Much the same thing can be said with equal force about *Land Use, Environment, and Social Change.* Richard White's great achievement was to discover in the past of this seemingly obscure pair of islands a series of changes that have extraordinarily broad implications for the history of the Pacific Northwest, the trans-Mississippi West, and even North America generally.

The stories of Whidbey and Camano islands are of course uniquely their own, and White is almost too scrupulous about making few general claims about their significance. Read at one level, the book can seem like a series of disconnected anecdotes about groups of Salish Indians digging camas roots over here, American farmers planting wheat and raising pigs over there, lumbermen cutting Douglas firs and complaining about taxes back up in the hills, cutover farmers going broke amid the stumps, and urban vacation-goers discovering the beauties of wild nature in the profoundly unwild landscape that resulted from this long, ironic human past.

Because White keeps his focus so sharply on Island County, it takes a subtle reader to appreciate the many echoes of other times and other places that occur everywhere on these pages. The epidemics and losses of land that happened to the Salish on these two islands are all too familiar in every corner of the continent. The shifting crops and fortunes of frontier farmers can be found as much in Vermont and Arkansas and Montana as in Island County, Washington. The struggle (and often the ultimate failure) of those who tried to raise crops on cutover forest lands is no less a part of Maine's and Wisconsin's histories than of Island County's. (Indeed, White's mentor at the University of Washington, Vernon Carstensen, wrote *Farms or Forests*, a study of northern Wisconsin's cutover lands which became an important model for this book.)

Readers who have already studied the history of environmental change in North America will recognize in these 160 pages many of the most important shifts that have occurred repeatedly in other parts of the continent. White is far too modest to make such an assertion on his own behalf, but it doesn't require much of an imaginative leap to read *Land Use, Environment, and Social Change* as if all the world were indeed Island County. Readers who approach the book with this larger vision in mind will learn far more from it than those who read it simply as the local history of two islands in Puget Sound—though the book is subtle enough to be read profitably in either way.

Without much fanfare, Richard White tried in this book to show that western history could be written without resorting to the narrative devices of traditional frontier historiography. By putting the ecology of a single small region at the center of his story, he escaped in a single stroke the east-to-west linearity that has bedeviled frontier history since the days of Frederick Jackson Turner. Frontiers do not open or close in this book. No great divide separates the nineteeth from the twentieth century. Indians and Chinese tenant farmers, although not so fully fleshed out as they would be in White's later work, share the stage unapologetically with white Euroamericans. The book offers no simple sequence of frontier types following a predestined path of community improvement and national progress. The result is a new version of western history that is far more complicated—and so both harder to follow and truer to the past— than many of its predecessors.

One reason too few people have read *Land Use, Environment, and Social Change*, then, is their failure to recognize its far-reaching implications. This is local history with a difference. When antiquarians write the stories of their home communities, they usually have trouble sorting out important from unimportant facts. The names and stories of a great many individual people loom large in such accounts. Every detail seems equally momentous, so that the menu at the church picnic, the election of the county sheriff, the actors in the school play, the strike at the factory, the construction of a new gazebo in the town square, the contributions of each storekeeper to the local retail festival—all seem equally significant to insiders, and equally *in*significant to outsiders. It's not that such details are intrinsically uninteresting or unimportant—far from it. But they gain their significance from the scholar's search to discover and understand their deeper meanings. It is meanings of just this sort that too many antiquarians take for granted and hence omit from their loving catalogs of the places they call home.

White's approach is quite different. Individual people show up in his text mainly for illustrative purposes, so that their names are much less important than the general activities in which they (and a thousand others) took part. The result is a rather impersonal history, in which large groups of people, working steadily to make their living in the world, profoundly alter the landscape around them. There are few climactic moments, few battles won or lost, few dramatic turning points, just lots of people doing lots of things with lots of consequences. It's not your ordinary history book, precisely because it spends so much time on processes and events that are the very core of ordinary life. In it, people catch fish, set fires, cut down trees, build houses, plow the soil, plant seeds, pull weeds, harvest crops, store food, sell produce, earn wages, pay taxes, seek respite— and transform the lands around them. Few things could be more basic to our human lives, and yet too often such activities fail to make an appearance in ordinary history books.

Like other environmental historians, White fills his text with nearly as many nonhuman actors as human ones. Few local histories devote as much time as this one does to Douglas fir trees, bracken ferns, camas roots, dogs, salmon, potatoes, sheep, timothy grass, Canadian thistles, and lady's slippers. To trace their stories, White had to use documents that rarely show up in the bibliographies of more traditional histories. The notes of this volume are littered with references to books and articles carrying titles such as "Increment Mortality in a Virgin Douglas Fir Forest," "Pleistocene Stratigraphy of Island County," "An Economic Study of Poultry Farming in Western Washington," and *Weeds of the Pacific Northwest*—hardly your usual historian's fare. And so another key contribution of this and other environmental histories has been to widen considerably the range of sources and theoretical tools that historians have at their command.

But perhaps the quality that most distinguishes *Land Use, Environment, and Social Change* is Richard White's trademark self-criticism and commitment to pursue scholarly rigor wherever it may lead. White is completely even-handed in his refusal to accept easy explanations, his suspicion of conventional wisdom, and his search for the ironic consequences of human intentions. Readers who imagine the western past as a sentimental or mythic landscape peopled by heroic figures of outsized proportions who struggle over great causes lost and won will receive no solace from this or any other work by Richard White. He peoples his book with Indians who live close to the land but profoundly alter it to serve their own ends, pioneering farmers who undermine their own cherished success, capitalist lumbermen who complain of taxation but destroy themselves with their own inadequate capital, urban tourists who seek to purchase access to a wild nature that conveniently conforms to their own artificial image of wilderness. Ironies abound. As those who know him can attest, White's favorite (perhaps even obsessive) way of describing the past is to say that it is "*complex.*" For him, complexity means that we inhabit a world of unexpected consequences, in which even our most well-intentioned actions can come back to haunt us in ways we never anticipated.

Therein may lie the deepest reason why this book has had fewer readers than it deserves. Its narrative of the many ways human beings have reshaped the landscapes of Whidbey and Camano islands is hardly reassuring, and offers little comfort to those who look for simple lessons from the past. White steadfastly refuses to identify the actions of any one group of people as unambiguously good or evil in this story. Heroes and villains are not easy to find here. Instead, he offers "complexity," and the bittersweet knowledge that people rarely have a very clear idea of how their actions will affect the world around them. It might be more satisfying to believe otherwise, but White's story has the ring of truth to it. Complexity, irony, and unexpected consequences mingle in this subtle and unsentimental book to offer profound lessons that are as relevant to our environmental future as to our environmental past. In his scrupulous and understated way,

Richard White has much to say not just about two islands in Puget Sound, but about all history and the human place in nature. *Land Use, Environment, and Social Change* reveals with extraordinary care the intricacy of our lives upon the land, and shows that in shaping the good earth we also shape ourselves. The book is a slender classic, and deserves to find its audience at last.

WILLIAM CRONON
Yale University
October 1991

PREFACE TO THE 1992 EDITION

As I started to write this preface, I was immediately struck by my own ambivalence in confronting a book that I had written in a different time. Not that I want to disavow the book—I don't. This book existed independently of me for so long, however, that I had begun to feel little or no responsibility for it. The reprinting of *Land Use, Environment, and Social Change* forces me to confront my authorship and to acknowledge that, if I wished, I could alter this book. I decided to leave it unchanged not because the book is flawless, but rather because in revising it I seemed more likely to diminish its virtues than to enhance them.

People reading this book for the first time should not think that my own unease arises from my belief that this book is now somehow "wrong." The problem is more complicated than that. It arises more from differences between what I tried to accomplish when I wrote the book and what I would try to accomplish now.

What I had tried to do in this book came into focus for me in a letter from a colleague, Tom Dunlap. He referred to *Land Use, Environment, and Social Change* as being "closer to the land and much closer to natural history and the narrative techniques of nature study" than other regional environmental histories. I had never thought about the book precisely this way, but what Tom Dunlap noted is, perhaps, what now seems to me most distinctive about the book. My model for this study was not an academic monograph but a classic piece of nature writing: H. Guthrie-Smith's *Tutira: The Story of a New Zealand Sheep Station*. And the research I did for the book involved at least as much time feeling out the seasonal changes and the textures of the coasts, fields, and forests of Whidbey Island as it did time in the archives and library.

As a narrative modeled after nature writing, this volume concentrates on human relations with the exterior world as well as with the more normal historical fare of relations between humans. It borrows heavily, as Tom Dunlap noted, from natural history and descriptive ecology. This direct engagement with the exterior world is the book's strength, and it is, perhaps, something I could not now duplicate.

My own interest in the natural world remains as strong today as when I wrote this book, but my understanding of that world has changed significantly. In *Land Use, Environment, and Social Change* I used ecological concepts like community, succession, climax, and ecosystem unproblematically even though within the discipline of ecology those ideas had already come under attack. Looking back now, I realize that this book and other historical studies were themselves undermining such ecological concepts even as they relied on them. Historians were describing a human impact upon the natural world so pervasive that it made questions of climax and succession seem abstractions with few equivalents in the actual landscape. The very scope of the change that I described in this book should have made me more suspicious of what I mistook for unquestioned ecological orthodoxy. Like most scholars, however, I was more polite and less belligerent when intruding upon disciplines other than my own.

My own concern with narrative and various aspects of critical theory would also betray me if I were to rewrite this book. Today, I would have devoted more attention to examining the meanings which the various human groups who inhabited the county imposed on the landscape. Questions of culture and meaning have come to dominate much historical study over the last ten years. Along with such questions has come greater concern among historians about their own constructions of the past and their own impositions of meaning. Issues of language, of discourse, of texts, and of creation of the subject that so occupy postmodernist scholarship are quite serious ones. They had not, however, occurred to me when I wrote this book. Rewriting *Land Use, Environment, and Social Change* with these issues in mind would make this a very different book.

But would such a rewriting make this a better book? I don't think so, for my newer concerns sometimes seem capable of growing only at the expense of what remains my major interest: How do human beings engage with and influence the external world, the nonhuman world in which they live? As a historian, I am interested in how we write history, in how we fashion the past into a meaningful narrative. I am also interested in material change, particularly in changes in the natural world. I realize that the natural world is a social construction and that histories such as this one are made and not discovered. Yet I also remain convinced that when we talk and write about changes in our material surroundings there is a reality beyond our discourse and that we can, if imperfectly, grasp that reality. If I were to begin rewriting this book, reconciling these two perspectives would become my major concern. In correcting what now seems the book's naivete I am afraid I might eliminate its greatest strength. When this book was published I could write about the physical environment with a directness and clarity that I would find more difficult to achieve today.

RICHARD WHITE
University of Washington
November, 1991

ACKNOWLEDGMENTS

Much of the credit for any merit this work may possess goes to Professor Vernon Carstensen, who originally suggested looking at the environmental history of an area as well as its social history. He has been generous with both his time and criticism and has immeasurably aided my research and writing. He has done his best to protect the English language from my worst barbarities. This book owes much to Professor Carstensen's own knowledge of the American West and American agriculture, as well as to his insistence on cogency and clarity. The volume's shortcomings would have been far greater without his aid.

Jimmie Jean Cook of the Island County Auditor's Office shared her own extensive knowledge of the county with me and was of invaluable help in locating materials in the county archives. Without her aid, researching this book would have been far more difficult. Both Andy Johnson and Susan Cunningham of the Pacific Northwest Collection went out of their way to help me find necessary materials and generously gave me both free access to the collection and a place to work. The entire staff of the Manuscript Collection of the University of Washington proved to be both helpful and good-humored, even in the face of my most impossible questions.

I am grateful to *Arizona and the West* and *Pacific Historical Review* for permission to reprint portions of two chapters.

Finally, Professors Dauril Alden and Claude Singer gave all or parts of the original manuscript careful and attentive reading, eliminating many outright errors and sloppy formulations.

LAND USE,
ENVIRONMENT,
AND SOCIAL CHANGE

The Shaping of Island County, Washington

INTRODUCTION

Beginning far to the south, then sweeping past the island nation that gives it its name, the Japanese Current crosses the Pacific and skirts the coast of Washington. Today the current still brings the flotsam and debris of other continents to deposit on the Pacific Coast of North America. A century and a half ago and before, it sometimes brought Japanese fishermen whose boats had been lost in storms and then swept away by the current, which eventually wrecked them on Cape Flattery. The Indians scavenged the boats and adopted or enslaved those men who had survived their forced ocean journey. Above all else, however, the current brings warmth. Its relatively mild waters moderate the coastal climates of the Pacific Northwest, where, based on the latitude, Europeans initially expected to find icebergs and freezing winters. They found instead a cool, wet, maritime climate and a land whose most notable feature was the massive forest that covered it.

Puget Sound opens onto the Pacific and the Japanese Current at the Strait of Juan de Fuca, which separates the Olympic Peninsula on the south from Vancouver Island on the north (see Map 1). Numerous islands dot the Sound, and two of the largest, Whidbey and Camano, now form Island County, a small county in western Washington. Second in size only to Long Island in the contiguous United States, Whidbey stretches thirty-eight miles from Deception Pass in the north to Cultus Bay in the south, with its southern terminus lying some thirty miles north of Seattle; Camano is about one-fifth its size. Whidbey curves around the northern and

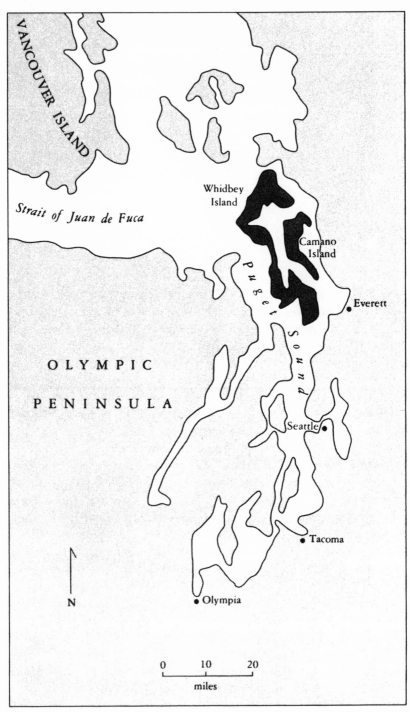

Map 1. Outline map of western Washington

southern edges of Camano with the smaller island curled like a fetus off Whidbey's eastern shore. Numerous coves and inlets cut the eastern coasts of both islands, and no place on these long, narrow pieces of land is more than a few miles from tidewater.

In all, Island County contains approximately 208 square miles. Its land ranges from the small, fertile prairies of northern Whidbey (approximately 5–10 percent of the total area) to the far more extensive and relatively infertile uplands that once supported the immense conifer forests. Much of the land is still forested. Although set in a region of high rainfall and abundant rivers, the county contains no stream of any size that runs year-round, and it has only a few small lakes.

Because of topography and climate, the islands can be divided into two fairly distinct areas (see Map 2). The Olympic Mountains shield north Whidbey from Pacific storms and so, although it shares the marine climate of most of the region, north Whidbey receives only about two-thirds of the annual rainfall of the rest of the county. The total rainfall of the area is substantial but seasonal: North Whidbey averages 20 inches a year, and the rest of the county averages about 30 inches annually. Usually only two to three inches of rain fall during the summer. As one travels south through the county, not only does the rainfall increase but the land rises. The prairies, swamps, and near-level forest of north Whidbey yield to the rolling hills and upland plateaus of south Whidbey and Camano. These range from 50 to 500 feet in height, resembling the mainland foothills of the Cascade Mountains a few miles away.[1]

People have lived in Island County for millennia; their history there has been inextricably tied with the islands and the waters that surround them. The real history of the area is not political history, nor in a strict sense, social history, although it contains elements of each. Instead it is the history of changes wrought in the natural environment by both Indian and white occupation and use of the land, and the consequences of these changes for the people who made them. Such a history is, of course, not peculiar to Island County, nor does the county serve as an obvious and vivid example of the ruthless exploitation of the resources of an area by its inhabitants. To a casual visitor the county displays no scars of flagrant misuse. Its history contains no arresting and appalling en-

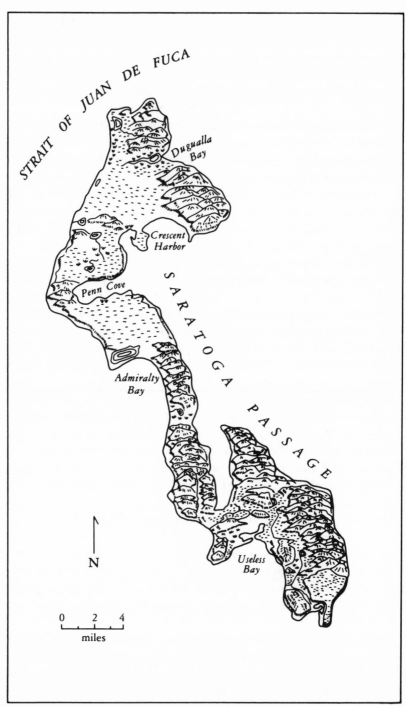

Map 2. Topography of Whidbey Island

vironmental disaster as might the history of a dust bowl or coal mining county. And, since Island County is not and has never been urban, the pressing environmental problems associated with big cities are absent. Although urban influences from the bordering Seattle-Tacoma-Everett area are far from negligible, in the twentieth century the county remained a quiet rural area located just beyond the urban fringe. It is this very absence of dramatic disasters that gives the county its significance.

Its quiet past is typical of other such areas in western Washington, Oregon, and northern California. People have logged and farmed the land and fished the adjoining waters. In this literal sense its environmental history is typical of a much wider area, and the attitudes that influenced human activities here are probably applicable to yet a wider area.

By attempting to trace the environmental impact of both Indian and (later) intruding peoples and to examine, within the limitations of the evidence, the consequences of this impact for their societies, this study departs somewhat from recent trends in environmental history. Most recent environmental history has been a variant of intellectual and political history. The literature is rich in histories of environmental thought and environmental politics, but studies of the history of man's relationship with the North American environment are scarce. The trail James Malin blazed thirty years ago in his studies of the Great Plains has been ignored by most historians, who apparently do not feel at ease with the kinds of data available to them.[2] Old scientific surveys, technical reports, surveyors' notes, census reports of crops and animals, and specialized scientific monographs may not seem promising materials to a historian who is not an expert in ecology, geography, botany, zoology, anthropology, and soil sciences. In any case, historians have by and large left the history of the impact of man upon the continent to scholars in other fields. These scholars, in their studies of both European and non-western cultures, have given the relationship of human societies with their environment a degree of complexity far removed from early determinist theories. Where such early works as Ellen Semple's *American History and Its Geographic Conditions,* Ellsworth Huntington's *The Red Man's Continent,* and even Walter Prescott Webb's *The Great Plains* indicated that environments shaped cultures, more recent studies have proceeded from George Perkins Marsh's insight that cultures very often shape their environments.[3]

The irony of the historians' neglect of this aspect of environmental history is that other scholars have explicitly recognized the historical elements present in any such study. Frank Fraser Darling, a leading ecologist, has called social history, political history, and natural history the three horses pulling the chariot of the study of human sociology and its relationship with the natural world. But historians have been reluctant to acknowledge their horses, let alone help harness them.[4]

The basic organization of this study of Island County is thematic. It is based on the premise that different types of land use have created different landscapes. The opening chapter examines Indian land use and its consequences. The displacement of the Indians by white farmers and the ecological changes that followed during the nineteenth century are the subjects of two succeeding chapters. Since bull team logging in Island County differed significantly in its environmental impact from later donkey engine logging, each of these developments is covered in a separate chapter. The final pair of chapters discuss two of the most important twentieth century developments in the county: the agricultural settlement of the logged-off lands, and the development of the islands for urban visitors seeking resorts and summer homes.

In Island County, the physical environment as humans would know it began to take shape 25,000 years ago, when the Vashon Glacier ended its slow advance from British Columbia. Inexorably it had moved through the deep drainage systems of the interglacial period and merged with smaller glaciers from the Olympic and Cascade mountains. The retreat of the glacier put the last major touches on the topography of Puget Sound. Melting at the average rate of one mile every twenty-five years, the Vashon ice sheet left huge glacial lakes in its wake.

From 12,500 to 13,000 years ago the retreating glacier reached the area that would become Island County. Here it deposited sand and till to depths of 100 feet and began the creation of Whidbey and Camano islands. But water and floating ice still covered all but the highest uplands of the present islands. From this floating ice, clay and silt filtered down, leaving additional deposits of from eight to twenty feet. As the glacier retreated even more and the

Strait of Juan de Fuca opened, salt water replaced fresh water and gradually the level of the Sound dropped and the islands appeared.

The islands emerged as glacial moraine—rolling masses of sand, gravel, and clay mixed with a few glacial stones. Underneath lay peat and lignite, remains of the life that had flourished on the surface between glacial periods. At Deception Pass the even older Eocene surface of the area rose above the glacial deposits. Gradually the glacial lakes and shallow lagoons filled with washings from the upper slopes of the islands, and as the glacial leavings mixed with organic matter, the small fertile prairies distinctive of Whidbey Island emerged. In scattered sections of the islands' uplands, and more extensively along the shores, other depressions filled with largely organic matter and became peat bogs and marshes that dotted the islands.[5]

Almost in the shadow of the glacier the forest returned to the land. Foresters have recorded the invasion by the use of pollen analysis. The lodgepole pine (*Pinus contorta* Doug.), aggressive and hardy, was the pioneer species. It thrived on the instability of the early post-glacial period; its early maturity, prolific seed bearing, and wide adaptability allowed it to survive when changes in ice position, flooding, or erosion destroyed other species before they had time to bear seeds. Only the white pine (*Pinus monticola* Doug.) could rival it as a pioneer, but the white pine, although amenable to a cool moist climate, adapted to change less readily than the lodgepole and took much longer to produce seeds.

As the glaciers disappeared and climatic conditions stabilized, new invaders appeared. The short life span of the lodgepole pine allowed longer lived species to outlast it, and the tree's intolerance of shade offset its prolific seeding. Gradually, over a period of 3,000 to 4,000 years, the Douglas fir (*Pseudotsuga menziesii* (Mirbel) Franco) replaced the lodgepole pine as the dominant species, and the pines almost disappeared from the islands. Only the white pine, longer lived than the lodgepole pine and more shade resistant, survived in spots.

Along with the Douglas fir came a scattering of western hemlocks (*Tsuga heterophylla* (Raf.) Sarg.) and later, red cedar (*Thuja plicata* Donn.). A brief period of desiccation checked these trees in turn, but when the climate became wetter they resumed their advance. During this period the Douglas fir achieved its greatest dominance, composing about 64 percent of the forest in the Puget Sound region.[6]

The very dominance of the Douglas fir assured its decline. The seedlings could not endure the dense shade of the mature trees. As the fir forests reached maturity, red cedar and western hemlock (species able to survive and prosper in the shade of the forest) became the new understory. The forests gradually came to consist of mature Douglas firs towering over several generations of hemlock and cedar. As the giant firs fell and new fir seedlings were choked off in the dense shade of the forest, cedar and hemlock regenerated successfully and came to constitute a greater proportion of the forest.

Eventually the whole region might have become a climax forest of cedar and hemlock, perpetuating itself indefinitely. On portions of the islands this did happen. Only natural catastrophes, especially fires, kept the Douglas fir vital and even dominant over most of the region. Irregularly fir trees produced immense crops of seeds. Favored by rodents above nearly all others, these seeds were cached and often forgotten. This fecundity was wasted, however, unless coupled with natural disaster; only then could the dominance of Douglas fir be maintained.

Flash fires killed hemlocks, not firs, but larger fires worked even more to the advantage of Douglas fir. When fires destroyed mature fir along with hemlock and cedar, they opened up the forest floor to the sun. Douglas fir seedlings then rose up in incredible numbers, often as many as 50,000 to 60,000 seedlings to the acre. The young trees thrived in the sunshine, competing largely against each other. After twenty years, competition had thinned the seedlings to about 20,000 firs to the acre. At fifty years of age, when the hemlock and cedar began to reappear in significant numbers, only about 500 fir trees remained out of the original 50,000 seedlings. If the new forest escaped fire, the old cycle reasserted itself, and after 500 to 600 years, the forest would become predominantly hemlock and cedar together with a few giant old firs.[7]

Along with these major invaders came other trees. The Sitka spruce (*Picea sitchensis* (Bong.) Carr.) dominated sections of the islands' bogs. Oak trees (*Quercus garryana* Dougl.) spread out onto the prairies of Oak Harbor, but oddly were found nowhere else on the islands. Red alder (*Alnus rubra* Bong.), ash (*Fraxinus oregona* Nutt.), and maple (*Acer* L.) found niches along stream banks, flood plains, and large sections of shoreline. Red alder even spread out onto some burned-over lands.[8]

Viewed in this way, the changes in the forest seem to have an inner logic with more than a touch of inevitability. In the Pacific Northwest the dominant species of this forest attained a size and longevity unrivaled elsewhere in the world. Deciduous trees, not conifers, dominate all other regions with climatic conditions similar to Puget Sound; yet broadleafs compose only about 6 percent of the trees that made up the forests of western Washington. Why this is so is not entirely clear. A. W. Kuchler has suggested that, for some unknown reason, the Klamath-Shasta Glacier of California descended prior to the Vashon Glacier of British Columbia and Washington. When the climate in the Pacific Northwest deteriorated further, the Shasta Glacier had already cut off the natural escape route to the south. Because of the glacier, the deciduous trees of the Northwest could not spread south into the regions now open to them through climatic change, and the hardier conifers survived in much greater numbers. Trapped in the Pacific Northwest, broadleafs largely disappeared. Rather than being inevitable, the forests themselves were an accident.[9] When the climate moderated, conifers dominated the region and there was no large deciduous forest in the south to expand north and displace them.

The forests would change the islands. Their death and decay created humus over the moraine and helped to develop the acidic podzol soils typical of conifer forests. The trees even influenced the climate somewhat; the thick growth created microclimates beneath their branches. And with the forests humans appeared. Over thousands of years men and forest would be the dominant components of the ecosystem of the islands. Each would influence the other. Men, too, would transform these islands, but they would do it—to varying degrees—consciously; observing, if not always comprehending, the changes.

Humans first arrived in the Puget Sound region 10,000–12,000 years ago.[10] At Cattle Point on the San Juan Islands, one of the oldest examined sites on the Sound, man appeared before the returning forest had had time to deposit the first lay of humus on the glacier-scoured landscape. The excavated site rests directly on glacial till.

In Island County humans left the earliest evidence of their arrival on the northern extremity of Whidbey Island, at Coronet Bay facing Deception Pass. Similarities to Cattle Point indicate that the two sites were probably occupied at roughly the same time, but who the occupants were and where they came from have not yet been determined. Philip Drucker has argued that the first inhabitants farther north, along the rugged coasts of British Columbia, must have arrived with a culture already well adapted to coastal maritime life or they could never have survived in the region. But in coastal Washington, Oregon, and northern California, with their gentler topography and climate, the first peoples could have migrated from the interior, and archaeological evidence in the Puget Sound region indicates that they did.[11]

Like many later immigrants, these first men came to a new land only to continue doing what they had done before. In a land that faced the sea, these people continued as hunters of land mammals and as gatherers. The oldest middens at Coronet Bay contain few shells, a scattering of fish bones, and the bones of many land animals. On the second of the three levels of excavation at Cattle Point, remains of shellfish begin to appear, but the bulk of them were mussels (*Mytilus edulis, Mytilus californianus,* and *Margaritana margaritifera*). Immigrants from the interior plateaus already would have had wide experience with river mussels. The appearance of shells in the middens is, nevertheless, significant because it shows the first reliance of these people upon the sea. The gradual appearance of simple bone and antler artifacts, fishhooks and harpoons, and the first woodworking tools provide further evidence of accommodation. The top levels of both the Cattle Point and Coronet Bay sites are composed of numerous varieties of shellfish (twenty on the highest level at Coronet Bay, compared with the seven kinds found immediately below it), along with fish bones and the remains of a number of sea mammals, including porpoises (*Lagenecrhynchus obliquidens* and *Phocoena vomerina*) and harbor seals (*Phoca vitulina richardii*). These middens seem to be the products of a culture that adapted to and became increasingly dependent on the sea that surrounded it.[12]

Whidbey and the San Juans formed only a peripheral area of a cultural region centered on the Fraser River. Fishermen had appeared on the Fraser as early as 6000 B.C., and by the seventh century B.C. a highly developed culture, identified as the Marpole culture after the major Fraser River site, had evolved. The Marpole was a river culture; the rivers provided both transportation through the dense forests for human inhabitants and migratory routes for the salmon, the major food resource of the area. Despite their own lack of rivers, Whidbey and Camano, facing the mouths of the Skagit and Snohomish rivers, filled the physical requirements for such a culture. It was at the river mouths, as A. L. Kroeber has suggested, that humans concentrated, only gradually spreading to the beaches and beyond.[13]

These early inhabitants of the islands and river estuaries were not the Salish, the group to which nearly all the historic Puget Sound Indians belonged. They were a physically distinct group, a long-headed people whose remains are easily distinguishable from the broad-headed Salish. The Salish were later immigrants, interior people who filtered into the Sound region and the Canadian coast, gradually replacing the people of the Marpole. In the Puget Sound region the Salish probably moved down the Skagit Valley and out onto north Whidbey. The invasion does not appear to have been a violent one. There was no sharp cultural break. The evolution of the large multifamily dwelling of the Salish appears to have continued uninterrupted from Marpole origins. The woodworking tools of the Salish, and even their distinctive art, also appear to have roots in the earlier culture. By A.D. 1300 the Salish were in firm control of the coast.[14]

Chapter I 🦌

SHAPING THE FACE OF THE LAND

Indian Land Use in Island County

🦌 From A.D. 1300 until white settlement in the 1850s, Salish villagers occupied Whidbey and Camano islands. When the whites arrived, four groups of Salish Indians—the Skagit, Snohomish, Kikialos, and Clallam—shared the islands. Far from being centralized political unions, these "tribes" amounted to little more than loose aggregations of villages united by language and kinship. Identification of Indians by culture group often told more about them than did identification by tribe. American settlers and later anthropologists classified the Indians as those who lived near the salt water, those who lived along the rivers, and those who lived on the inland prairies. They ascribed to each a specific economy and set of cultural characteristics. Using such a system, all four tribal groups in Island County would be classified as saltwater or canoe Indians. The villagers differed in language, kinship, and minor cultural traits, but on the whole they were very similar.[1]

In the eyes of the Salish, not only humans, plants, and animals occupied this land, but also a vast array of spirits associated with specific animals or natural phenomena. This added dimension gave the land an ambience and meaning it largely lacked for whites. Plants and animals took on a religious as well as an economic significance. Whites saw this cultural outlook as mere superstition, but within their system of beliefs the Salish proved to be acute students of the natural world. Their knowledge of plant life, for instance, was both thorough and refined. They knew, named, and classified plants, observing subtle differences in taxonomy and

14

habitat. This knowledge was not solely utilitarian; they observed and studied many plants for which they had no use.[2]

The saltwater Indians of Island County relied heavily on salmon—the chinook (Oncorhynchus tshawytscha), the coho (O. kisutch), the pink (O. gorbuscha), the chum (O. keta), and the sockeye (O. nerka). These fish were the most important and most dependable food source of the region. Salmon oriented the tribes toward the rivers, and boundaries in Island County, an area without any rivers, were the logical continuations of mainland river systems. South Whidbey and south Camano, abreast of the Snohomish River, became an extension of that river and a territory of the Snohomish, the people who lived along it. North Camano was isolated from the Snohomish River. It faced the Skagit River, and its northern boundary was almost indistinguishable from the mouth of the Stillaguamish River. The people of north Camano, the Kikialos, were separate and distinct. North Whidbey lay immediately offshore from the Skagit River delta, and the northern boundary of the island, Deception Pass, was the natural route of salmon returning to the Skagit. These links with the Skagit River made north Whidbey the territory of the Skagit Indians.

Only the Clallam territory fails to fit this classification, largely because the Clallam Indians arrived on Whidbey much later than the other tribes. In the 1840s they seized part of Ebeys Prairie to grow potatoes and built a formidable wooden fort. Potato land, not the salmon, set this boundary.[3] These tribes coexisted peacefully on the islands, except for some sporadic fighting between the Skagit and Clallam, and at least in the early historic period, lived in common fear of the aggressive Canadian tribes to the north.

Although, on the whole, Salish relations remained peaceful enough and their tribal organization stayed loose, these boundaries were quite real. Fishing, hunting, and berry grounds belonged to tribal groups, and permission for outsiders to use them had to be obtained from the claimant tribe. It was the Salish who first imposed abstract territorial boundaries upon the land and preserved them in continuous human memory.[4]

At the peak of Salish population, around 1780, these territories contained from 1,500 to 2,500 people, occupying more than 93 village sites. Although the vast majority of these sites were summer camping grounds inhabited seasonally for fishing, hunting, and berry or root gathering, the Indians built at least fifteen permanent villages on the islands. In each village a single row of three to five large cedar houses, together with smaller buildings, faced the water with the forest looming at their backs. Often from 100 to 200 feet long, these buildings normally housed several families who partitioned the interiors into separate living quarters. The Salish located these villages quite precisely. They needed safe, protected anchorages for their canoes and they wanted abundant local supplies of fish and shellfish. The sites that met these requirements clustered on the northern beaches of the islands and, as a result, so did the Salish. (See Map 3.) The Skagit settled in three permanent villages on the shores of Penn Cove (the center of population), built a fourth village at Oak Harbor, a fifth at Crescent Harbor, and perhaps several more scattered elsewhere on northeastern Whidbey. The Snohomish occupied three villages on south Whidbey: one at Camano Head, their main village on the southern tip of Cultus Bay, and a village at Sandy Point, which George Vancouver described as sizable. The Kikialos had six permanent village sites scattered along the western and northern beaches of Camano, but none have been excavated. Most of southern Whidbey and southern Camano had no permanent occupants.[5]

The population of the islands fluctuated from season to season. When Indians departed to fish the mainland rivers, they deserted the permanent villages and temporarily depopulated the islands. At other times of the year, however, the population mushroomed as mainland tribal members joined the inhabitants of the islands for hunting or gathering, the residents and visitors occupied many of the eighty or so seasonal sites scattered around Whidbey and Camano. The Salish food cycle of hunting, gathering, and fishing varied slightly from tribe to tribe, but all over the Puget Sound country the Salish moved regularly through their territories to harvest wild foods as they became available.

Salish fishermen left their winter villages in January when the steelhead (*Salmo gairdneri*), an oceangoing rainbow trout, migrated up the mainland rivers, but most of the population remained in the cedar houses until April and May, when they could gather cattail (*Typha latifolia* L.) and salmonberry (*Rubus spectabilis* Pursh.) sprouts in surrounding woods and marshes. In late May and early June salmonberries and strawberries ripened (*Frageria* sp.), and the

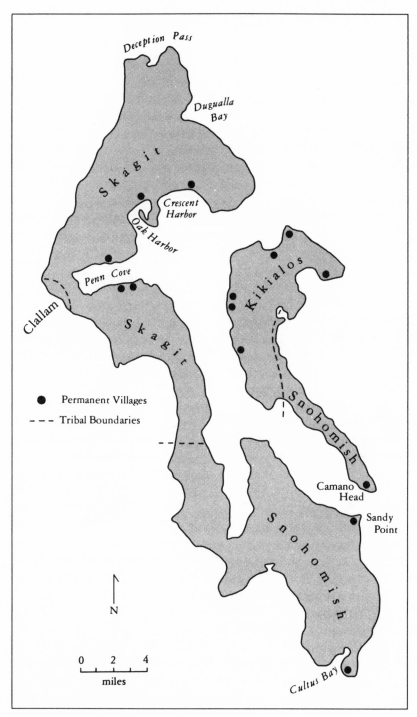

Map 3. Salish boundaries and village sites

camas (*Camassia quamash* (Pursh) Greene), a small bulb eaten much like the potato, was ready for digging. The prairies of Whidbey Island produced camas in great abundance. Indians dried the root and used it as a staple, year-round food; like dried salmon, it was a major commodity in Indian commerce. From June through August the Salish collected berries: salal berry (*Gaultheria shallon* Pursh), blackberry (*Rubus macropetalus* (Dougl.) Brown and *Rubus laciniatus* Willd.), blackcaps (*Rubus leucodermis* Dougl.), serviceberry (*Amelanchier florida* Lindl.), cranberry (Vaccinium oxycoccus L.), thimbleberry (*Rubus parviflorus* Nutt.), and huckleberry (*Vaccinium parvifolium* Smith, *Vaccinium ovalifolium* Smith). They also dug the bracken fern (*Pteridium aquilinum* (L.) Kuhn) and collected wood ferns (*Dryopteris dilatata* (Hoffm.) Gray), sword ferns (*Polystichum munitum* (Kaulf.) Presl.), wild carrots (*Daucus carota* L.), rose hips (*Rosa* sp.), tiger lilies (*Trillium ovatum* Pursh), acorns (from *Quercus garryana* Dougl.), hazelnuts (*Corylus californica* (A. Dc.)), and crab apples (*Pyrus diversifolia* Bong.). Erna Gunther, an anthropologist who studied the Salish, listed fifty plants (not including trees) used by the Skagit alone, and such a list is certainly incomplete.[6]

In the spring the Salish also dug for shellfish, and throughout the spring and summer they hunted and fished. They trolled for salmon, flounder (Pleuronectidae), perch (Embiotocidae), dogfish (Squalidae), rockfish (Scorpoanidae), and lingcod (Ophiodon), as well as an occasional sturgeon (Acipenseridae) or sculpin (Cottidae). Most of the big game hunting on the islands was done by upriver mainland Indians, who would later trade the elk (*Cervus canadensis*) and deer (*Ococoileus hemionius*) meat and hides along the shores of Puget Sound.

Early in September when the first salmon of the great fall runs moved up the rivers, the Indians gathered on the banks to take them. For months salmon crowded the streams and the Indians caught them in such immense numbers that early white settlers thought the salmon were the Indians' only source of food. Of course, salmon were of fundamental importance to the Salish, but the Indians of Island County did not starve when the salmon failed to appear. Unlike the upriver Indians, who suffered badly in those years when the salmon did not run, the lower Skagit and Kikialos could simply shift to other sources of food. The recollections of

John Fornsby, an upriver Skagit, may be exaggerated, but they certainly contained a core of truth: [7] "The lower Skagit always had something to eat—duck. There were lots of deer on Whidby Island. They pretty near ate fresh meat every day." [8]

In 1855 a brief Indian war flared up in Washington territory, and the Americans confined the bulk of the Indians on Puget Sound to island reservations. For the tribes immediately to the south of Island County, the Nisqually, Puyallup, and Squaxin, the result of confinement was hunger, suffering, and a staggering death rate. The Americans concentrated the Snohomish, Kikialos, and Skagit on Whidbey Island reservations, and these peoples also suffered, sickened, and died, but not on the massive scale of the tribes to the south. Food remained relatively plentiful. This was partially because supplies provided by the government arrived sporadically. But more crucially, despite limited fishing on the rivers, poor salmon runs in 1855 and 1856, and confiscation of the Indians' guns, ample food could be obtained from Whidbey and Camano and the neighboring waters. The upriver Indians complained about their diet of clams and saltwater fish, but their very complaints are evidence that local resources remained sufficient to support large numbers of people, even with access to such major food supplies as salmon and game animals restricted. [9]

This Indian food cycle led early white observers to hold contradictory views of Salish culture. At times they described the Indians as nomadic, but this was hard to reconcile with the obvious Salish reverence for their village and homeland and their attachment to the graves of their ancestors. The tenacity of this devotion both impressed and bewildered the Americans who sought to displace them. The Salish did not drift over the surface of the land. Their devotion to their homes and their lands was as formidable as the huge cedar houses in which they lived. The permanent village and the seasonal journeys in search of food coexisted easily and logically; together they defined the relationship of the Salish to their land. Both the village and the food cycle were basic. [10]

Anthropologists have described the Salish as living off the "spontaneous product of nature" for generation after generation until they were displaced by the whites. They have been viewed as having moved easily across the face of the land, leaving no trace of their presence. The whites supposedly inherited the land much as the first Indians had found it.[11] Settlers, and some anthropologists, have presumed that the components of the Salish food cycle were the result of virgin nature, not the product of Salish occupation. But the plant communities that existed at the time of white settlement are themselves evidence of substantial Salish influence on the environment. Three plants in particular—bracken, camas, and nettles—which surveyors and settlers found in abundance, were closely tied to Salish cultural practices.

Prolonged human occupation of a site often leads to a local enrichment of the soil. Generations of Indians living at the same village site inevitably produced considerable amounts of waste. The shells and bones, the plant refuse, the ashes from fires, the excrement of humans and animals gradually rotted and provided the surrounding soils with significant amounts of potash, phosphorous, and nitrogen. The accumulations harbored many of the ancestors of human food crops.[12]

The nettle (*Urtica dioica* ssp. *gracilis* var. *lyalli* (Wats) Hitchc.), with a preference for rich soils, has historically been associated with human occupation. The plant probably spread from its native prairie into the vicinity of the Salish villages. Constant proximity brought familiarity and, eventually, the discovery of a variety of uses for the plant. The Indians of Puget Sound made medicines and dyes from the nettle, and they peeled, dried, and rolled its bark into the two-ply string they used for their fishing and duck nets. Moreover, since the existence of a nettle patch indicated rich ground, the Indians later used the plant as a guide in locating potential potato patches. According to the testimony of the Skagit Indians, they cared for the nettle in a manner closely resembling cultivation. They kept the prairie patches of nettle free of weeds and burned the plant refuse in the fall after harvesting. The Salish clearly encouraged the nettle over other plant species of the prairies.[13]

The Salish used fire not only to maintain their nettle grounds, but also as an instrument for shaping the ecology of the entire prairie. That the Skagits on Whidbey burned the prairies is certain; testimony by both Indians and whites is quite explicit on this point. The results of the practice, however, were more apparent than the initial motivation. Indians burned vegetation elsewhere on the continent to increase the grazing and browsing areas of either large game animals or of the tribes' own horses. But the island Skagit had no horses, nor were they very dependent on large herbivores for food. Even deer, a relatively minor source of food, were browsers that did not rely on extensive grasslands for feed. Browsing animals, like deer and elk, eat mainly on herbaceous vegetation and the leaves of shrubs and trees. They lack the specialized dentition of grazing animals, like horses, that allows these animals to subsist on the majority of grasses, which contain some silica. If browsers had to rely on such grasses, they would wear their teeth to the gums. If the Salish wanted to improve the land for game animals, therefore, burning the forest would have increased deer and elk numbers far more effectively than burning the prairies. Undoubtedly, burning helped game animals somewhat by maintaining ecotones between forest and prairies and, when the fires spread into neighboring woodlands, by opening up some of the forest floor for new secondary growth on which deer browsed, but this was probably a side effect of the process, not its rationale. More likely the original impetus came from the increase in vegetable products that followed fires.[14]

The best evidence for this was the abundance of two plants when the Americans first settled on the prairies: bracken, a fern that reached heights of seven feet on the prairies, and camas, which dominated large expanses of open land. Both plants were staples of the Indian diet. The Salish ground bracken roots and baked the flour into bread, and they boiled camas (eating it fresh like a potato), as well as drying and preserving the bulb. The abundance of bracken and camas on the prairies of Whidbey Island was probably not fortuitous. Rather than being major Indian food sources because they dominated the prairies, camas and bracken more likely dominated the prairies because they were major Indian food sources. As Carl Sauer, the noted geographer, pointed out, the very existence of people like the Salish depended on "acting intelligently within the range of their experience." Observing the changes brought by fire and using them to their own advantage was the kind of "advantageous behavior" that enabled the Salish to survive. In cloudy, moist climates, such as that of Puget Sound, bracken has often moved into open areas where plant life has been disturbed. Fire, by inhibiting the dense growth of native grasses, facilitated its spread.[15]

In the Puget Sound region bracken was, and remains, one of the major pioneer invaders of disturbed and burned-over lands. Once established, the dense root network of the plant and the death of its topgrowth in the fall protected it from fatal damage by fire and gave it an advantage over less resilient rivals. Ecologists and shepherds in areas with climates similar to that of Island County have noted that continued burning and heavy grazing of open land lead to immense increases in the amount of bracken. Since bracken is a poor feed after its first growth, this increase is lamented by pastoral peoples. But the Salish were not herdsmen. They valued the fern as an important source of food, and therefore set fires to increase the yield of the plant. Evidence from other prairies in western Washington seems to substantiate this pattern.[16]

Camas benefited less directly from burning. Like bracken, its topgrowth died off in late summer, and fall prairie fires did it little harm. Unlike bracken, however, the mere destruction of competing plants did not ensure an expansion of its range. Only direct human or animal intervention enabled the plant to expand significantly. The Skagits moved the bulbs into fresh areas—at first unwittingly, perhaps, but later with zeal and care. Harvesting enabled the plant to increase: dropped, split, and discarded bulbs spread camas to fresh areas. Gathering the crop with a digging stick became, as Carl Sauer has said of root digging in general, "unplanned tillage." According to Indian and white testimony, the Salish eventually supplemented the digging of the mature bulbs with cultivation to secure a better harvest. Such a technique approached true farming, as did other practices of the Salish. They dug in plant refuse around the tiger lily, and the Indians of the upper Skagit, and almost certainly the Whidbey Skagit, came close to actual cultivation of the lily and wild carrot. When the potato was brought into the Puget Sound region, all Salish tribes moved easily and rapidly to the cultivation of that crop without any direct instruction by the whites.[17]

The Indians significantly modified the vegetational community of the prairies. Indian land use involved purposeful manipulation of the environment, and this manipulation had profound ecological effects. Burning destroyed seedlings and shrubs that encroached on the prairies. If unwanted invaders survived, they were often pulled out. Fire encouraged the bracken that came to be the dominant vegetation of the prairies, and other Salish practices helped spread nettles and camas. Human activities (primarily burning, but also collection and cultivation) created new environmental factors that placed certain plants at a disadvantage while aiding others. Some species were encouraged while the range of others was drastically curtailed. When the whites arrived, they regarded the prairies as wild, the creations of either nature or God, but certainly not a product of human design. They damned bracken for making plowing difficult, cursed the painful sting of the nettle, and praised camas as pig food. As settlers fulfilled the biblical injunctions of sinking plowshares into the earth, they imagined that they were putting the stamp of man upon the land. But the stamp of man was already firmly present.[18]

The influence of the Salish extended beyond the limits of the prairies into the forests that surrounded them. Indians used the trees of the forest extensively, not only cedar, but also fir, hemlock, and alder. Yet considering the abundance of the forests and the massive size of individual trees, Salish harvesting for canoes or houses probably had little impact on forest ecology. The firs and cedars of Whidbey and Camano were huge. It took the neighboring Makah Indians two weeks to fell a Sitka spruce by fire and axe, and the conifers of Island County demanded similar labor. The felling of one of these giants would have made only a minuscule difference in the forest as a whole.[19]

But for the Salish wood was only one product of the forest. The woods also yielded berries and game. None of these favored deep forest, but all thrived in the clearings and young successful forests that followed fires. The upriver Indians, fearing its immediate threat to existing game, were very wary of fire, but the saltwater peoples of the lowlands apparently burned over berry fields without much hesitation. They were interested in the fireweed and berries that formed part of the normal successional pattern on such burned lands. Berries were an important food, and the Salish used fireweed (*Epilobium angustifolium L.*) with other materials to weave their blankets. The very name "fireweed" indicated how obvious the connection between the plant and burning was to the whites who later came to the area.[20]

The first United States land surveys of Whidbey and Camano islands in the late 1850s suggested how extensively the forests had been burned. There had not yet been a decade of American settlement, and most of the islands were unoccupied and practically unexplored by whites. The surveyors made two critical observations. One was that Douglas fir was the dominant species, closely followed by hemlock and locally abundant Sitka spruce and cedar. Since fir, in a region of hemlock–cedar climax forests such as Island County, depended for propagation on the destruction not only of hemlock and cedar but also of the mature fir itself, the climax forest had either been destroyed or had never existed. This destruction was clearly not the result of harvesting, nor is there any evidence of extensive destruction by disease or insects. The most likely cause of destruction was fire, but electrical storms produce virtually all natural fires, and there are few thunderstorms in western Washington. There are thunderstorms in the mountains, but fires started by lightning in the mountains would have to be of staggering proportions to reach Puget Sound. Furthermore, mainland forest fires could never have reached Island County simply because Whidbey and Camano were islands. Yet the surveyors recorded that large portions of the islands had been burned. It was this burning that gave the Douglas fir its advantage and enabled the tree to dominate the forests of the islands.[21]

North of Crescent Harbor almost to Dugualla Bay the surveyors reported the bulk of the forest killed by fire. West of Holmes Harbor to Admiralty Inlet much of the timber had been burned, and the surveyors reported substantial damage on the southern end of Whidbey Island. On the west coast of Camano, from Point Lowell to north of Point Onamec, fire had destroyed much of the timber several years prior to the survey. On northern Camano, where whites would take out some of the finest timber in the world, fires had done substantial damage before 1859, and in one partial township on the east coast of the island, out of ten sections only one, the site of a Kikialos village, had escaped burning. Of the sixteen townships surveyed in the 1850s, surveyors reported that six had burned-over forests, and in five of these damage seems to have been substantial.[22]

This destruction probably resulted from a combination of prairie fires that accidentally spread to the neighboring forests and from fires deliberately set to extend berry grounds. With the brisk winds that blew across the islands, a small fire could have spread rapidly. If these Indian fires started most of the forest fires in the Puget Sound country, and particularly in Island County, then the species composition of the forests can only be attributed to Indian occupation and land use. The large numbers of Douglas fir in the lowland forests of Puget Sound, as well as the early successional growth of groundsel (*Senecio* L.); fireweed; berries; bracken; and fir, alder, and hemlock seedlings, owed their existence to fire, and fire was significant because of the Salish.[23]

In the northern conifer forests generally, burning has for centuries shaped woodland ecology. That on the shores of Puget Sound men largely caused the fires did not make burning any less crucial. Fire not only released mineral nutrients accumulated in the litter, humus, wood, and foliage of old forest, it simultaneously prepared seedbeds and triggered the release of some seed supplies. The periodic destruction of old forests kept a significant proportion of each region in young trees and thus reduced the susceptibility of the forest to insects and disease. In a sense, fires were so common and critical that the species composition that would have developed without fire would have been unnatural.[24]

Just as fire shaped the forests, it shaped the populations of the animals that inhabited the woodlands. The deer and elk, abundant in Island County when whites first arrived, were "best adapted to recent burns and early succession forests—not climax forests." By providing fires, the Salish provided these animals with their habitat and increased their numbers as well as the numbers of their predators, the wolves.[25]

Changes such as these were not readily apparent to the casual observer. Unless the environment bore obvious marks of human handiwork, the first whites dismissed it as wilderness, natural and untouched. But wilderness has little meaning when applied to Island County and areas like it. This was a land shaped by its inhabitants to fit their own purposes. They populated this land with spirits and powers, but they did not restrict their manipulation to magic. Through observation and tradition, Indians altered natural communities to fit their needs without, in the process, destroying the ability of those communities to sustain the cultures that had created them. Their technology was limited, but they used it effectively. The accomplishment of the villagers in creating and maintaining this ecosystem was impressive. Because of the world the Indians created, the Salish population of 1780 would be larger than any human population on the islands before 1910. Unlike the Indians of the upper river, this population was plagued by neither seasonal scarcities nor periodic famines. Indeed, in terms of camas, berries, bracken, deer, and elk, the islands were a food exporting region. Far from being creatures of their environment, these people had shaped their world and made it what it was when whites first arrived.[26]

With the arrival of the whites, however, two ecosystems separated for thousands of years came into contact, and members of one ecosystem entered into the other. The magnitude of the resulting process of readjustment has been, until recently, a neglected aspect of American Indian history. Of all the biological fellow travelers that accompanied the whites onto the North American continent, their diseases spread the most quickly and had the most obvious impact. European diseases quickly pushed beyond the frontiers of white settlement into areas where, very often, Indians had never even seen a white man.

Of these diseases, smallpox was probably the most deadly. In Europe, long exposure to smallpox had eliminated the least-resistant members of the population during childhood and created antibodies and some degree of immunity among the remaining population. The infection remained serious and deadly, but it was largely confined to children. Among the Indians no such selection had taken place; there was no resistance, and they died by the millions.[27]

Smallpox pushed into the interior of the continent well ahead of the Europeans, probably reaching Puget Sound in 1782 or 1783. When George Vancouver first sailed into Puget Sound in 1793, smallpox scars, the "indelible mark" of that "deplored disease," were already borne by many. A sense of the ravages and horror of this disease dominate sections of his *Voyages*. There was an aura of death over the new land. Near Port Discovery on the Olympic Peninsula, Vancouver described a deserted village "capable of containing a hundred inhabitants," but

> The habitations had now fallen into decay; their inside, as well as a small surrounding space that appeared to have been formerly occupied, were overrun with weeds; amongst which were found several human skulls, and other bones, promiscuously scattered about.

The whole area took on the aspect of a vast graveyard. Throughout the vicinity of Port Discovery:

> scull [sic], limbs, ribs, and backbones or some other vestiges of the human body were found promiscuously . . . . scattered about the beach, in great numbers. Similar relics were also frequently met with during our survey in the boats; and I was informed by the officers that in their several perambulations the like appearances had presented themselves so repeatedly, and in such abundance, as to produce an idea that the environs of Port Discovery were a general cemetery for the whole of the surrounding country.

Vancouver guessed correctly that "at no very remote period this country had been far more populous than at present."[28]

The arrival of the explorers and the opening of the sea otter trade that followed brought more extended white contact and with it exposure to other European diseases. Syphilis, probably contracted from the sailors who manned the trading ships on the Columbia River, spread rapidly and was well established among the Chinooks at the time of Lewis and Clark's visit in 1805–06. By the 1850s Isaac Stevens would blame syphilis for carrying off hundreds in the Puget Sound region every year. In the 1820s and 1830s intermittent fever (probably malaria) virtually depopulated the Willamette Valley, and although it apparently did not reach the Sound, a disease similar to it struck in 1836. A measles epidemic broke out in the Sound area in 1847 and the Snohomish, believing it to have been deliberately introduced by the whites, planned to burn the Hudson Bay Company Fort at Nisqually. Tuberculosis appeared, also in epidemic form, and smallpox recurred sporadically. Estimates are that by 1840 the population of the Puget Sound region had been cut in half.

Still the death rate continued high. In 1853 and 1854 the last great smallpox epidemic struck the Puget Sound Indians. Skagit folktales credited a disease (identified as chicken pox, but probably smallpox) with depopulating whole villages. The Makahs at Cape Flattery on the Olympic Peninsula lost half of their population, and farther south smallpox, syphilis, and tuberculosis reduced the once numerous Chinooks and Cowlitz to pitiful remnants before they ever had experienced extensive white settlement. Island County did not escape these epidemics, and the new diseases continued to take their toll into the 1850s. Venereal diseases were so extensive that children contracted them at birth, and whooping cough killed more Indian children. In 1855 the Island Skagits were reported decreasing in numbers and influence, and in 1857 the Indian agent for the Skagits, Snohomish, and Kikialos reported influenza and venereal diseases rampant. The agent had seen ten deaths in seven days and twenty-two in a month, and guessed the total number was double that. In 1858 there was extensive sickness, mainly tuberculosis, syphilis, and influenza, and many died.

Early settlers on the islands reported the Indians dying in great numbers and predicted extinction for many tribes. This prediction was not often viewed with sorrow. "The Rambler" traveling on Whidbey Island in 1854 wrote to the *Pioneer and Democrat,* "I saw a set of bipeds represented to be human beings, the 'red men of the forest' " and that the sooner they disappeared "the better as it will save sympathy on the part of the whites and degradation and misery on themselves." [29]

The Indian was helpless in the face of most of these exotic diseases. Their own medicines were ineffective, and, except for the smallpox vaccinations provided after 1855, so were white medicines. As Indian population diminished, so too did the pressure they put on the land to provide food and shelter. Peoples reduced by disease abandoned villages and camping sites, and the vegetation once banished from them returned. The Indian adjustment to the land was fundamentally altered. Practices once beneficial became harmful. The huge cedar houses, once admirable adaptations to the environment, became death traps. Tuberculosis and scorfula, the infection of the lymph glands by the tubercle bacillus, thrived in the dark of the big village houses. The houses were windowless, meaningless enough originally, but now the lack of sunlight favored the disease. Similarly the dirt floors, once harmless, now collected infested spittle and mucus that was fed on by flies that infected food. Other practices also spread the disease. Consumptive women wetted fibers in their mouth to make the Indian baskets that were used to store food supplies, and the communal living arrangements provided nearly maximum contact between the diseased and other members of the village. The invasion of the bacillus immediately altered adaptations to the land centuries in the making. Nearly overnight the village passed from reasonably sanitary to being dangerously destructive. Primarily an urban disease in most of the world, tuberculosis gained its strongest hold on rural Indian populations. As late as 1907–08, the incidence of tuberculosis remained as high as 36.2 people per thousand among the Quinault Indians of western Washington.[30]

Disease and death on this scale almost inevitably produced a cultural crisis and loss of confidence. Early whites repeatedly mentioned the conviction of the Salish that they were a dying people, although admittedly the whites used this to justify their own seizure of Salish resources. White religion, especially Catholicism, made rapid, if superficial, inroads among the Skagits in the 1840s. It imposed another world view—a view that, as has often been mentioned, sees nature largely in terms of human domination, upon the Salish's own beliefs. The new outlook was usually only lightly held, but it had some influence.[31]

In the older Salish world the idea of powers that were associated with specific animals had blurred the boundaries between men and animals. To possess a power was to have a desirable trait of the animals with which that power was associated. For the hunter to kill an animal he had to possess either its power or that of one of its predators. Animals were not a lower order created for man, but rather a repository of spirits and beings with natures similar to man's own. Fraught not only with economic but also with religious significance, animals were not to be lightly persecuted. They were to be treated with respect and were not even to be laughed at, let alone tormented or killed without need.[32]

In their preservation of game animals the upriver peoples, particularly, developed quite a definite set of rules. Young animals were never to be killed, nor were more animals to be killed than could be used, and meat was never to be wasted. Shooting undersized or young animals made the hunter feel "cheap," and social pressures were exerted to limit the hunt to adult animals. The upper Nisqually were said to keep such a close track of their hunting territory that they limited their yearly kill in order to keep game abundant.

These attitudes toward game animals do not seem to have been as strong in the saltwater region, however, as they were on the upper rivers. For whatever reason—the greater abundance of game, or the saltwater Salish's lesser dependence on it, or simply less skill at hunting—these rules do not seem to have been consistently observed. On the Sound the Indians often killed animals en masse. The skeletal remains of deer (*Odocoileus hemionus*) and elk (*Cervus canadensis roosevelti*) at Penn Cove villages are complete, an unlikely occurrence if animals were killed inland and butchered on the spot since the hunter would discard the heavier bones at the site of the killing. But, as Alan Bryan points out, if the lower Skagit hunted these animals using cliff drives and nets, the carcasses could be moved easily from beach-side cliffs by canoe.

There is at least one record of such a drive. In 1845 Patkanim, a Snoqualmie chief, organized a large hunt on Ebeys Prairie to provide food for a meeting of several tribes to consider closing Whidbey Island to white settlement. The Snoqualmie constructed a large corral near Penn Cove with wings extending outward and drove the game into it with dogs. They captured and killed over sixty deer. By their very nature, deer or elk drives lessened the chances of selective hunting. Likewise, the prohibition against killing young animals does not appear to have been extended to sea mammals by the Indians of the islands. Immature and fetal seal bones (*Phoca vitulina richardii*) were common in the middens, suggesting that "young mammals and pregant females were preferred or more easily caught."[33]

It was within this cultural framework, disrupted by disease but still viable, that British and American fur traders placed another value on animal life by offering to exchange manufactured goods for furs. The most lucrative trade was in pelts of the coastal sea otters (*Enhydra lutris*), but the Salish of Whidbey and Camano were too far distant to participate in the hunts that eventually eliminated the sea otter from the region. Instead their involvement in the fur trade centered on the beaver (*Castor canadensis*), but initially they reacted quite coolly to British solicitations to engage in commercial hunting. Despite gifts of ammunition and money for the game, the Salish refused to hunt for the British when the Hudson's Bay Company established Fort Nisqually on upper Puget Sound in 1833. And later that year, rather than rushing to cash in on the steady market for furs, the Salish boycotted the trade for months because the British would not meet their price.

Even when the fur trade was at its height, it appears to have been absorbed partially into older Salish commercial patterns. The upper Skagit had long sold elk and deer hides to the saltwater peoples, and now they merely added the beaver. Snatelum, the head-men of the village at Snatelum Point, was a major mover in this trade, acting as middleman between the Hudson's Bay Company (H.B.C.) and the upriver Indians, a practice the British en-couraged. The middens of Whidbey Island show relatively few beaver remains, indicating that the lower Skagit did little beaver hunting, but the journal at Fort Nisqually shows repeated trips by Snatelum to trade furs. June Collins, in her study of the upper Skagit, mentions Snatelum as the major middleman in the trade, and such a conclusion seems unavoidable. But even at its height this trade in furs was not extensive; the Indians traded 1,075 beaver at Fort Nisqually in 1836, but there was a sharp drop to 759 in 1837. When the Hudson's Bay Company changed its opera-tion at Fort Nisqually to farming and ceased extensive partici-pation in the fur trade, the beaver population, whose actual de-cline is not known, rose rapidly. George Gibbs, a government official and ethnologist, claimed that there were as many beaver in the 1850s as there had ever been.[34]

The long-term effects of Salish trapping upon the fur-bearing animals were minimal, but the consequences of the trade itself were immense. The trade gave the Salish access to a new technol-ogy. Initially the Indians merely adapted guns, metal tools, trade blankets, and potato cultivation into their own culture, but gradu-ally white tools began to make dramatic changes in the culture it-self.[35] And, as the culture changed, the natural world it had helped create changed with it.

The only domesticated animal of the Salish was a dog they raised primarily for its hair. The animals were small, about the size of Pomeranians (according to Vancouver), with thick coats. The Indians wove their hair, mixed with mountain goat wool, duck down, and fireweed cotton, into blankets. Joseph Whidbey reported meeting a herd of about forty of these, "shorn close to the skin like sheep," near the Snohomish village at Sandy Point. The dog was present only among the saltwater peoples of the northern Sound. With the trade blanket, however, the specially bred dogs of the Salish became superfluous. Blankets could be obtained more easily by trade and paid labor than they could be manufactured by native techniques. As a result the dog, one of the unique animals in the Salish ecosystem, was already vanishing by the 1850s. It was an example of the way technical importations could affect biological populations.[36]

The impact of the gun was more direct and more immediate. With the musket the Salish began to rely more extensively on game animals for food. In archaeological excavations, the animal bones gathered at the upper or most recent level of occupation at the Snatelum Point village are greater in number than the animal bones from all other levels combined. Since the upper level represents Salish occupation after white contact in the 1790s, the logical conclusion is that the gun, mainly the H.B.C. musket, greatly increased the hunting of land mammals. As a result elk, once described as numerous, had almost vanished when the whites settled the island in the 1850s.[37]

The potato was as significant an addition as the gun to Salish culture. Not a European native at all, the potato had developed on the Pacific coast of South America, was carried across the Atlantic to Europe, and had now reached the Pacific again, thousands of miles north of its place of origin.[38] The date of its first appearance in the Pacific Northwest is unknown. The Spanish might have planted it in their short-lived settlement at Neah Bay on the Olympic Peninsula, but such a beginning would have been abortive, as would have been its introduction in the garden Vancouver hurriedly planted and abandoned near Port Discovery.

By the 1830s, the British at Fort Nisqually had definitely introduced the potato on the upper Sound, and the Skagit probably acquired it from the British at the fort, from traders on Vancouver Island, or through Indian intermediaries. In any case, they rapidly adopted the vegetable without any direct instruction in its care and planting. The ease and rapidity with which Indians accepted the potato probably reflects the extent to which their gathering practices had already approached true agriculture. With their climate unsuited to such standard native American crops as corn and squash, and cut off from other agricultural peoples, it is possible that the Salish, especially the Skagit, were in the process of turning their native bracken, camas, and nettles into domesticated food crops. The Salish possessed tools, especially the digging stick, that they could easily adapt to potato culture; they lived in permanent villages well suited for agriculture, and Salish women already gathered and cultivated such root crops as the tiger lily

(*Lilium columbianum* Hanson), camas, and wapato (*Sagittaria* L.). The potato was a simple crop. Replanting the potato simply involved replacing in the spring what had been uprooted in the fall.[39]

The potato became a significant addition to Indian food supplies. White missionaries, explorers, and settlers repeatedly mentioned its importance in the Indian economy. As early as 1840, when Father Blanchet first visited the Skagit at Penn Cove, the Salish had land planted to potatoes. In 1842 Wilkes reported the Indians on Whidbey raised "extremely fine" potatoes in great abundance. They had three or four acres enclosed and had added beans, probably obtained from Blanchet, to their food crops. In 1851 Charles Wilson, an early settler, went to Penn Cove to buy potatoes from the Skagit, and in 1853 George Gibbs described their crop as "considerable."

The potato became a valuable food and tied the Salish even more firmly to their land. The Skagits and Clallams fought over the fertile potato lands of Ebeys Prairie, and in their treaty negotiations with the whites the Salish asked that good potato lands be reserved for their use. It is ironic that such a major food, one that helped boost populations elsewhere in the world, should have been brought into western Washington at a time of drastic population decline.[40]

White settlement brought a decline, too, in Salish farming. Cows and hogs introduced to the islands by whites not only threatened to destroy the camas, but also invaded Indian potato grounds. They destroyed the Clallam's patches near Ebeys Landing and threatened the Skagit crop near Penn Cove. But even more than the pig and cow, the white man himself destroyed Indian agriculture. White claims of prairie land forced the Skagit off, and by 1855–56 even the island Skagit were apparently planting on the mainland. Constant use had reduced the fertility of this land, however, and sporadic flooding would periodically destroy much of the crop. For a brief time in the late fifties, the Skagit appear to have returned to a small reservation on Penn Cove and put in ten acres of potatoes, but that was the end. Soon Skagit agriculture would be practically eliminated in the county. Indians still worked the fields, but now for white farmers.

By the mid-fifties the Salish had effectively yielded the land.

The treaty of Point Elliot in 1855 ceded title to the county to the whites, although (as often occurred in negotiations in western Washington) the Indians did not fully understand the terms of the treaty. Even after signing, they would return to the island and demand rent from the white settlers. It would, of course, be indignantly refused.

The coming of the white man had shaken the Salish profoundly. The new tools, the new plants and animals, the new possibilities may have changed the way they saw the islands, but, if they did, the change was as much a product of the weakening of the old ways through death, disease, and loss of confidence as it was a conversion to the white's vision of the land. We will give you the forests, a Snoqualmie chief in council on southern Whidbey would say, but leave us the game and fish, the good potato lands, and the graves of our fathers. Needless to say, they would be left nothing of the sort.[41]

Chapter II

THE GARDEN
AND THE WILDERNESS

The Frontier Farmer on the Land

Americans have celebrated the frontier farmer as, among other things, a bearer of "civilization," a founder of new communities, and a conqueror of the wilderness, but the farmer served one purpose that they have usually neglected. Along with the explorer and trader, the farmer composed the vanguard of the ecological invasion of North America. He introduced to the continent, both intentionally and accidentally, the exotic plants and animals that have permanently altered the natural systems of the New World. Some farmers, at least in Island County, explicitly recognized their ecological function. As Walter Crockett, an early settler, wrote, the main object of the farmer in settling new land was:

> . . . to get the land subdued and the wilde nature out of it. When that is accomplished we can increase our crops to a very large amount and the high prices of every thing that is raised heare will make the cultivation of the soil a very profitable business (sic).[1]

Subduing the land and getting the "wilde nature out of it" meant replacement of native flora and fauna on a massive scale. Crockett and his neighboring farmers did not begin the ecological invasion of Island County. The European diseases that had riddled the Salish, demoralizing and destroying them, and the potatoes and beans that the Indians had brought to the islands before the whites arrived had already invaded and altered the Salish ecosystem. Farmers did not initiate the assault on the natural world of

the Salish, but they increased its scale and magnified its consequences.

Changes in the natural environment by the Salish had basically
involved shifts in the proportions of native flora and fauna. Of
necessity Salish land use had consisted of the manipulation of a set
number of native plants. Some plants had diminished, others had
increased. American farmers attempted something entirely different. Their first fields were beachheads for exotic plants: wheat,
oats, barley, peas, corn, cabbage, carrots, turnips, beets, toma-
toes, melons, squashes, parsnips, and a host of others. The survival of these plants depended on the farmer just as surely as his
survival depended upon them.

The process of invasion seemed at once simple and straight-
forward and laborious and tedious to men like Crockett. The
farmer would clear existing "useless" vegetation and replace it
with useful vegetation.[2] He would eliminate wild herbivores and
introduce domestic herbivores. He would plow up bracken and
plant wheat. He would eliminate elk and introduce cattle. When
he was done, wild nature would be gone and a farm would be established. Ecologically this view may have been dangerously sim-
pleminded, but in the nineteenth century as well as in the twentieth, this outlook remained common.

Like the Salish before them, the farmers created their own landscapes. But since the farmer undertook more ambitious changes
than the Salish ever had, the consequences were more far-reaching,
the interrelationships more complex, and the chances for mis-
calculation far greater. The arrival of the white farmer spurred
what one botanist has described as the most cataclysmic series of
events in the natural history of the area since the Ice Age.[3]

The farmers came to the county as part of the much larger
Oregon and California migrations of the 1840s and 1850s. Americans had spilled north of the Columbia River, entering the Puget
Sound region by the mid-1840s and settling on lands the British
had believed they would retain when diplomats determined the
final status of the Oregon country. The Americans found these
lands less fertile and less inviting than those to the south, but they
nevertheless came in sufficient numbers to undermine British
hegemony. The land north of the Columbia became American, not
British, and by 1854 these lands formed the base of the new terri-

tory of Washington. But the migration into the Puget Sound region remained a mere rivulet when compared with the rivers of people that flowed to Oregon's Willamette Valley.

The first white farmer to arrive in Island County came in 1850. Isaac Neff Ebey, then thirty-two years of age, had been born in Ohio during what amounted to a pause in the life-long migration of his Pennsylvania-born parents. He went with them to Illinois in 1832 and afterwards to Missouri. In Missouri Ebey married and fathered two sons before going on alone to the Oregon country in 1847. Briefly diverted to California by the gold rush, he came north to Olympia on Puget Sound and then to Whidbey Island. In 1851 he sent for his wife and children. Parents, brothers, sisters, cousins, and in-laws followed.[4] Besides the Ebeys, other extended families came to Whidbey. The Crocketts, Hills, Millers, and Alexanders all brought friends, old neighbors, and in-laws to settle and to dominate the county. Settlement was never random; the census of 1860 shows that one-third of the settlers on Whidbey Island during the 1850s had been born in New York, Pennsylvania, and Virginia.[5] They arrived in a burst of settlement that continued from the late summer of 1852 to the late spring of 1853. In the fall of 1853 the white population of the county was 195. It would rise to only 294 by 1860.[6]

These people settled almost entirely on the prairie land. By the early 1850s Whidbey Island had already gained a reputation as the "garden spot of Oregon," the best agricultural land in the Pacific Northwest, or at least in what was to become Washington Territory. Even men so skeptical of farmland of the Puget Sound region as to compare it with the notoriously poor land of New England exempted Whidbey Island. For a moment the island landscape and the settlers' interests coincided. The prairies had attracted these men, and they covered the prairies with claims that followed the natural boundaries of the land. By the spring of 1853 little unclaimed prairie land remained on the island.[7]

These first settlers filed their claims under either the Donation Land Laws of Oregon and Washington or the Preemption Act. The Donation Land Law, passed by Congress in 1850 and extended explicitly to Washington after creation of that territory in 1853, granted 320 acres to each male settler over eighteen who was, or intended to become, a citizen, and who had arrived in the territory before December 1, 1850. If the settler married before December 1, 1851, his wife also was entitled to 320 acres. To perfect title the settler had to occupy and cultivate his land for four consecutive years. Settlers who arrived after December 1, 1850, but before December 1, 1854, could claim 160 acres under the same terms. Under the Preemption Act of 1841, 160 acres of surveyed land could be acquired for $1.25 an acre, and the Donation Land Law, as amended in July of 1854, extended the Preemption Act provisions to unsurveyed land.[8]

Settlers marked out their donation claims on Whidbey before the surveyors arrived (see Map 4). Isaac Ebey, coming first, simply took a square mile out of the heart of the prairie that would bear his name. But others, coming in later and thus entitled to smaller claims, or simply not having such broad prairies to carve, took their claims in triangles like W. C. Engle's, rough backward L's such as J. C. Kellog's, or even the impossible twelve-sided parcel William Wallace claimed. These claims meshed with their neighbors to form clusters in the major prairies. Since the prairies were confined largely to north central Whidbey, so were the settlements. South and north Whidbey and most of Camano remained nearly devoid of white settlers and virtually unexplored. The Donation Law contained no provision for reconciling claim boundaries with survey lines, and, as a result, the prairies never achieved the checkerboard uniformity found in most of the West.

One cluster of claims began with the Alexander and Coupe claims at Coupeville and ended with the Kellog and Seabert claims near Crocketts Lake. Another covered the west and north shores of Penn Cove, with an arm taking in the small prairie north of Point Partridge. The Freund, Sumner, and Tafteson claims were the core of a third group around Oak Harbor, and northeast of them a last group stretched back from the shores of Crescent Harbor. By 1860, settlers had claimed 15,381 acres, nearly all of them on or bordering the prairies.[9]

Within these clusters of claims the infrastructure of white settlement emerged. The prairies quickly became a collection of farms; only Coveland and Coupeville, both on Penn Cove, could even pretend to be villages. During the fall of 1853, farmers laid out a road from Coveland to Ebeys Prairie and another to R. C. Fay's claim on a smaller prairie to the north. In the summer of

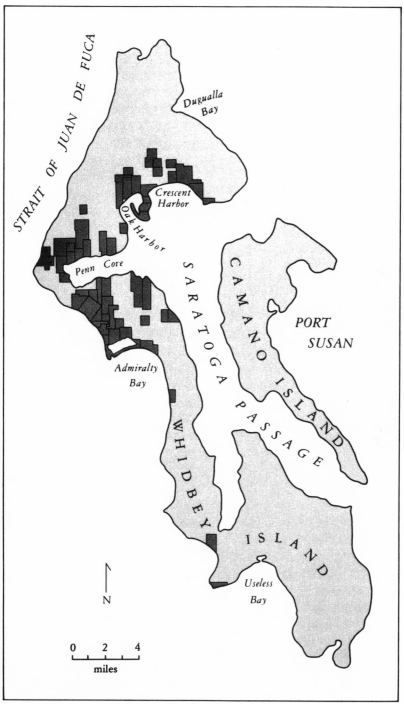

Map 4. Donation land claims

1854 they marked out a road from Ebeys Prairie to Snatelum Point east of Coupeville, the site of a Salish village. In the fall they surveyed a fourth road from Coveland to Crescent Harbor, the edge of settlement north of Penn Cove; and in the spring of 1855, they approved a road to connect Oak Harbor and Coveland. By the summer of 1855 they had connected the major clusters of settlement, at least on paper.[10]

These early roads conformed to natural boundaries, yet their impact on natural systems was considerable. Road builders avoided hills and swamps, and, on at least one occasion, they used burned-over land to make a route through the forest. Although the roads were serviceable enough in summer, winter rains turned them into quagmires. But no matter how primitive these tracks were, they became avenues for invading plants by stripping away native vegetation and thus brought changes in the natural landscape. Builders opened the forest and created new microclimates on the forest floor that would change the distribution of plant species. Immediately the total impact was slight; the prairies remained small islands in a sea of forest. But, at least potentially, these roads provided an opportunity for the spread of floral invaders from one cluster of settlement to another. Plants as well as wagons could move along these ribbons of disturbed land from one group of cleared fields to the next.[11]

In 1860, a decade after the arrival of the white farmer, census takers found seventy-four farms clustered on the prairie. They missed perhaps half a dozen others. The two major prairie townships with their hearts in Ebeys Prairie and the prairies north of Penn Cove and Oak Harbor held fifty-four of these farms. In neither township had farmers subdued much of the land. The census reported 781 improved acres (13.5 percent of the total land within farm boundaries) in San de Fuca (T 32N, R1E) and 716 acres (13.9 percent of the total farmland) in Ebeys Prairie (T 31N, R1E). Farmers did not cultivate all improved land; permanent pasture was listed as improved.[12]

The tools that these settlers used to make their roads, farms, and villages were not impressive. But as the Salish had shown, far-reaching effects can be obtained from relatively unsophisticated technology. When Isaac Ebey's estate was inventoried after his murder by Canadian Indians, his farming equipment consisted of a set of double harnesses, a breaking plow, a cast iron plow, a harrow, four hoes, two picks, two shovels, and two scythes, the whole valued at $79. These tools, along with the axe, the maul, and the adze, were the instruments with which white men sought to conquer the land.[13]

Except for the plow, the tools the American farmers brought to the land did not differ drastically from those of the Salish. At the time of white settlement, the two peoples differed not so much in technology as perception. Americans reduced the complex view of the Indians to a few simple categories. The new farmers saw most native plants as simply "weeds" or "brush." Land that grew these plants was, in the words of the census, "unimproved." Land on which native plants had been eliminated and replaced by domestic plants was "improved." For all practical purposes most native plants vanished from the everyday landscape of the new settlers, disappearing into the undifferentiated flora of the prairies. The intimate and detailed knowledge of the natural world that was widespread among the Salish became a specialized realm of esoteric knowledge among the whites.[14]

The settler's perception of the natural world and his technology found symbolic expression in the fence. The utilitarian function of the worm or snake fence was obvious: It enclosed crops and kept cattle out. The fence became both an actual and a symbolic boundary line. It separated improved land from the Salish prairie, and it also marked the boundary of the farmer's conscious control. To the settler this fence seemed the natural division that the river was to the Salish. The fence reduced the prairie to human size, and within its boundaries the farmer replaced the ecosystem of the prairies with the cultivated field or the permanent pasture.[15]

The fence also marked the line between two different kinds of perception. Inside the fence the farmer observed closely; he was inquisitive and experimental. But outside the fence the farmer's perception narrowed. He took only limited interest in the undifferentiated "brush" of the prairies. He left knowledge of most native flora to specialists. One of these specialists was James Swan, ethnologist, Indian Agent, and botanist.[16] Swan's own interest in the natural world was catholic, taking in both the "useful and the useless." His descriptions of the prairies are unique in their specificity.

The ground over which we walked was a perfect carpet of flowers. Conspicuous among these were the beautiful rhododendron with its rich cluster of blossoms, the blue flowers of the camonass, the bright red of the bartsia and columbine. The white blossom of the fragrant seringa, the variegated lupine, the purple of wild peas and iris intermaking a floral display equal to any I ever witnessed in California and one that would delight the heart of every true lover of nature [sic].[17]

The farmers recognized the beauty of these prairies, but beauty was expendable. They sought utility. When Swan sought uses for native plants, farmers could appreciate his concerns. They were sympathetic when Swan attempted to promote the nettle as a plant that could be domesticated and made into a source of fiber, or when he reported to the Smithsonian on the attempts of a farmer in Whatcom County to domesticate native grasses.[18] In Island County farmers took a similar if limited interest in wild plants that might find a market. A brisk trade in wild cranberries (*Vaccinium oxycoccus* L., var. *ovalifolium* Smith) developed, so brisk that attempts were made to domesticate and cultivate them. And Rebecca Ebey did begin to domesticate the wild gooseberry (*Ribes* L.) by the simple expedient of uprooting a young bush and replanting it within the confines of her garden. But of the hundreds of plants known by the Salish, relatively few, besides trees, had economic value for the whites. Cattle grazed wild grasses and farmers cut them for hay; settlers picked several kinds of berries, and pigs ate the camas. The remaining native flora, outside the forest, was useless—mere brush and weeds—and Swan's curiosity about these plants remained foreign to most American settlers.[19]

The farmer treated the world outside the fence differently from the world within, and different treatment yielded different results. Plowing was the first, and most significant, alteration that the farmer made in the land within the fence. But when in March, before the first flowers bloomed, the farmer's plow bit into the prairie, the dense root network of the bracken fern often snagged and stopped it. As Walter Crockett wrote, bracken made the land "quite hard to get into cultivation." It was quickly learned that only heavy breaking plows drawn by four or five yoke of oxen could cut through these roots. Oxen, however, because they were essential not only for land breaking but also for logging, were in much demand; they were expensive and hard to obtain. In 1852 the Crocketts offered oxen for sale at $150 a yoke. A year later Isaac Ebey wrote that oxen cost $300 a yoke, and the same year Nathaniel Hill had to go all the way to Olympia to buy a yoke for $205. If a man could not afford to buy oxen at these prices, he might hire them. Isaac Ebey estimated in 1853 that men with oxen and breaking plows could contract to break 1,000 acres of Whidbey prairie that spring and summer at from $10 to $15 an acre. But the hired teams never appeared, and little land was broken.[20]

Bracken roots made plowing the prairies slow and laborious, but even worse, plowing did not kill the roots. When split and turned under by the plow, the rhizomes promptly sprouted. Crockett guessed in 1853 that it would take four or five years of cultivation to eliminate the fern, but thought that it would not damage the crops. Even in the late 1850s Winfield Scott Ebey complained of bracken in his father's wheat and potatoes, and this was on land that had been under cultivation since 1852 or 1853. Throughout the century bracken would remain in fields planted to timothy, and its presence in hay reduced the value of the crop.[21]

Plowing was necessary for farming, but it had consequences the farmer never intended. When settlers turned under acres of bracken and grass, they were destroying the native cover of the prairies. Evaporation rates then increased and water needed during the dry summer months was lost. Repeated plowing broke down the granular texture of the virgin soils that enabled them to retain water, thus reducing the water-holding capacity of the soil still further. The results of this process varied from one soil type to another. The soils of Ebeys Prairie continued to produce well year after year, but the Townsend Loam soils of north Penn Cove, which initially produced quite well, suffered a cumulative degradation during the nineteenth century. (See Table 19.) The amount of water retained by these soils declined until most crops grown on them suffered from lack of moisture. From being the most productive soils in the county, they deteriorated until by the twentieth century they could only be used for pasture.[22]

The effects of new environmental conditions upon the imported plants were as hard to predict as the eventual consequences of plowing on prairie soils. Every movement of farming peoples into new areas changed the rules of farming because physical conditions changed. Not all the plants farmers brought with them flourished. In each new region farmers began afresh, and they had to discover from experience the limits of the new land and climate. So it was on Whidbey Island.

During the first decade of settlement farmers tried, and failed, to produce plants that ranged from such semi-tropical species as the eggplant and tomato to the pioneer staple, corn. A letter Nathaniel Hill wrote home on his way to Whidbey Island in 1852 requesting, among other things, tomato, gumbo, melon, sweet potato, and eggplant seeds, shows the deficient understanding some early farmers originally had of the climatic conditions of western Washington. The cool summers and long, wet winters of the region doomed any plant requiring either a long, hot growing season or warm summer nights.[23]

Once climate had winnowed potential food crops and those suitable to the conditions of western Washington had been selected, farmers seem to have shown no particular attachment to the crops they had grown in other places at other times. In Island County there was no strong correlation between the farmer's place of birth and the crops he grew. Farmers from the middle Atlantic states and Virginia, the leading grain producers of the period, did tend to raise more grain than other Island County farmers, but farmers from New York and Pennsylvania, the leading potato producing regions of the 1850s, actually tended to raise fewer potatoes than county farmers in general. Even in wheat and potato production, the relationship was a modest one and can obviously be the result of many causes outside of place of birth, especially since many of these men had moved several times.[24] (See Table 20.)

Once the farmers had discovered the limitations of climate, markets largely determined what they produced. In the 1850s villages, logging camps, crews of ships, and the military provided a ready market for nearly any crop the farmer chose to raise. High prices were paid for grain, potatoes, and hay throughout the decade. Flour sold as high as $20 per 100-lb. barrel on Whidbey in 1853 and $16 a barrel in Olympia in 1858. In the 1850s markets left farmers free to grow almost any crop climatically suited to the region.[25] On Whidbey Island they concentrated on three staple crops: potatoes, oats, and wheat. In their uneven experience with these crops lies an illustration of some of the complexities of crop selection on an agricultural frontier.

The Salish had grown potatoes on Whidbey Island since 1840, and the Indians and the British supplied American settlers with their first seed potatoes. These potatoes were tasty, but very small, and almost immediately the settlers began to import larger strains from California. Potatoes became the most widely grown crop on the island. In 1860, 50 percent of the farmers planted them and produced crops ranging from 20 to 4,000 bushels, with 70 percent of the farms producing from 20 to 500 bushels. In a sense, the potato supported early white settlement in much the same manner corn did elsewhere. Already adapted to the climate and soil of the county, small acreages produced large yields. With either wild meat or salmon as a source of protein, it formed the bulk of the settlers' diet, one almost identical to the staples of the Salish.[26]

The American settlers themselves introduced oats to the prairies, and the plant seems to have adapted to the environment as quickly and easily as the potato. In the 1850s neither farmers nor newspapers mentioned any particular problems with the crop. In terms of bushels produced, oats were the second largest crop in the county in 1860, and in terms of acres planted, they probably ranked first.[27]

Of the triumvirate of staple crops, only wheat failed to adapt to the prairies. On Whidbey during the 1850s, farmers constantly expected bumper crops of wheat, and they were just as constantly disappointed. Isaac Ebey called the first wheat crop sown in the spring of 1853 the most promising crop he had seen in the Oregon country. When harvested, however, yields proved uneven: Walter Crockett obtained twenty bushels to the acre, but Nathaniel Hill, less than a mile away, had a total crop failure.[28] For the rest of the decade consistent wheat yields proved unattainable. Indian war and blights (probably smut) accounted for some of the difficulties, but even in years with no social, economic, or ecological upheavels harvests were disappointing. By 1860 only 16 percent of the farmers in the county produced 200 bushels or more of wheat, and 60 percent of the farmers in the county produced no wheat at all.[29]

Why wheat was not successfully raised is unclear. The climate was suitable; farmers on Whidbey Island would later claim world record yields. There was an ample market for wheat at high prices. Failure probably stemmed from a combination of factors: lack of rain following late spring planting, competition from bracken, lack of a suitable wheat strain, and contamination of at least part of their seed wheat with smut. Furthermore, the botanist for the Railroad Expedition who visited the islands in the mid-1850s attributed difficulty with the crop to an excessively fertile soil that caused the wheat to grow rankly and subsequently lodge, or fall over. But no matter what its cause, the failure of wheat to adapt to an environment apparently well suited to it demonstrates the sometimes mystifyingly thin line that separated the success or failure of a new crop in a new land.[30]

The inability of some desirable crops to adapt was one side of the farmer's problems with ecological imports; the other side was his almost total inability to prevent the entry of unwanted invaders. Weeds are an inevitable result of any human attempt to restrict large areas of land to a single plant. But what is often ignored is that many common weeds are not native plants, but, like the farmers and the crops they cultivate, invaders from Europe. Current ecological opinion holds that most European weeds are plants that have developed a close association with man. They are adapted to open land and, without the intervention of men, open land rarely occurs in nature. Floods and fires are the only other forces that produce it.[31]

By plowing the prairies and by cutting roads, man opened the way for invasion by these weeds. In New Zealand, H. Guthrie-Smith could watch the annual movement of the invaders along the roads from ports where they had arrived.[32] There was no Guthrie-Smith to chronicle the invasion of Whidbey, but settlers in the 1850s noticed that invaders appeared largely in fields and along the roads. The fields, where a single species maintained by human labor had replaced a complex natural community, became an especially easy target for invaders.

The introduction of weeds into a new area was usually accidental. Seeds adhered to men or their vehicles; the seeds of weeds were mixed with crop seeds or dispersed among packing materials or the ballast of ships. In 1865 Granville Haller, who owned a farm near Oak Harbor, examined 391 lbs. of seed wheat. He estimated it to be one-third wastage, "barley, oats, buckwheat, and peas besides an abundance of cheet and smut."[33] By 1855 many common European, North American, and South American weeds had established themselves on the islands. European foxtails (*Alopecurus carolinianus* Walt. and *Hordeum* L.) and shepherd's purse (*Capsella bursa-pastoris* (L.)) moved in on roadsides and spread to other open lands: abandoned gardens, fields, and overgrazed prairies. The sow thistle (*Sonchus oleraceus* L.), a competitor with food plants in cultivated fields and gardens, was already a troublesome weed at the time of the Railroad Survey in 1853–54, and American black nightshade (*Solanum nodiflorum* Jacq.), now an ubiquitous weed in the Puget Sound region, was at home in cultivated ground. Another invader, knotweed or willowweed (*Polygonum lapathifolium* L.), was also a garden weed, but it did not adapt as well as its companions. Dock or sorrel (*Rumex acetosella* L. or *Rumex crispus* L.) had appeared in cultivated sections of the prairies, and it had the capability of spreading outward along roads onto relatively undisturbed lands where it eliminated other, more valuable species. All of these were troublesome and harmful, but Canadian thistle became by far the most damaging.[34]

Canadian thistle (*Cirsium arvense* (L.) Scop.) apparently reached Whidbey Island in the spring of 1856, probably mixed with crop seed. When settlers discovered and identified the plants, they undertook an immediate campaign of eradication. The Davises of Ebeys Prairie apparently had the heaviest infestation, and they took the lead in trying to destroy the thistles. By the spring of 1857 it looked as though they had been successful. However, before the plant had been recognized, a farmer named Stewart had taken a single stock of it and cultivated it for its flower. He let the plant go to seed, and that fall or winter he abandoned his claim and his garden. By June when W. S. Ebey visited the claim, he found that the garden was "litterly [sic] covered with it (thistles)," and the seeds had already ripened. Ebey cut the stalks and burned the garden, but it was too late; the plant was securely established.[35] Undoubtedly later additions to the thistle population were made, but from the beginning the plant became one of the most harmful weeds on the island. Spreading both by seed and by its underground root network, it damaged both cultivated and pasture land. The failure of the settlers to control the thistle held a warning of how, once begun, ecological change could prove irreversible.

On the prairies, outside the fences, the ecological impact of settlement was the result not of plowing and planting, but of rooting, browsing, and grazing by domestic animals—especially pigs, cattle, and sheep. John Alexander imported the first bargeload of domestic animals to Whidbey Island in 1852. The arrival of cattle helped spark the eruption of worm fences that soon covered the prairies, but cattle ruined unfenced Clallam potato fields. As the importation of exotic animals progressed and cattle and hogs destroyed more and more Salish food plants, the coexistence of the Salish and white systems of land use became increasingly difficult. Only the rapid decline of Salish population prevented a direct clash.[36]

Domestic animals, especially hogs, multiplied rapidly. Camas, in the words of Rebecca Ebey, "excellent both for Indians and hogs," provided abundant food for the pigs that the settlers released to forage on the prairies. Initially, in the early 1850s, wolves (*Canis lupus*) preyed upon these pigs. Nathaniel Hill noted that of the twenty-five pigs his sows had borne, all but six were dead. When B. P. Barstow died, his estate contained eight pigs; the wolves quickly ate half of them.[37]

The total amount of damage wolves did to livestock in the county is hard to assess. The settlers blamed all stock losses on the wolves, probably even the damage done by their own and Indian dogs. The settlers' hatred of the wolf was automatic, almost instinctive. Here, as elsewhere, the wolf had to be destroyed to make the county safe for cattle, sheep, and swine. Hunting them down was too slow, and settlers resorted to shooting deer, lacing their carcasses with strychnine, and leaving them for the wolves. The county government encouraged extermination by paying a $3 bounty after 1855. The wolves that howled near W. S. Ebey's cabin in 1856 had, by the end of the decade, been destroyed or driven from the county.[38]

Just as it is hard to estimate the amount of livestock killed by the wolves, so it is hard to gauge the part they played in keeping the pigs in check. But it is clear that the pig population rose as the number of wolves declined. These pigs ate inordinate amounts of camas, and that plant, still abundant in the early 1850s, was soon so reduced that it ceased to be a major Indian food on the islands.[39] Nor did hogs confine their feeding to wild plants. The pigs squirmed through or pushed under worm fences into fields, where they rooted potatoes and trampled grain. They were blamed for the destruction of two-thirds of the Ebeys' oats in 1857 and the whole of Captain Coupe's oat crop in 1859.

To protect their crops, farmers began shooting the hogs when they found them in their fields. On occasion they did not even bother to use the meat. By 1859, W. S. Ebey was so desperate he abandoned the worm fence and built an expensive plank fence. When it failed to hold out the hogs, Ebey went back to the gun. By July his neighbors, the Hills, complained that he had killed eighty of their hogs. They sued him for damages and won $15 plus court costs, but Ebey noted in his diary that it was still less expensive to lose a suit than to have his whole crop destroyed by pigs.[40]

The pigs adapted to the island at least as well and as quickly as the whites who brought them. They became something of an ecological Frankenstein. To preserve the pig, the wolf had been killed, but farmers eventually sought to exterminate wild pigs. They drove the animals into the forests, but here they survived and farmers continued to hunt them until the end of the century.

Cattle, unlike pigs, remained a marketable commodity and an economic asset, but otherwise the treatment of the two animals was similar. The first animals brought to Whidbey Island consisted of a mixture of Spanish and American stock. Americans turned cattle loose, as they did pigs, and they too became feral. Only some oxen and milk cows were pastured inside fenced fields. The settlers hunted down the wild cattle as they needed them and sold the beef to the shipowners, merchants, lumber camps, and the military who provided a steady market by the late 1850s.[41]

Prairies, marshes, and tide flats supplied abundant feed for cattle. The prairies had Junegrass (*Koeleria cristata* Pers.), bromegrass (*Bromus carinatus* var. *martimis* (Piper) Hitchc.), ryegrass (*Elymus mollis* Trin.), reedgrass (*Calamagrostis inexpansa* Gray), and clover (*Trifolium microcephalum* Pursh). In addition, the tide flats and marshes produced sedges (*Carex lyngbyei* Hornem., *Carex stichensis* Prescott, *Carex macrocephala* Willd.), hair grass (*Deschampsia elongata* (Hook.)), and the much less valuable salt grass (*Distichlis spicata* (L.)). But there was also a native foxtail (*Hordeum jubatum*) that was harmful to livestock, and this was soon supplemented by several introduced foxtails (*Alpecurus cardinianus* Walt. and probably *Hordeum geniculatum* All., *Hordeum leporinum* Link, and *Hordeum murinum* L.). The omnipresent bracken could be a deadly feed: In the last stage of growth it could be cumulatively poisonous to livestock.[42] This relative abundance of food on the prairies, marshes, and tide flats, and the relative scarcity of food in the forests pushed cattle, like men, onto the open land.

By the mid-1860s, the cattle range had expanded from Crescent Harbor in the north to Useless Bay in the south, well beyond the boundaries of white settlement. During the 1850s settlers claimed some prairie land, not for farming but for grazing. W. S. Ebey, for example, claimed Waterloo Marsh because of its excellent grass. And when a decision in a surveying dispute threatened to deprive William Robertson of his fifteen acres of prairie land, he was angered over the loss of grazing land, not over the loss of potential farming land.[43]

Farmers made few attempts in the 1850s to supplement the feed these wild grasslands provided. They harvested little hay. Not one quarter of the farmers cut hay in 1860; indeed, four farmers provided the bulk of hay cut in the county. Furthermore, little clearing of forest lands took place; only I. B. Powers is mentioned as attempting to clear forest to open up grazing land.[44]

American farmers did eliminate part of the native fauna that relied on the grasslands for feed. Elk and deer were the primary herbivores of the islands, although neither relied exclusively on the prairies for food. At the time of white settlement the number of elk on the islands was already dwindling. Their decline had begun with the introduction of the gun among the Salish, but white hunters completed the destruction of the animal in the 1850s. They hunted elk for food, and direct competition between cattle and elk for feeding areas probably had little to do with the elimination of the animal on the islands.[45]

The introduction of cattle and the elimination of elk represented more than simple replacement of one large herbivore with another. Elk and deer were primarily browsing animals, while cattle and sheep were primarily grazing animals. The substitution of cattle for elk meant that different prairie plants were eaten. Furthermore, since the number of cattle soon far exceeded the number of elk they had replaced, the amount of vegetation eaten also increased. Further ecological changes inevitably followed.

The native grasses of Whidbey upon which cattle relied for feed were tall grasses. During the 1850s heavy grazing weakened these grasses and more recumbent grasses, or plants that cattle would not willingly eat, replaced them. Gradually, as the native flora declined, such exotic plants as Canadian thistle (*Cirsium arvense* (L.) Scop.), shepherd's purse, mint (*Mentha canadensis* L.), and foxtails began to appear. Of these, the foxtails gave the most trouble. The bristles could damage the mouth and nose of cattle and might cause abscesses in the stomach. South of the county, on Hudson's Bay Company grazing lands near Fort Nisqually, overgrazing had already seriously damaged the prairies. Dock or sorrel, introduced in the 1830s, had taken over much of the Nisqually prairies and *Festuca megalura* Nutt., an annual fescue that is almost always a sign of overgrazing, also appeared. Together these invasions had rendered the land nearly worthless for livestock.[46] During the 1850s both plants appeared on the prairies of Whidbey.

By 1860 the census reported 1,158 head of cattle on Whidbey Island, along with 3,409 hogs and a few sheep. These animals constituted a substantial addition to the animal population of the islands, and by the 1860s it appeared that the natural vegetation of the island could no longer sustain them. In 1863 W. S. Ebey sold off his cattle, complaining that they were scrawny and underfed, and that the range was too poor to maintain them.[47]

With native vegetation unable to support the number of domestic animals that relied upon it, farmers began to depend on domesticated plants to feed their cattle. As early as the 1850s the Crocketts and others had begun to replace native grasses with timothy, and these efforts increased in the 1860s. Furthermore, by 1860 the major livestock raisers had become major oat growers, feeding much of their crop to their animals. Even W. S. Ebey's diary occasionally mentioned fattened hogs and steers and some feeding in severe weather.[48]

Not all native fauna melted away with white settlement. Americans destroyed the wolf and elk, but deer survived and might actually have increased in numbers. An animal of secondary growth rather than open or forested land, the ecological changes brought by white settlers bothered it little, and the destruction of the wolf eliminated its major predator. The farmers became the new predator of deer on the islands, but they were not nearly as effective as wolves. Marksmanship was not a necessary qualification for frontier farming. By later accounts venison was the meat most often on settlers' tables, but much of it must have been obtained from market hunters or Indians. A brief notation in Nathaniel Hill's diary sums up the woodsmanship of many farmers, "shot at a dear and missed as usual."[49] Not even the market hunters and the remaining Indian hunters could seriously deplete the deer population. A. J. Deming supposedly paid for a yoke of oxen with the proceeds of his deer hunting, and with oxen selling at $200 a yoke and venison at a few cents a pound, this would have represented a substantial kill. Yet deer still thrived. They rivaled the wild hogs in destroying or damaging crops and young orchards.[50]

Hunting and fishing imposed distinctive patterns on the island. People would later recall that the island was divided by diet: The west lived on venison, pork, and potatoes; the east on salmon, pork, and potatoes. The meager contemporary evidence available gives this some support. The Hill and Ebey diaries on west Whidbey mentioned venison frequently, for example, but only rarely mentioned salmon and then it was apparently dried or salted. Later diaries from Coupeville, only a few miles to the east, mentioned salmon as something of a staple. The wildness Walter Crockett was determined to drive out still dominated his dinner table.[51]

Indeed, the net impact of the whites during the first decade of settlement was not what Walter Crockett had envisioned. Driving wild nature from the land was not the simple process he had imagined. The farmer had set in motion a series of changes whose consequences he only vaguely glimpsed. His desire to produce wheat, beef, and pork clashed fundamentally, if not dramatically, with what has been called the evolutionary goal of the biosphere for "maximum production . . . (the) maximum support of complex biomass structure."[52] Man wanted what was immediately usable; the natural world struggled to maintain a protective variety. In this struggle settlers observed signs of the changes they had set in motion, but the relationship between their actions and these changes was not always clear to them.

The farmer found he could not do whatever he wished with the land, and sometimes he saw his successes undermine his own prosperity. The failure of some exotic plants to adapt quickly, as in the case of wheat, and the too successful adaptation of other imports, such as the pig, both proved detrimental to the farmer's hopes. Some soils deteriorated, others remained fertile; some crops grew luxuriantly, others failed to grow at all, and noxious weeds took over productive lands. Even Walter Crockett's faith in the omnipotence of the plow and the gun must have waned sometimes.

New land settlement in Island County, and probably elsewhere, represented neither the righteous and fruitful use of bountiful nature that settlers would have liked to remember later, nor the rape of a continent it is sometimes now represented to be. These people often thought of themselves as creators; their perception of the land as "improved" or "unimproved," the garden and the wilderness, all made them see only progress flowing from their actions. When obviously undesirable, but also undramatic, changes took place, it was often hard for farmers to connect these changes with their actions. The farmer, for all his desire for change, never fully realized how central he was to the changes, both beneficial and harmful, that were taking place all around him. The dominant invader in a massive ecological invasion, the farmer was at once a commander, a beneficiary, and a victim of the natural world he, in the best of conscience, sought to exploit.

Chapter III

A SEARCH FOR STABILITY:

The Social and Environmental Consequences of Market Agriculture, 1860–1900

Historians have generally viewed new land settlement in the United States as a social movement of vast scale and a political movement of immense significance. But this human migration onto the land had a complexity that extends beyond the land system, the economic system, the social structure, and the political forms that accompanied it and developed within it. It also embraced a massive invasion of new flora and fauna. The relationship of the social, political, and ecological aspects of this and other migrations has received little attention. F. Fraser Darling's complaint about the neglect of these factors in understanding the Scottish Highlands deserves a wider application.

> An assessment of the state of these five and one-half million acres cannot disregard history, which is, in fact, natural history, where a man is one of the animal species, behaving positively or negatively, bringing about consequences which he did not imagine at the time and tends not to recognize now. This natural history of causes and consequences of organisms in relation to their environment is quite different from the political history of the problem . . . although the two are coeval and to some extent interdependent. The social history . . . is the third horse in the chariot, influenced in character by the other two and exerting its own effects on them. . . .
>
> . . . the extremely practical and significant natural history of the Highlands has not been written, nor scarcely considered in relation to its fellow steeds and the state of the chariot which is governed by all three.[1]

In Island County, too, the social and political history of the islands is intertwined with the natural history of the land. The terrain of the islands, with its combination of infertile forest land and unusually rich prairie land, shaped the pattern of early settlement. The first settlers correctly recognized the prairies as excellent farmland, and they quickly laid claim to them. This land, acquired free or for a $1.25 an acre, would sell for nearly $100 an acre in the 1880s, and some farms would be valued at $25,000 or $30,000.[2]

This increase in value often benefited the original claimants or their descendants. Island County became known as a place of old settlers and longtime residents. Of the fifty-two donation claims finally patented in Island County, the original owners still held thirty-seven of them in 1860. Of the seventy-four farms listed in the 1860 census, most of which had been filed on in the early 1850s, 50 percent remained in the hands of the original claimants in 1879. In 1880, almost thirty years after first settlement, the original owners or their descendants still owned 30 percent of the farms claimed in the 1850s. This stability varied little between native and foreign-born farmers. Of the fifty-four American-born farm owners of 1860, twenty-six were still present in 1870, and of the seventeen foreign-born farmers present in 1860, nine were still farming in the county in 1870.[3]

The tendency of original families to remain in the county seems to be most directly related to the fertility of the land they settled. According to the U.S. Soil Survey maps, nine original settlers on Ebeys Prairie occupied the Coupeville Loam series, the most fertile land on the island. Nine more occupied the fertile, but excessively drained, Townsend Loam soils north of Penn Cove near San de Fuca. Eight of the nine original families were still present on Ebeys Prairie in 1870, and six of the nine original families near San de Fuca are recorded in the 1870 census.[4]

Because the first settlers had claimed nearly all the prairie land by 1860, later settlers had only limited access to the best and most easily cultivated land. The newcomers either had to buy land from the original settlers, claim marsh land, tideland, or forest land, or else rent or sharecrop. Between 1870 and 1880 farmers apparently began to move in some numbers onto inferior farmlands. In 1870, for example, only two farms out of ninety-four reported crops valued under $100, but in 1880 twenty farms out of the 117 visited by census takers reported a production under $100. It is likely that these farms were located on woodlands adjoining the prairies, but the evidence here is not conclusive. In the prairie townships of San de Fuca and Ebeys Prairie and in the prairies adjoining Oak Harbor and Crescent Harbor, the number of farms had increased substantially (see Table 1). This probably resulted from the subdivision of existing farms and the creation of new farms in wooded areas. Outside the large prairie townships the increase in the number of farms was small.[5]

TABLE 1. INCREASE IN FARMS ON PRAIRIE TOWNSHIPS,
ISLAND COUNTY

Township	1870	1880	Net Increase/Decrease
31N, R1E (Ebeys Prairie)	22	35	13
32N, R1E (San de Fuca)	32	27	−5
33N, R2E (Crescent Harbor)	8	13	5
Others	33	42	9

SOURCE: Manuscript Census, Agriculture, 1870, 1880.

Settlers on the forest lands, marshland, and tidelands that made up most of the county faced formidable difficulties. On the forest lands a settler had to clear the ground of the big trees and grub out the stumps before cultivation was possible. The labor involved in removing fir and cedar was immense. In the twentieth century, with dynamite, the removal of the stumps alone took a man with a horse 400 hours of labor per acre. With prices for farm products low and labor expensive, there was relatively little incentive to bring these lands into production. The Immigration Aid Society of Northwestern Washington wrote in 1880 that the forested uplands of Island County would "no doubt . . . be largely utilized in the future, but they are at present regarded as practically worthless except for their timber." The land of the freshwater marshes of the prairies was more promising, but again much physical labor was required to drain them. Farmers used most marshland only for grazing until the 1880s, when they began to undertake limited reclamation.[6]

Tidelands in Island County remained virtually unexploited for most of the nineteenth century. Of the 4,000 acres of tide marsh, land covered by the tide at its highest stages, farmers had only successfully diked and drained 485 acres by 1885. Diking proved to be expensive and uncertain. In the mid-1880s Granville Haller began to dike a slough at Meadowside, his farm near Oak Harbor. A year-long effort yielded only a gravelly basin covered with driftwood and still usually inundated by high tides. Other farmers who did dike their land successfully often found that the winter rains did not fully leach the salt from the soil and that the potatoes grown on this land had a tendency to scab.[7]

Rather than face the difficulties presented by forest lands, marshlands, and tidelands, many farmers who arrived in the county during the 1870s chose to rent or sharecrop improved land. Tenants ran 22 percent of the farms in Island County in 1880. These farms were predominantly located on the fertile prairie townships of Ebeys Prairie and San de Fuca. Although these two townships had only 54 percent of the farms in the county in 1880, they had 71 percent of the sharecroppers and 89 percent of the renters. Renters and sharecroppers worked over one-third of the farms on Ebeys Prairie and almost one-third of the farms in the townships around San de Fuca in 1880. Almost one-third of the farmers who migrated into the county during the 1870s and remained until 1880 rented or sharecropped fertile lands instead of acquiring marginal lands outside the prairies. The decision of so many settlers to sharecrop or rent despite an abundance of free land in the county was eminently rational. The landscape of the islands steered them toward the prairies just as it had the first settlers. That only one-third of them chose tenancy on good land over ownership of poor land, however, testifies to the strength of cultural and institutional factors pushing people toward freeholding even when, as Table 2 shows, freeholds held no immediate economic advantage.[8]

Among the migrants of the 1870s, sharecroppers and renters did significantly better than farmer owners. The mean production of the farms run by sharecroppers in 1880 was $1,367, compared with a mean production of $557 for the farms of the 1870s migrants in general. Indeed, farms run by these sharecroppers were more productive than those of the farmers who had settled in the 1850s. Although the sharecropper did not keep all that he produced, it appears likely that he obtained a better living than

TABLE 2. FARMERS ARRIVING IN ISLAND COUNTY DURING THE 1870S
AND REMAINING UNTIL 1880, TENURE

1880	No.	Production in Dollars		
		0–500	500–900	1,000 or more
Owners	49	25	13	11
		51 %	26.5%	22.4%
Renters	8	1	5	2
		12.5%	62.5%	25 %
Sharecroppers	15	5	1	9
		33.3%	6.7%	60 %

SOURCE: Manuscript Census, Agriculture, Island County, 1870,
1880. Manuscript Census, Population, Island County, 1870, 1880.

the farmowners who arrived with him. The fertility of the land
proved a better guide to the productivity of a farm, and probably
the prosperity of the farmer, than did the tenure of the farm opera-
tor.[9]

That anyone chose to settle the forest lands is surprising, but
many contemporary observers remained blind to the limits of the
land. In the eyes of local boosters, the limited settlement of forest
lands resulted not from the nature of the land itself, but from the
supposed control of such land by speculators. Port Townsend
newspapers attacked speculators who, they asserted, held good
farmland off the market, waiting for higher prices. Their greed
caused the economic stagnation of the county. In the relatively
brief period between 1869 and 1872, speculators had obtained
large holdings in Island County. During 1869, rumors that the
Northern Pacific Railroad would locate its western terminus at
Coupeville on Penn Cove gained credibility from the purchase of
nearly 20,000 acres in Island County by John Sprague, head of the
western division of the Northern Pacific. Sprague's purchases
equaled the total amount of land entered in the county up to that
time. Almost immediately other speculators appeared. Between
1869 and 1873, when the Northern Pacific finally located its terminus in Tacoma, speculators purchased 58,600 acres of land on
Whidbey and Camano from the government. Eventually much of

this land, 38,151 acres in 1883–84 alone, would revert to the county for nonpayment of taxes. Although owners eventually redeemed 14,591 acres of the 1883–84 tax reversions, on most of this land taxes remained unpaid.[10]

Critics rightly observed that state law offered little incentive for farmers to buy and improve the land taken by the county for taxes. Laws that, on the surface, seemed designed to protect struggling freeholders unable to meet tax payments actually protected speculators against the settler. The potential settler could buy tax land at auction, often for virtually nothing, but he received only a certificate of sale (in effect a lien on the land), not a deed. At the end of three years he could pay the back taxes and get a valid deed. But, at any time during these three years, the original owner could reclaim the land from the purchaser by paying him the amount of taxes owed plus interest at 20 percent per year. In its 1885–86 session, the legislature strengthened the rights of delinquent taxpayers by requiring the owner of tax certificates to locate, if possible, and notify the original owner of the impending loss of his land at least sixty days before the expiration of the three-year waiting period. Thus, for three years after purchase of a tax certificate, any settler who acquired land at a tax sale and attempted to farm it faced the possibility of losing his improvements to the original owner of the land—without compensation. Few farmers chose to take the risk.[11]

Extensive speculation in land in Island County did not end until the late 1890s, but it is doubtful that speculation seriously retarded the settlement of forest lands. The apparent failure of the farmers who did push into the forest lands in the 1870s indicated the difficulty of farming this land in the late nineteenth century. Furthermore, if the land was actually as fertile as boosters sometimes claimed, then it seems unlikely that speculators would have abandoned such vast amounts of it.

The new farmers who did migrate to the county between 1860 and 1880 were far less stable and far less prosperous than the first settlers. Of the fifty-eight farmowners who arrived in the 1860s and appeared in the 1870 census, only 36 percent of them or their descendants still farmed in the county in 1880. (For comparison, 50 percent of the farmers who appeared in the 1860 census had remained until 1870.) By 1870 the average value of the farms of

TABLE 3. AMOUNT OF LAND HELD BY SETTLERS AND THE PRODUCTIVITY OF THEIR FARMS BY THE DECADE OF THEIR ARRIVAL IN ISLAND COUNTY, 1880

Settled in	No.	Acreage			Value ($)	Total Prod. ($)	
		Improved	Woodland	Unimproved			
1850s	22	3,259	2,479	2,053	105,500	22,290	Total
		99.25	87.50	67.50	4,500	1,043	Median
1860s	21	2,457	2,173	1,405	69,600	15,400	Total
		107.75	96.75	12.30	2,830	675	Median
1870s	73	8,780	5,251	3,020	170,100	54,510	Total
		81.25	85.50	3.38	1,550	557	Median

SOURCE: Manuscript Census, Island County, Agriculture, 1880.

the original settlers was twice that of the settlers of the 1860s, and in 1880 the farms of the people who settled in the 1850s remained the most valuable in the county (see Table 3).[12]

In Island County, after 1860 most settlers were market farmers. The twenty farms that produced less than $100 worth of crops in 1880 were, for all practical purposes, subsistence farms, but these farms were definitely a minority. For most farmers in the county, the price they would receive for their crops (see Table 4) was as important as the condition of the crops themselves. The agricultural market influenced what they grew, how much they grew, and how they grew it.

TABLE 4. AGRICULTURAL EXPANSION IN ISLAND COUNTY, 1860–1900

	1860	1870	1880	1890	1900
No. of Farms	74	94	117	93	254
Acreage in Farms	15,251	22,555	32,413	22,248	30,705
Improved Acreage	2,057	7,275	14,615	9,112	9,368
Farm Products in Dollars	8,490	79,318	94,951	150,110	197,044*

*Not fed to livestock. Compiled from U.S. Census.

SOURCE: Manuscript Census, Agriculture, 1860; Ninth Census, Agriculture, 3:274–75; Tenth Census, Agriculture, 3:138; Eleventh Census, Agriculture, 5:233, Twelfth Census, Agriculture, 5, pt. 1:304.

The gradual expansion of the scale and productivity of agriculture in Island County was part of a far larger expansion in the United States as a whole between 1860 and 1900. During these years the number of farms in the United States increased from 2 million in 1860 to 5.7 million in 1900. Revolutions in technology gave the farmer new reapers, the binder, and improved plows, and allowed him to plant and harvest more acres with less labor than ever before. The spread of the railroads connected the farmers with new markets and brought farms hundreds and even thousands of miles away into direct competition.

By the 1860s, competition from California was having an impact on the farmers of Whidbey Island. The ships of the mill companies, rather than return empty from California, began to carry cargoes of California vegetables and grain back to Washington at low freight rates. As California produce appeared in the lumber camps, mill towns, and cities that formed the local market, Washington farmers could not compete. By the 1870s, Eason Ebey wrote to relatives that "I could not conscientiously advise you and Mr. Enos to come here to stay unless you have means enough to live entirely without depending on the farm for a living." To meet competition, first from California and later from eastern Washington, Island County farmers had to change both their methods of farming and the kinds of crops and animals they produced. Each change in farming was reflected in changes in the prairie landscape. For most of the nineteenth century the agricultural market was an element of major importance in shaping social and ecological change in Island County.[13] There were three discernible shifts in farming in Island County during the nineteenth century. The first involved sheep raising, the second a shift back to the production of grain and potatoes, and the third was spread of intensive farming by Chinese tenants.

Sheep raising increased in general throughout western Washington and Oregon during the 1860s, but in Island County it exhibited two notable features: Large prairie farmers took it up the most enthusiastically, and it persisted as an important feature of agriculture in Island County for twenty years, long after it had faded from most regions west of the Cascades (see Table 5). Es-

TABLE 5. Changes in Sheep and Crop Production
(Bushels) in Island County, 1870

Township	Date	Sheep	Wheat	Oats	Barley	Potatoes
San de Fuca	1860	27	2,820	11,090	400	14,740
(T32N, R1E)	1870	1,123	470	1,920	5,750	6,010
Ebeys Prairie	1860	46	3,120	5,260	540	5,230
(T31N, R1E)	1870	1,102	2,510	2,270	6,820	1,600
Island County	1860	73	6,390	19,167	. . .	27,260
(Total)	1870	3,099	3,271	4,856	13,069	15,043

Source: Manuscript Census, Agriculture, Island County, 1860, 1870.

tablished farmers who had settled during the 1850s adopted sheep raising on the largest scale. Eleven of the thirteen farmers who reported ownership of more than one hundred sheep in 1870 had entered the county in the 1850s. These men largely stopped raising grain and potatoes; they either put the land in pasture or raised hay.[14] Farmers on the best land with the largest acreage and most capital responded to market pressures the most quickly.

To feed their sheep, farmers planted timothy and clover extensively during the late 1860s and early 1870s. Improved land continued to increase in the county, but such land no longer produced staple crops. In the San de Fuca township, for example, the amount of improved land increased from 71 acres in 1860 to 2,953 acres in 1870, while wheat, oat, and potato production declined dramatically. By 1869 an estimate put the amount of land in timothy in the county at 1,199 acres out of 2,132 acres in cultivation. This increase in improved land made deep inroads into the vegetation of the prairie. Native plants, especially bracken, resisted, but by the late 1860s the old splendor of the prairies was gone.[15]

Timothy and clover did not remain confined to the prairies, however. By the 1870s farmers had begun planting both on forest land within farm boundaries. In the San de Fuca township the number of sheep owned by farmers in 1880 was roughly the same as in 1870, and the total amount of land in farms remained virtually unchanged (8,046 in 1870 and 8,118 in 1880). The amount of improved land, however, had increased from 2,444 to 3,679 acres, and the acreage in woodlands had dropped from 4,681 to 3,310 acres in 1880. Furthermore, the production of staple crops had increased substantially. Apparently, farmers had cleared some of the forest land for sheep pasture and planted the old sheep pasture to field crops. Farmers cleared the forest by burning, then allowing the land to go to clover (the natural succession crop on some soils) or seeding it to timothy or clover. Grazing in combination with burning kept the forest from returning, at least temporarily.[16]

During the 1880s the number of sheep in the county fell off drastically, until by 1890 there were less than half the number there had been in 1870. With the decline in the number of sheep, the amount of "improved" land in the county also decreased.

Farmers abandoned their woodland pasture. Apparently sheep had been as instrumental in "improving" land as the plow.[17]

The return of the prairies to field crops in the 1870s introduced a period of instability in crop production that would last for the next thirty years. Between 1880 and 1890 the production of all field crops in the county except hay and fruit declined. The fall in production of potatoes and barley was especially precipitous. In 1880 farmers in Island County had produced more potatoes than the farmers of any other county in the territory, but by 1890 their production was insignificant. During the 1890s farmers increased potato production once more, and they also planted over 3,000 acres to grain and produced nearly 150,000 bushels.[18]

In the 1890s, horticulture became a significant part of agriculture in the county for the first time. Farmers had planted small orchards on Whidbey since the 1850s, but lack of markets for fruit led to a long period of neglect. The growing urban population of the Puget Sound region in the late nineteenth century created new markets, and 375 acres had been planted to fruit trees by 1896.[19]

The census reflects only the shifts in production that occurred over a decade (see Table 6), but in Island County abandonment of one crop and the planting of another was almost an annual occurrence. In 1870, for example, a blight reduced the California potato crop. News reached Island County in time for a large planting and a record crop. But the boom was only temporary. When California farmers overcame the blight, potatoes rotted in the fields of Whidbey Island for lack of markets, and farmers renewed their search for a profitable crop.[20]

In part to escape the vagaries of the market and in part of secure high rents, large prairie farmers began renting their land to Chinese tenants in the late nineteenth century. Initially the Chinese in Island County had been farm laborers, not tenants. In 1880, of the Chinese men listing occupations, twenty were farm laborers, 45 percent of all farm laborers in the county. Only four rented land. By 1900, eighteen of the fifty-three Chinese in the county were tenants. Although the Chinese population of the county was never high, it was virtually all male, and by the turn of the century the Chinese constituted 28 percent of all renters and sharecroppers (see Table 7).[21]

TABLE 6. CROP PRODUCTION IN ISLAND COUNTY, 1870–1900

Census	Wheat	Oats	Potatoes	Barley	Hay	Orchard Fruits
1870	3,271	4,856	15,043	13,069	1,942	$ 5,015
1880	22,223	38,451	202,010	13,259	1,925	$ 5,535
1890	16,170	35,968	60,222	1,075	3,256	. . .
						19,834 b.
1900	41,890	106,010	115,486	1,720	4,906	$12,028
						16,215 b.

All figures in bushels (b.) except for hay, which is in tons, and apples, which are in value of orchard products for 1870 and 1880, in bushels for 1890, and in both bushels and value for 1900 because of changes in census categories. Apples composed the great bulk of orchard production. The hay figure for 1900 was derived by adding cultivated grasses and grains cut green.

SOURCE: Ninth Census, Agriculture, 3:274–75; Tenth Census, Agriculture, 3:210, 322, 323; Eleventh Census, Agriculture, 5:389, 456, 495, 535; Twelfth Census, Agriculture, 6, pt. 2: 189, 266, 396, 694–98.

These Chinese tenants intensively farmed small plots of fertile land, capitalizing on the knowledge of Whidbey Island soil types that the prairie farmers had already acquired. They were able to produce huge and profitable yields of potatoes by carefully selecting the sites best suited for early potatoes and by farming only the soils that produced the largest potato crops.[22]

White merchants and residents of the small villages of Oak Harbor and Coupeville viewed the increase in Chinese tenants with far more alarm than did county farmers. The merchants resorted to

TABLE 7. CHINESE POPULATION, ISLAND COUNTY

1870	1880	1890	1900	1910	1920
7	45	76	53	28	8

SOURCE: Twelfth Census, Population, 1:570; Fourteenth Census, Population, 3:1085.

arguments common on the Pacific Coast during the late nineteenth century: They claimed that the Chinese refused to spend their money locally, that they farmed land that would otherwise be farmed by whites, and that they so reduced the standard of living on farms that white immigrants avoided the county. In 1891, the *Island County Times* asserted that the Chinese controlled 750 acres of fertile land that produced seven tons of potatoes per acre, which sold for $10 a ton, giving the Chinese a gross income of $52,500. The Chinese spent $3,750 in the county; the rest they sent back to China or spent and invested elsewhere. These reports, almost certainly exaggerated, were initially directed against the landlords of the prairies, who preferred Chinese tenants because they paid higher rents and took better care of the land. When prairie landlords refused to stop renting to the Chinese, the Island County Board of Trade attempted an economic boycott against everyone who employed or rented to the Chinese. The boycott failed.[23]

In the late 1890s merchants renewed the agitation against the Chinese and, in one of the last outbreaks of anti-Chinese violence on the coast, townspeople resorted to terrorism. They dynamited potato pits of the Chinese near Oak Harbor, destroying their contents. By 1900 they had forced Chinese tenants from the Oak Harbor area, and when other immigrants tried to reenter the area, armed vigilantes met them and drove them off. Ebeys Prairie became the last center of Chinese tenancy, and whites blamed the sixty or so Chinese there in the spring of 1900 for the economic stagnation of the entire county. Many people in Coupeville believed that if the Chinese tenants could be driven off, white farmers would gladly take their place, buy and sell locally, and return prosperity to the county. In January of 1901 these whites formed a vigilance committee, and Chinese residents reported that they had been told to be out of the county by February 1. Reports of these threats in the Seattle papers brought indignant denials in Coupeville. The purpose of the vigilance committee, the *Island County Times* claimed, was not to threaten the Chinese, but rather to convince white landowners not to rent to them. The persuasion of the vigilantes, reportedly backed by threats of burning barns, proved effective. By 1901 most prairie landlords had signed agreements refusing to rent to Chinese. The number of Chinese in the county fell to twenty-eight in 1910 and to eight in 1920. Working the land for a profit in Island County became a business for white men only.[24]

The constant fluctuation of prices, crops, and farming systems in Island County during the nineteenth century made "good farming" difficult. Rural editors, at least in Island County, had very definite ideas about "good farming" and its practitioners. They almost always placed their ideal rural landscape in northern Europe. They believed English and continental farms had endured for centuries with few traumatic changes by creating a landscape that successfully mixed farming, crop rotation, varied domestic fowl and animals, and even limited wildlife. This idealization of northern Europe provides a revealing glimpse of the implicit ecological assumptions upon which "good farming" was based. Good farming was above all stable farming, and although stability admittedly meant economic or social stability, good farming always presumed an ecological stability also—a firm and smoothly functioning rural landscape.[25]

The reliance of the farmers on ecological stability was implicit in common economic and social expectations. The new settlers in Island County hoped for good weather, good soil, and good crops. They presumed that native and exotic weeds and wild animals would not overwhelm their crops and take over their pastures. They assumed that land, once cleared, would grow only what they planted and would continue to be productive for many years. Excessive soil erosion and exhaustion would, obviously, undermine these hopes.

The ecological and social stability reformers desired depended on stable markets. A stable market meant stable production of staple crops. It meant a relatively orderly system of cropping and land use. Great fluctuations between grazing and cropping and sudden shifts in the production of staple crops could be avoided. Agricultural progress would be found in the steady addition of new fields and new farms. A stable market with good prices did not ensure good farming, but it did make it possible. An unstable market brought fluctuations in crops as great as the fluctuations in prices, and planned production gave way to frantic yearly attempts to select and plant crops that would sell. Such a situation would make orderly and good farming difficult, if not impossible. Yet this was essentially the situation farmers in Island County faced.

This relationship between ecological change and agricultural change in Island County was reciprocal. All the major changes in farming in Island County had their ecological consequences, but some also had their ecological causes. The replacement of native vegetation in the 1860s with thousands of acres of timothy and clover, and the stocking of these new fields and pastures with sheep created a new pattern of ecological succession. Many owners apparently let their sheep graze timothy until the ground was bare. Granville Haller, for example, complained that, on the farm he rented to a tenant, sheep had eaten the timothy so close that Canadian thistle had invaded his pastures, rendering many of them worthless. Canadian thistle spread by both seed and an underground root network that permitted it to cover acres of land. Since sheep would not touch the plant, once it had replaced domesticated grasses the land became incapable of supporting livestock.[26]

In 1880, the editor of the *Puget Sound Argus* of Port Townsend began a campaign to get a law passed to eradicate the thistle. The attempt produced little more than bad jokes, but by 1882 thistles had become such a formidable threat to Puget Sound farmers that a new campaign was undertaken. In 1883 the legislature passed a law that made it a misdemeanor for a property owner to let Canadian thistle grow or go to seed on his land and that required road superintendents to eradicate the plant from the roadsides. Legislators apparently formulated the law in absolute ignorance of how Canadian thistle grew. When chopped up, each portion of the thistle is capable of establishing a new plant. Road crews and farmers who diligently chopped up thistles were as likely to seed the next year's crop as to destroy the current one.[27]

Another new, and equally dangerous, component of the altered successional pattern was velvet grass (*Holcus lanatus* L). This exotic plant apparently entered western Washington as an introduced meadow grass, although it is a poor feed and some farmers claimed that if sheep were forced to subsist on it they would die. Once established, the grass became the natural successor to timothy on most pastures that went two years without replanting. By the late nineteenth century the prevalence of the plant in sheep pastures and hay fields made it "a curse to the Sound country" and drastically reduced the usefulness of the land it dominated for grazing.

The Canadian thistle and velvet grass quickly became economic problems. In Island County permanent pasture was too often only a euphemism for land gone to weeds. To maintain their pastures, farmers had to replow and replant almost annually. This raised the cost of their operations and increased their need for additional land to feed sheep while they rehabilitated pastures. How much the decline in sheep raising in Island County owes to these factors is hard to say. Granville Haller, following his complaints about overgrazing and the inroads of the Canadian thistle, began removing the sheep from his farms. Whether Haller's action was typical or not is unclear, but the weeds that destroyed county pastures made competition with the sheep raisers of the far more extensive, if less fertile, grasslands of eastern Washington and Oregon more costly and difficult.[28]

The decline of sheep raising and the substitution of staple crops only altered the nature of environmental change, they did not halt it. A kaleidoscope of exotic plants and animals established themselves in the county as the farmers attempted to meet market demands. The invaders profited not only from the farmer's poor planning but also from poor tillage, which, according to rural editors, was its inevitable companion. Editors castigated the farmers, but their own advice was often capricious. One issue of a paper could contain an editorial condemning farmers for raising too many potatoes alongside an article declaring that high potato prices showed that "farmers cannot raise too many of them." Island County agriculture swung from plantings of a regular annual crop to rapid shifts from one crop to another. The extremes dominated. There was rarely any middle ground.[29]

European invaders joined holdovers from the Salish ecosystem, such as bracken, in competing with the farmer's crops. Canadian thistle, mustards (*Brassica* L.), and poverty grasses like velvet grass joined the other invaders of the 1850s and 1860s, such as sorrel (*Rumex acetosella* L.) in the farmer's fields. In addition, dandelions (*Taraxaeum* Hall.), introduced as a green, spread rapidly along roads and into waste places. In the orchards in the 1890s the woolly aphis, which infected the older orchards during the long years of neglect, spread to the young trees and became a major pest. Even on the ponds the water lily (*Nymphaea odorata* Ait.), introduced in the 1870s, began to take hold. Unused or abandoned fields often contained little more than collections of European weeds.[30]

Such landlords as the Ebeys, Almira Enos, and Granville Haller tended to blame this poor farming exclusively on their tenants, excepting only the Chinese. They complained that their tenants put the land repeatedly in grain and potatoes; that they never rotated crops; that they never fertilized the soil; that they did not maintain buildings and fences; and, finally, that tenants allowed livestock to overgraze the pastures and orchards. Landlords saw their tenants as arrant profiteers, "men getting the cream off the place," as Jacob Ebey put it in the 1880s, and ruining the land in the process. The Ebeys, in particular, had complained about their tenants since 1867, when Eason denounced a renter for overstocking and ruining his pastures, forcing him to sell off livestock for want of feed.[31]

Tenants, however, probably did not abuse farmland any more than did the farmowners themselves. If they didn't manure land, neither did many owners. The total expenditure for fertilizer in the county in 1900 was reported to be fifty dollars. In 1900 the 4,687 white tenants of Washington actually spent more money on fertilizers ($15,425) than did the state's 23,346 white farmowners ($12,089). The statistics do not reflect the manure that farmers gathered and spread on their fields, but, in Island County rural editors complained that all farmers, not just tenants, neglected to spread manure from their livestock onto their fields. The practice of not housing stock made it difficult to gather manure for fertilizer. And if tenants planted the same crops year after year, so apparently did other farmers whenever the market warranted it. Prairie farmers on some soils may even have made conscious attempts to reduce fertility in order to keep wheat from lodging.[32]

The results of this type of farming began to show up as early as 1875, when there were reports of decreasing crop yields. By the 1880s even some of the most fertile prairie lands began to show signs of misuse. Jacob Ebey reported that Meadowside, a farm on the sloping upper reaches of Ebeys Prairie, was "settling" two inches every year and logs, once buried, were now on the surface. The land was not settling, it was washing away. By 1901, while sections of the county were producing world record wheat yields, there were also accounts of land abandonment.[33]

By the late nineteenth century, farmers had nearly erased the ecological communities the Salish had established on the prairies, but the Salish themselves clung tenaciously to the land (see Table 8). In 1880 Island County had proportionately the highest off-reservation Indian population in the territory. There were 295 Indians (27 percent of the total population), and they had lived with the whites on Whidbey and Camano for thirty years.[34]

TABLE 8. INDIAN POPULATION, ISLAND COUNTY

1880	1890	1900	1910	1920
295	141	44	108	38

SOURCE: U.S. Census, Statistics of Population, Twelfth Census, 1:562; Fourteenth Census, 3:1085.

In 1880 many Indians still followed traditional pursuits. Of the twenty-eight fishermen in the county in 1880, twenty-three were Indians. There were two Indian hunters and two shamans or Indian doctors, but these were mostly old men. Only a few of the fishermen were under fifty, and not one was under thirty. In one village, census takers reported the ages of the six fishermen as ninety, eighty, seventy, sixty (two), and fifty. The Indian doctors, too, were old men, and although one hunter was only thirty, the other was over fifty.[35]

It was largely the younger men and women who took the jobs the new agricultural economy offered. Nineteen Indian men listed their occupation as farm laborer, one as woodcutter, and fifteen as laborer. Many of the Salish women married white farmers, and they and their mixed-blood children formed one-quarter of the Indian population.[36]

Superficially, these figures seem to show a culture unable to hold together its old and young. The old men conformed to the demands of a vanishing economy, while the younger men and women were forced to accommodate to the requirements of the farmer's world. But such a split is too dramatic. What is more likely is that the young men and women of the Salish participated in both cultures. Everyone fished when the salmon ran, but at other times the younger men would work as field hands or in the woods. This accommodation to the agricultural world of the whites was not what Indian agents and missionaries wanted, but for a time it was a viable compromise. By the mid-1870s, however, mechanical harvesters had been brought to Whidbey and gradually increasing mechanization cut the demand for farm labor. The Salish, the largest group of farm laborers in the county, suffered most.

Even old tasks, like hunting, took on new meanings within the world created by white farmers. Most Indians probably hunted only for domestic use, but a few, such as the two who listed their occupation as hunter on the census of 1880, became market hunters. These hunters usually killed deer and sold the venison and hides. And other hunting, such as the capture of fur seals, brought Indian hunters up to forty dollars a day for limited periods during the 1870s. A law prohibiting commercial hunting out of season was passed in 1877, but it was never really enforced. As late as 1895 two Indians from Whidbey delivered forty-seven deer to an Everett market. Many whites did a similar business.[37]

Any increased Indian income from hunting was more than offset by reduced access to salmon. In the early twentieth century whites introduced fish traps to Island County. These devices, a complex arrangement of nets and scaffolding, called for substantial investments. The Apex Fish Company had its traps assessed at $15,750 in 1911, a figure well beyond Indian resources. The county licensed each fish trap and gave its owner sole use of a location. In 1905, the first year of licensing, there were forty-two of these traps, and during the next thirty years licenses would be issued for 443 locations. Eventually fishermen almost circled Whidbey Island with fish traps, and they formed a legal and physical barrier to Indian fishermen. In a society in which law, rather than tradition or religion, increasingly defined man's relationship with the land and sea, the Salish became a people literally without rights. They were cut off by law from centuries-old fishing grounds, and the state allotted their catch to white commercial fishermen.[38]

For more than a generation, significant numbers of Salish had declined to go to the reservations. By the 1890s, however, they had begun to leave. They had clung to the islands until changes in the land itself deprived them of their hold. Almost half a century after the treaties, the Salish had at last moved to the reservations. The move was both bitter and ironic. The architects of American Indian policy had assumed that forty years after the treaties took effect acculturation would be largely completed; Indians would be moving off reservations, not onto them. They could not have been more wrong. For a generation, on their own and with little government aid, the Salish had made a private, precarious adjustment to white society. It was an adjustment undermined both accidentally with new technology and purposefully through fish and game laws. Changed circumstance forced the Indians out of the larger society; the reservation became more a refuge than the school for acculturation that policymakers had intended.

One glimpse of the society the Salish were departing is contained in a turn-of-the-century photograph taken from the old graveyard that sat on a small hill north of Ebeys Prairie (see in section of illustrations). It is a picture of barns and fields, horses, and fences. In it the fences, some of them old wooden worm fences, divide the fields into an uneven patchwork. Fields and farm buildings mark the farmsteads imposed on the prairies. The landscape is tidy, well ordered, and seemingly prosperous. Even the forest, which frames the picture, looks domesticated, not at all like the vast and almost impenetrable forests that settlers had encountered fifty years before.

The prairie had taken on human dimensions. Although no human being appears in the picture, the barns, the fields, and the fences are all human creations; the whole landscape is a human creation. But the picture, precisely because it is so vivid, so concretely a picture of a late summer afternoon three-quarters of a century ago, is finally deceptive. It displays an ideal, a harmony, that was never really attained. The bucolic paradise it seems to capture never existed. The actual adjustment of men and women to the landscape the farmer had created in Island County had a complexity not suggested by this photograph at the turn of the century.

The picture never suggested the long parade of human, animal, and floral populations that moved across the prairies. Tenants replaced freeholders; machines replaced Salish laborers; Chinese tenants replaced whites, and whites returned to replace Chinese. In the fields potatoes replaced wheat, sheep replaced potatoes, apples replaced sheep, and then men destroyed the orchards and planted wheat once again.

Under market agriculture, farmers simplified the ecology of the prairies and made both the natural and exotic communities dependent on new forces thousands of miles away. The new plant and animal communities the land supported had relatively few components; they existed only so long as humans labored to protect them. Compared with their predecessors, the communities that the farmers maintained were incredibly precarious, unable to sustain themselves even briefly without man. It was in this respect a simple system, but it was also a system tied in with similar farming systems hundreds and thousands of miles away. What happened in California could, and did, influence what grew on Whidbey. The prairies of 1900 were gardens in the sense that they were the cultural creations of Europeans and were occupied by men, plants, and animals whose own ancestry was mostly European, but the mythic corollaries did not automatically follow.

In many ways, the relationship between the new inhabitants and the land they occupied came to be a legal one. Law mediated, often unsuccessfully, between the invading Americans and the natural world. The land was divided by law; hunting of game was nominally regulated by law; and residents attempted to deal with such undesirable exotics as Canadian thistle through law. Even if many laws were rarely enforced, they still represented a new approach to the natural landscape of the islands, and this approach would continue to dominate in the twentieth century.

Within the realities of market farming, even the older myths of rural stability took on new and paradoxical meanings. Such historians as Richard Hofstadter and Henry Nash Smith have portrayed the myth of the yeoman in the garden, with its emphasis on the farmer as the backbone of his community and the republic as a defensive, reactionary response by the farmer to a new economic and social order. But in Island County the myth of the yeoman was a weapon not of the farmer, but of the town against the country. In part the battle against Chinese renters was racial, but in part it was a conflict between farmer landlords of the prairies and the businessmen of the towns, with both groups operating within the confines of the larger agricultural market. The merchants turned agrarian assumptions about the value of freeholders against the farmer. It was the merchants and vigilantes of the towns who claimed that freeholding farmers on the prairies were the backbone of the community and the basis of its prosperity. They hated the Chinese not only for their race, but also because they had failed to fulfill a basic physiocratic assumption: that prosperous farmers would produce prosperous communities. The Chinese appeared to prosper, the landlords appeared to prosper, but the towns stagnated.

The response of the townspeople—the glorification of the white freeholder and the attack on the Chinese tenants—was obviously self-serving, but that is the point. Devotion to the rural freeholder was used against a group of farmers and their tenants, not by them.[39]

By 1900 the economy, society, and ecology of the prairies had merged into a pattern whose complexities could no longer be fully comprehended by isolating any single element. Men and women, the land and its plants and animals, and the social and economic institutions men had created formed a system whose governing rule had come to be rapid change. And change gave the land, as well as its inhabitants, a history. The landscape could in effect be read as an historical document. A pasture of velvet grass was more than a physical fact. It could be better understood as a result of thirty years of social, economic, and ecological history. Velvet grass was present because farmers had introduced it in the mistaken belief that it provided good feed for sheep. But mere introduction did not ensure its spread. That took the series of events that had encouraged farmers to undertake large-scale sheep raising on the prairies, as well as the farmers' devotion to timothy as feed for their stock. Sheep had then overgrazed the timothy, and farmers had failed to replant regularly. This created the opportunity for velvet grass to spread and become the main successional species on timothy pastures. Velvet grass, Canadian thistle, sorrel, and all the other invaders had histories that were closely tied to the white invaders. By 1900 for an observer to understand ecological change on the prairies, he would have to understand not only the plants themselves, but also the cultures of the people who farmed the land, their histories, their farming techniques and tools, and the conditions of the markets they supplied.

But the influence of social and economic factors on ecology was not one-sided. Extensive acreages of velvet grass and Canadian thistle, for example, had, in turn, helped make sheep raising more expensive and more laborious. Bracken, too, had cut the value of hay and, thus, both the farmer's income and his ability to compete with other farmers. Rural editors who denounced existing farming practices failed to grasp the complexity of the context in which farming took place. They saw only bad farming. But, with the farmer already an ecological invader in a changing landscape, his dependence on a competitive and unstable market made good farming close to impossible. As the 1850s had shown, the very presence of farms had ensured change, and when the farmers had to change crops annually to meet competition and altered markets, the care of the land could seem only a minor concern. The degradation of the landscape, whether in the form of erosion, soil exhaustion, or the loss of land to European weeds, seemed only the unavoidable price to be paid for getting a living from the land.

Chapter IV

THE OX AND THE AXE

Forest Economy and Ecology in the Nineteenth Century

🗲 In the 1850s, Americans on Whidbey and Camano islands began to log the vast forests that surrounded them. Primarily interested in producing marketable timber, not in clearing land, these men had, by the 1860s, made lumbering a major part of the county's economy. The infant industry developed under a set of laws that presumed the highest use of any land was for farming. Although American land law made the acquisition of farming land relatively easy, the laws made the acquisition of land for lumbering correspondingly difficult. To acquire timber, therefore, the early loggers either broke or evaded the federal laws designed to distribute the public domain. Fraud and theft became accepted, and even necessary, aspects of the industry. Inevitably, the exploitation of the forest that grew out of this situation was chaotic and haphazard.

The forest that loggers found in Island County was, and is, part of the western hemlock zone of western Washington and Oregon. Although the zone was named for the theoretical climax species of the area, the hemlock, in fact the Douglas fir dominated the zone, and Sitka spruce, white fir, and cedar, as well as hemlock, were abundant. Except for spruce, which seems to have been confined largely to central and northern Whidbey, each species grew throughout the county. These forests were largely conifer, but deciduous trees dominated specific niches on the islands. Oaks grew on the prairies around Oak Harbor, and alders and maples lined the stream banks, shorelines, and wet bottom lands.[1]

The stands of fir that composed the bulk of the forest ranged from four hundred to six hundred years old. These species, too, were long-lived with a life span of from four hundred years for the hemlock to over a thousand for the red cedar. But more immediately apparent than the age of these trees was their size. Except for the redwood forests of California, the conifer forests of Oregon and Washington were the most productive on earth, with accumulations of living matter far exceeding any other forests in the world. Ecologists have estimated the biomass of fir forests per hectare at 2,437 metric tons, and the size of individual trees was equally staggering. The biggest trees in the county grew on southern Whidbey and on Camano, but virtually all mature trees were immense. The hemlock's average diameter at maturity on good sites was from 3 to 4 feet, and its height from 125 to 200 feet; the diameter of the cedar was from 4 to 6 feet and its height was in the vicinity of 200 feet; the spruce had a diameter of from 6 to 7 feet and stood from 230 to 245 feet tall. The fir was the largest of all, with a diameter of from 5 to 7 feet and heights ranging from 245 to 330 feet. Such forests will probably never exist again.[2]

The understory of this forest grew so densely as to be impenetrable; such shrubs as vine maple (*Acer circinatum* Pursh), salal (*Gaultheria shallon* Pursh), rhododendron (*Rhododendron macrophyllum* G. Don), chinquapin (*Castanopsis chyrsophylla* Dougl.), salmonberry, and Oregon grape (*Berberis aguifolium* Pursh) merged with young hemlock, cedar, and willow, as well as the omnipresent swordfern and bracken, to form a luxuriant growth on the forest floor. Young trees springing up on burned land would often grow with such fecundity as to choke off the undergrowth, but these saplings themselves became so closely packed that travel through them was almost impossible. In the 1880s, government surveyors described the northern townships of Whidbey as having "a thick undergrowth of willow, salal and salmonberry and fern," and they described the shores of Holmes Harbor as "brushy." The first settlers gave much the same description. The survey of John Kineth's claim near Penn's Cove listed hemlock, cedar, vine maple, willow, salal, ferns, and briers in the forest understory.[3]

Along with shrubs, vines, and young trees, dead trees and fallen limbs littered the forest floor, and the first white hunters found the woods almost impassable; they often had to walk on fallen logs to obtain a view over the tangle of debris and undergrowth. Cattle, apparently, were no more adept at penetrating the forest. When W. S. Ebey found good grazing land in an alder bottom a mile back from Useless Bay, he had to cut a trail to allow his cattle to gain access to it.[4]

Occasionally old settlers, in reminiscing, described a different kind of forest. John Kineth, whose original claim survey has already been cited, remembered a forest where "you could ride horseback anywhere among the big trees." If such a parklike forest existed outside of romantic memory, it was the result of the sheep grazing in the 1870s and 1880s. Annual burning may have killed off understory plants without harming the more resistant fir, and sheep would have kept succession plants down. Certainly there is no record of such a forest at the time of settlement.[5]

The forest of the 1850s, however, for all its size, darkness, and impenetrability, was in no sense primal. It owed much of its composition to the Salish. The fires they set were neither systematic enough nor frequent enough to create Kineth's park, but they did occur regularly enough to keep the forest from attaining its hypothetical climax. By killing off less-resistant young and small trees, these fires may have helped produce the immense timber the whites found. On the burnt-over land, which was interspersed with the old mature timber, whites, like the Salish, initially found good hunting grounds and abundant berries. But if repeated firing did not occur, impenetrable undergrowth of hemlock, fir, willow, and alder sprang up.[6]

Farm makers ignored most of this woodland. Forests like those on Whidbey and Camano represented a special failure of the American land system. Designed to turn public lands into farms, American land laws succeeded well enough when distributing fertile agricultural lands, but lawmakers, with few exceptions, never really considered the forests themselves a thing of value. The laws assumed that trees were an impediment to progress, an obstacle to be removed. The federal laws thus bore little relation to the realities of western Washington, where the land itself had little agricultural potential, but the forests were the areas of real wealth. The lawmakers did not entertain the concept that the removal of timber could decrease, rather than increase, the land's value.[7]

By the 1850s, timbermen elsewhere in the country had shown

great resourcefulness in turning laws passed for farm makers to their own advantage. Surveyed lands could be purchased for $1.25 an acre, and after 1841, 160 acres of unoffered land could be acquired under the Preemption Act, with only the claimant's work necessary to prove six months' residence, for $1.25 an acre. Enterprising lumbermen paraded dummy entrymen into land offices, paid them for their efforts, and took title. Timberlands that actually brought $1.25 an acre in these forests were rare. In most cases lumbermen bought the land either with warrants or with scrip purchased at well below its face value, or, during the 1860s, with greenbacks worth forty cents on the dollar. Through mass purchases and fraud, timbermen acquired huge holdings in the public land states of the Midwest.[8]

Lumbermen in Washington eagerly sought to imitate their midwestern counterparts, but the slowness of the surveys during the 1850s frustrated their ambitions. The government offered land for sale only after it had been surveyed. The eight dollars per mile appropriated by Congress for surveying proved totally inadequate in the dense forest of western Washington, where actual costs ran closer to twelve dollars to twenty dollars a mile.[9] As a result, the government opened relatively little land—some three million acres—for purchase. So, as they had from colonial times, the loggers moved into the forests ahead of the surveyors. Between 1859 and 1870 the relation between land ownership and lumbering on forest lands remained quite tenuous. Men who cut timber often did not have a shadow of title to it. Settlers took timber for homes and fences, loggers cut whole sections to supply the mills, and farmers burned parts of the forest to create pasture.[10]

During the 1850s, the forest yielded a ready cash crop in the form of pilings and spars for ships. Whidbey farmers cut much of this timber, taking out the trees along the shores of Penn Cove and Puget Sound. In February 1853 ships were loading piles and squared timber at Coveland; that spring Samuel Hancock hauled out piles in the vicinity of his claim near Crockett Lake, and H. B. Lovejoy and Captain Kinney cut spars near Snatelum Point. In January 1854, Nathaniel Hill signed a contract to supply a cargo of piles to Captains Robertson and Coupe of Coupeville, and his piles were probably among the lumber shipped from Coupeville and Oak Harbor in 1854.[11]

The impact on the forest of this pile and spar minimal. When Thomas Cranney, later to become a berman in the county, began removing spars in 18 yoke of oxen, it took him two to three days to cut and haul it to tidewater. Later, at his best, he got out two spars on a good day. Farmers working with few oxen and little help probably produced far less. Since spars and piles were taken from mature timber containing twenty to seventy-five fir trees an acre, even Cranney's peak pace would clear only an acre a month. In practice, however, the early loggers cut only tall, straight, healthy trees. They felled a few giants, but the forest as a whole remained hardly altered.[12]

The first lumber company to operate in the county on any scale was Grennan and Cranney, a partnership between two local residents that was begun in 1856. Both Lawrence Grennan and Thomas Cranney were born in New Brunswick, Canada, and possessed some previous experience in the lumber business. Their company began by cutting piles for the San Francisco market during the 1850s, but spars and masts for the shipyards of England, France, and Spain soon dominated their production. They specialized in immense timbers. When Cunard of Great Britain needed spars for the *Great Eastern,* the largest steamer of the time, they got them from Grennan and Cranney. And, in 1866, the company produced a perfect two-hundred-foot pole for the flagstaff at the Paris exhibition, but since no available ship could transport timber of this size, fifty feet had to be cut off.

The size of the individual timbers they provided allowed Grennan and Cranney to fill orders by cutting only a few huge trees. A shipload of masts and spars for the Spanish Navy cost $18,000 and took thirty-five days to load in 1862, but since some of these masts were 125 feet long with 40-inch diameters, it took only 200 trees to complete the cargo. The 402,000 board feet of timber shipped to Chile in 1860 probably represented one of the company's largest orders. A more typical load would have been the 76,000 board feet shipped by schooner in 1861.[13]

As Grennan and Cranney prospered, they constructed the first mill in Island County at Utsalady on Camano Island. By 1860 their operation had spawned a milltown of several hundred people. In the late fifties, the creation of a small shipbuilding industry on northern Whidbey and on Camano prompted a further expansion of the lumber industry. The combination of excellent spar and mast timber with the oak groves near Oak Harbor made shipyards seem a natural development. The oak trees of Oak Harbor, a relatively scarce species, were crucial to the new industry. Americans recognized oak as a traditional ship-building timber at a time when men still questioned the usefulness of the abundant fir, hemlock, spruce, and cedar for anything besides "spars, yards, piles and the frame of buildings." Between 1858 and 1861, workers constructed at least five vessels at Utsalady and Oak Harbor.[14] This brief rush to exploit oak when surrounded by the finest conifer forests in the world is revealing. It demonstrated not only the economic adjustments necessary before the forest could be fully exploited, but also the perceptual adjustments necessary before men abandoned what was scarce, although familiar, and turned to what was abundant but strange.

During the 1850s and early 1860s the fledgling lumber industry expanded, and the establishment of sawmills around Puget Sound in the late 1850s increased the scale of the cutting on the public domain. The government, still unwilling to complete the surveys and open the land for purchase, responded with a compromise. By arrangement with the lumbermen, local officials extralegally reconciled the practice of cutting timber on the public lands with federal statutes. The agreement simply called for timbermen to report the amount they cut to the district court of the territory. The court then fined the timbermen fifty cents per tree. Later the government increased the penalty to fifteen cents per thousand board feet.[15]

Once begun, however, cutting timber on public lands easily slid into a habit, and even into something of a right. Even as the land office pushed the surveys to completion and the Northern Pacific claimed millions of acres of forest as part of its railroad land grant, the cutting continued. Many timbermen remained as oblivious as before to any obligation to buy the land that held the timber. In 1877, investigators claimed that half the timber cut in the Puget Sound region had been illegally taken from government or railroad land, and in 1881 the charge was repeated and the depredations put at millions of board feet.[16] Increasingly, in the 1870s and 1880s, this timber theft was the work of independent loggers.

Mill companies bought land as it became available, but they rarely logged it. They preferred to hold it for the future while they bought logs from independent operators.[17]

The purchase of even this surveyed land by mill companies often had to be done illegally. The passage of the Homestead Act in 1863 brought increasing pressure to retain land for actual settlers and caused much surveyed public land to be withheld from sale. The mill companies responded by recruiting fraudulent entrymen, to whom they paid one hundred dollars apiece to file preemption claims on the withheld lands and then sell their claims to the companies. The Timber and Stone Act of 1878 expanded the opportunities for acquisitions by providing for the sale of land chiefly valuable for timber or stone in quantities not to exceed 160 acres for $2.50 an acre. Unlike the Homestead and Preemption Acts, the new law required no residence or improvements on the land and thus eliminated the necessity for perjury on the part of the claimants acting for the mill companies. This law, ostensibly intended for actual users, had loopholes so large that entire crews of sailing ships walked through them and filed on timber claims that they immediately sold to the mill companies. When sailors were unavailable, the Puget Mill Company took to hiring boats to carry men from Seattle to Olympia to claim land for the company. Under the provisions of the Timber and Stone Act, some of the best timberland in Washington passed into the hands of the mill companies.[18]

Island County, however, only partially shared this general pattern. Fraud and timber theft occurred, but the relatively rapid completion of the surveys in the county during the early 1860s diminished both the opportunity and the necessity for either fraud or theft. By 1863, only two townships near Holmes Harbor and the area bordering Deception Pass had not been opened for sale. And even before the completion of the surveys, timberlands had been legally acquired from the University Land Grant. The federal government made this 46,000-acre grant to provide an endowment for the University of Washington. The law allowed officials to locate the land anywhere in the territory, but it merely reserved the land; it did not give university officials the power to dispose of it. Nevertheless, the territorial legislature authorized Daniel Bagley, a university land commissioner, to begin locating and selling land in 1861. Bagley offered such land for sale at $1.50 an acre. Mill companies made the bulk of the purchases; Puget Mill, the largest buyer, acquired 17,450 acres for $26,175 in greenbacks. In Island County during the 1860s, 3,712.35 acres passed into private hands from the University grant. The Port Ludlow Mill Company, with 595 acres, was the largest purchaser.[19]

When public lands came up for sale, Pope and Talbot, the owners of the Puget Mill Company, immediately made some purchases with Mexican War scrip that would expire in June 1863, and they acquired other tracts over the next five years. Grennan and Cranney also began to legitimize their operation by buying 1,268 acres, principally on Camano Island. Grennan and Cranney, residents of the county and familiar with its timberland, made their purchases directly, but most of the mills that acquired land used purchasing agents.

These agents knew not only lumbering but also the timberlands of the Puget Sound region. Jared Hurd, for instance, served as a government surveyor and also purchased land for Puget Mill. He identified 2,516 acres of prime timberland, purchased the tracts, and immediately transferred title to Puget Mill.[20] Two other Puget Mill Company agents, Fred and Michael Drew, had worked in the woods of Maine and Minnesota before coming to Washington. Fred was the chief cruiser for Puget Mill, and Michael was the assistant foreman. Both located and filed on lands in the county for the company. The Port Ludlow Mill Company bought land under its own name, and through one of the mill's owners, Arthur Phinney, but Port Ludlow also used employees to make purchases. Robert Attridge and his brother Richard had cut spars on Whidbey before joining the Mill Company, and, presumably, used their knowledge of Island County timberland to purchase 199 acres in the county for the company.[21]

In 1861 mill companies and timber speculators, fearing that withdrawals for the Northern Pacific Land Grant would remove huge tracts of prime timberland from the public domain, joined in the land rush that followed the large purchase of land in the county by agents of the Northern Pacific Railroad. They hoped to acquire cheap timberland on the islands while it was still available. Of the roughly 130,000 acres in the county, 88,820 were in private hands by the end of 1871. Most of what remained was either reserved for schools or the military, or was located in the two townships not surveyed until 1870 and thus not available for disposal.[22]

After 1871, considerable consolidation of forest land holdings occurred in the county. The Puget Sound and Lake Superior Land Company (a subsidiary of the Northern Pacific Railroad), which retained nearly all its holdings, remained the biggest landowner. Meanwhile, the Puget Mill Company gradually emerged as the dominant mill company in the county. When Grennan and Cranney went bankrupt, Puget Mill acquired the bulk of their land. Puget Mill also bought up other holdings, and when Arthur Phinney died, the company added the Port Ludlow Mill to its properties. The Washington Mill Company also expanded its holdings until a disastrous fire in 1886 destroyed both the mill and the company. By the 1880s only two mill companies, Puget Mill, with over 10,000 acres, and the Port Blakely Mill Company (with approximately 840 acres), still owned land in the county.[23]

The large purchases of land by the Northern Pacific Railroad and the Puget Mill Company marked the passing of local control of land use in Island County. Market agriculture had certainly begun the erosion of such local control, narrowing the farmer's range of decision over what to grow and how to grow it. Still, on the prairies the farmer made the final decision, no matter how restricted, on what to do with the land. In the forests, however, such decisions would now be made by agents of men thousands of miles away in Minneapolis or San Francisco, who had never seen the forests of the islands. Only Grennan and Cranney, for a brief period before their bankruptcy, and two minor speculators, Henry Maryott and Nicolas Code, both lived in the county and owned a significant amount of forest land there in 1870. By 1880 only Maryott retained his holdings.[24] (See Table 21.)

The outside companies, however, did not act totally as an economic army of occupation.[25] They established definite economic ties with local residents. Few mill companies actually did their own logging in the nineteenth century; they bought most of their timber from independent loggers working government or speculative lands. These loggers necessarily became dependent on mill companies for markets, and they were also often in debt to them for equipment. Farmers as well as loggers became dependents of the companies. In an era when markets were scarce, lumber camps and mill towns provided potential, if often unreliable, markets for farmers. Finally, the companies attached elements of the local business community in the towns and villages to their interests by company purchases and favors. The Port Blakely Mill Company retained Daniel Pearson, an old county settler and merchant, as its unofficial agent for the surrounding area. In return for substantial mill company patronage at his store, Pearson kept alert for available timberland and recruited dummy entrymen when they were needed for government lands. Granville Haller and Peter d'Jourup apparently performed similar services for the Washington Mill Company and the Puget Mill Company. This economic order, once established, depended on the mill companies and railroads as conduits of capital for "developing" Island County. Local control over land use may have passed, but local desires for growth and development remained unchanged. As long as outside corporations seemed likely means to such ends, local residents tolerated a certain degree of economic colonialism.[26]

The rise of absentee land ownership in the county by large private corporations did not automatically impose order on the cutting of the forest. The order in which loggers harvested the forests, however, did become a corollary of land ownership. Loggers cut the public domain townships in the county first, and by 1870 they had finished cutting the two townships near Holmes Harbor (T29N, R3E and T29N, R2E). After 1870 loggers worked the timber on private holdings, usually the smaller speculative tracts on north Whidbey and north Camano. They either bought timber at from fifty cents to a dollar per thousand board feet or simply took it with the practiced disregard for title developed on the public domain. Occasionally loggers bought land themselves, usually at tax sales. But of the thirteen loggers who are known to have operated in the county between 1878 and 1880, only three owned land, and of the nineteen operating between 1890 and 1895, only three owned any of the land they logged. By the late 1880s, loggers were working the lands of the Port Blakely Mill Company, and during the 1890s the Puget Mill Company sold some of its stumpage on central Whidbey to independent loggers.[27]

Both the number of camps and the number of areas logged

increased steadily after 1870. In the summer of 1878 four camps were reported running on south Whidbey. During the next year, lien and mortgage records indicate that the number of camps expanded at least to thirteen. Not all of these camps ran simultaneously and few, if any, ran during the winter rainy season. The census of 1880 lists only three camps operating, all on south Whidbey, but there were probably several more unreported on Camano. Lumbermen logged the land behind Triangle Cove and Livingston Bay on east Camano in the 1870s, as well as the land on the north coast from Utsalady to Rocky Point. Logging of north Whidbey began in earnest in the 1880s when the Lake Superior and Puget Sound Land Company began to sell off stumpage from its holdings. By the mid-1880s, when Braum and McKenzie opened a camp on Dugualla Bay, loggers had reached the extreme north end of Whidbey Island.[28]

These early loggers depended on a very primitive technology to cut and remove their trees. Initially, loggers felled trees with axes and then cut them into sections with crosscut saws. Once the trees were felled and cut, the loggers hitched them to a bull team and pulled them to water along a skid road, a corduroy track heavily greased with dogfish oil. A good six-yoke bull team took out 10,000 to 12,000 board feet of timber in a trip and made four one-mile-long trips a day.

Relatively minor technical innovations increased the productivity of these camps as the century wore on. In the 1880s, loggers learned that the use of the crosscut saw in conjunction with the axe speeded up the felling of trees, and the replacement of bull teams by faster horses moved the timber out of the woods more quickly. As important as these technical improvements, however, was the simple increase in the number of men working in each camp. Small camps continued to operate in Island County, and even farmers continued to cut a few logs to sell to the mills, but it was the big camps that dominated production. Camps operating on the shores of Holmes Harbor during 1891 sent booms of nearly a million board feet to the mills. Others a few miles away had to merge their production with neighboring camps to produce even a single boom of a few hundred thousand board feet. In 1896, the only year for which a figure is available, there were 115 men working in the woods of Island County.[29] (See Table 22.)

The primitive technology of bull team logging and the market it served had definite consequences for forest ecology. Because oxen were so slow, loggers contended that they were useful only on land a mile or two from water. Beyond that, bull team logging ceased to be profitable. In Island County this limitation was not as significant as elsewhere, since many areas of the county were within two miles of tidewater. But even in the areas bull team loggers could reach they could not market all the trees that composed the forest. During the 1860s and 1870s timbermen took only fir. By the 1880s they cut some cedar, but it was only a minor component of the total production. Loggers regarded hemlock as worthless, a garbage wood, throughout the period. Records of the booms shipped from Holmes Harbor and Utsalady to the Puget Mill Company between September 18, 1891, and December 3, 1891, for example, show that they contained 5,553 logs, of which only 70 were cedar, 28 were hemlock, 23 were spruce, and 13 were white fir. The remainder were Douglas fir.[30]

Loggers would not take all the mature Douglas fir on a site. Mills could not handle the biggest trees, and loggers ignored the diseased or conky trees that abounded in Island County. The forest logged in Island County during the late nineteenth century was mature, and one of the characteristics of mature forests in the region, and in Island County in particular, was the large proportion of trees infected with red ring rot. Rot usually appeared in trees over 160 years old, and it became progressively more widespread as a stand aged. Red ring rot and associated rots progress slowly but can eventually affect up to 65 percent of the timber in a stand. At 300 to 350 years of age, the growth of rot could equal the trees's own annual growth and after that point could exceed it. The tree itself could live for hundreds of years after becoming infected, but eventually it would be weakened enough to fall. For the logger, such trees were worthless. If felled, they were abandoned, and if spotted, as they often could be by the protrusions (conks) on their trunks, they were left standing.[31]

Bull team loggers wasted immense amounts of timber. When they cut a healthy Douglas fir, they sent only part of it to the mills. Loggers cut the fir from ten to twenty feet above the ground to avoid the thick and pitchy base, and they discarded everything above the first branches, usually forty to fifty feet of the total length of the tree. If the tree fell into a ravine or onto broken ground, or if it shattered when it fell, the whole trunk would be left to rot. Loggers left an incredible amount of timber—butts, tops, and limbs—on the forest floor at the end of a logging operation. If waste is calculated in terms of the number of board feet of each felled tree left in the woods, bull team logging was even more wasteful than later donkey engine logging. In the nineteenth century lumber industry, however, waste had little economic meaning. The mill owners and lumbermen assumed the forests to be inexhaustible, and the industry was chronically plagued by glutted markets. Hence, for them, more efficient logging would only provide more costly wood for an already oversupplied market.[32]

If waste had little economic meaning, it did have environmental consequences. The danger of waste was not that loggers killed an unnecessarily large number of trees, but rather that the debris loggers left might itself hamper the replacement of felled trees. The massive amounts of slash left on the forest floor increased the danger of fire, and fire, by killing seedlings, could prevent the return of the forest or alter its composition.

One example of the way waste left after a logging operation seeded further destruction and ecological change is found in the brief notations of a government surveyor, George Whitworth, in 1871. The logging of the public domain around Holmes Harbor during the 1860s left the usual abundance of slash and stumps, and in the dry summer weather fires followed. Whitworth indicated that there had been not just one fire in these townships during the late 1860s, but several, and that "a large amount (of timber) has been destroyed . . . some recently." As a consequence, the nature of the forest had changed. The original Douglas fir that had brought the loggers had probably regenerated successfully enough once, or even twice, but the repeated fires killed it. Since most of the remaining seed trees would have been hemlock, fir was "succeeded by a growth of small hemlock which in some places constitutes an impenetrable thicket." Logging, then, not only brought fires that killed standing timber, it changed the local species composition of the forest.[33]

The logging fires, that Whitworth noticed in 1871 began on cutover lands, but they could easily spread into adjoining standing

timber. In 1890, local officials had the 4,276 acres of land contained in the school sections of Island County cruised and ap-
praised. By federal law, sections sixteen and thirty-six had been
given to the territory with the provision that any proceeds derived
from them were to be used for the public schools. Because of the
irregular geography of Island County, sections sixteen and thirty-
six were often under water, and, even when they were not, they
had usually been claimed by settlers in the prairie townships before the arrival of surveyors. Because these school sections were un-
available, the territory was entitled to indemnity sections. In 1870
officials made their indemnity sections, and they almost invariably
took sections in the forests. Territorial law prohibited the removal
of timber from this school land but provided for grazing leases
that were not to exceed six years. When these lands were cruised
in 1890, therefore, ostensibly they had never been logged, although many had been leased for grazing.[34]

Cruises of these school lands in 1890 found evidence of fire
damage. All the land examined in the school section appraisement
of 1890 was on Whidbey Island. With doubtful sections eliminated, 50 percent of the sections on south Whidbey and 25 percent of the sections on north Whidbey had been burned. Since
damage was highest in the logging regions of north and south
Whidbey and least in the central farming regions, the fires probably resulted from logging operations rather than burning by
farmers seeking to create pasture. Unfortunately, the appraisers
gave no indication of the frequency of these fires nor of when they
had occurred.[35] (See Table 23.)

Good management could reduce the danger of fire in the mature
forests, and slash fires did not affect timberlands equally. By the
late nineteenth century, the Puget Mill Company already patrolled
its own lands to prevent fires and also kept an eye on neighboring
operations that might threaten its holdings. This policy was apparently successful. When, in 1889, the Puget Mill Company
cruised seven sections on south Whidbey, they found fire damage
on only one, and even there only forty acres had been affected.
This was substantially less damage than was found on the school
sections in this region. On Camano Island, the cruisers examined
three sections on the west coast and only one had been burned.
Since the timber cruisers reported logging on neighboring lands in

nearly all these sections, damage from logging fires seems to have been quite moderate on Puget Mill lands.[36]

Fires on logged-off land represented a new factor in forest ecology, one that would eventually have severe consequences for the regeneration of the forests. Such slash fires, however, became immensely more common and destructive with the introduction of steam technology into the woods and are best discussed later. Slash fires occurred with bull team logging, but other logging practices compensated for the damage they caused. Loggers left all but the best trees standing, a practice that was frequently denounced as wasteful by their critics. These cull trees, however, provided abundant sources of seed for the cutover areas. If slash fires destroyed new seedlings, cull trees could usually provide another seed crop to replace them, although in some places the seed might be disproportionately hemlock. A Forest Service survey of the 1930s found that 38,740 acres of land, because of either logging or fires, produced new growth during the period between 1860 and 1890. Virtually all of this land, 91.7 percent, regenerated successfully and produced good stands of timber by Forest Service definition.[37]

The changes that bull team logging brought to the forest—increased fire damage, local alterations in species composition, larger faunal populations that came with clearing, perhaps even increased erosion—did not mean serious deterioration of forest ecology. Selective logging and successful regeneration restored the forest landscape so quickly that, within a few years of the end of a logging operation, the face of the forest looked untouched to a casual observer. Thirty to forty years after logging, sections of northern Camano cut during the 1870s and 1880s appeared never to have felt the axe. Old-growth cedar, hemlock, and culled fir interspersed with new growth made the forest appear virgin. Only the scattered old stumps rising above the brush revealed that logging had once taken place. After twenty-five years of logging, a traveler described Whidbey in 1884 as "a nearly unbroken wilderness of forest."

Bull team logging was ecologically benign, but some opposition developed to it nevertheless. Such opposition (while limited) is revealing, however, both of the differences between conservationist and ecological views of nature and of splits within the conservation movement itself. The wastefulness of bull team logging, not its consequences for forest ecology, raised scattered local opposition. Logically enough, this opposition grounded its argument on economic and developmental concerns, not environmental ones. Occasionally ecological arguments did surface, as when, in 1877, the *Puget Sound Argus* reprinted an address by Elwood Evans before the Academy of Sciences at Olympia on forest preservation. Most of Evans' text closely followed the argument of George Perkins Marsh on erosion, stream flow, and retention of water in the soil. Evans, however, made little attempt to couple these popular environmental doctrines with observations on local conditions. He imported his ideas and they remained as exotic as any biological invader. The core of local opposition rose from other, more native roots. Most local opponents of the logging industry were conservationists in Samuel Hays's sense of the word—people who opposed waste and wanted rational use of resources. Important differences separated these local conservationists, however, from the national conservationists Hays discussed.

Unlike national conservationists, whose tendencies were toward central, bureaucratic, planned development, the regional conservationists shared the common entrepreneurial western bias in favor of local development. National conservation tended to favor large corporations since they seemed the most likely source, next to the government, of large-scale, rationalized, national development. The conservationists of areas like Puget Sound tended to oppose precisely these same corporations, since their actual wastefulness provided few benefits for the local economy and since, by using up limited resources, they threatened future local development. Thus, although the language of the two groups was often similar, their ultimate concerns were not.

The *Puget Sound Argus* best stated the objections of local conservationists to lumber companies in an attack on both the lumber industry and popular attitudes toward the forest in 1879. "Perhaps no greater drain on our resources could be imagined than that of the lumber business," the *Argus* editorialized, and it followed with a list of specific grievances: Logging was wasteful; only the best timber was taken, the rest was left to rot or burn; lumbermen bled Washington dry for the benefit of San Francisco, squandering its timber and taking the profits out of the state. According to the *Argus,* the timber companies were destroying the forest itself and taking no steps to replace it. Similar sentiments would reappear in the paper over the next decade until, by 1889, the *Argus* demanded that the forest be withdrawn from entry and placed under the custody of the army.[38]

Such denunciations of the timber companies for exploiting the territory echoed older agrarian resentments of the lumber industry voiced in Island County, just across Admiralty Inlet from Port Townsend, where the *Argus* was published. In the 1860s George Beam, a cousin of the Ebeys, had denounced mill companies for taking timber out of the territory without bringing anything in. And in the same decade Granville Haller, who later became an agent of the mill companies, complained that the mills were a bane to agriculture in the territory. They used their empty lumber ships to bring back California produce that kept prices low and deprived farmers of markets.[39]

It must be emphasized that the real concern here is not with saving the forest, but with developing the territory. What these relatively feeble complaints by local newspapers and settlers meant was that the forests had not yielded all the economic benefits that residents of Island and neighboring counties had expected. What profits had come from lumbering had gone to men who did not even live in the territory, let alone the county. Local people were more concerned with the allocation of the proceeds that came from the cutting of the forest than with the way loggers treated the forest. County residents were not so much concerned that waste had occurred, as that it had not benefited them.

These complaints about the social and economic failings of bull team logging were justified, but they cannot be confused with the condition of the forest itself. Loggers, despite appearances, did little harm to the forest environment during the nineteenth century. In the face of greed, waste, and corruption, the forest was able to regenerate quite successfully. Human moral, social, and economic failings were, after all, not automatically fatal to a Douglas fir.

Chapter V

THE CREATION OF A NEW FOREST

Technology, Ecology, and Social Change

It is often stated as a truism that the impact of a human society upon the natural world varies with the sophistication of that society's technology. This kind of generalization (sometimes offered in connection with a condemnation of technology), however, tells us relatively little about environmental change. As the Salish demonstrated, a simple technology does not necessarily mean limited impact upon natural systems. The consequences of Salish technology, all out of proportion to its constituent parts, warns against easy assumptions about the impact of humans on natural systems. If primitive technologies can have great impact on the environment, then it might be equally possible for sophisticated technologies to have only a limited impact. Why a given technology is being used and how it is used are sometimes as important as the mechanism itself.

The environmental consequences of a technology do not rest like some ghost within the machine, ready to be released by the flick of a switch. They are the result of factors and relationships beyond the machine itself. The forests of Island County can be studied as a microcosm in which social, technological, and economic systems of varying sophistication operated during the twentieth century to influence the natural environment. It is the interrelationship of these elements that holds the key to environmental change.

The whole pattern of logging changed in Island County during the early twentieth century. By 1900, fifty years of logging had carved the forests of the islands into a patchwork of virgin timber, second growth, and burned lands. Although no section of the county remained untouched by the axe, substantial amounts of prime timber still existed. During the next thirty years, but primarily between 1900 and 1920, loggers cut or recut about 70,000 acres of land and took out over one billion board feet of timber. These twentieth century loggers, however, cut different kinds of timber, from different kinds of holdings, and they harvested trees in new ways. In this lay the seeds of great change for the forest.

Nineteenth century bull team loggers had already taken much of the best Douglas fir; twentieth century loggers now took cedar, the remaining fir, and even hemlock, and then turned to second growth, which smaller operations harvested for mining poles, railway ties, and cordwood. The development of the shingle industry even made some slash and stumps marketable, and scavengers followed the loggers to sift their debris for discarded cedar that could be made into the bolts used to manufacture shingles.[1] After 1900 the bulk of the logging operations shifted from Whidbey to Camano. Scattered operations continued on Whidbey as camps operated at Dugualla Bay until 1903, and loggers took virgin cedar out of the Holmes Harbor region between 1912 and 1915, but the operations on Camano dwarfed these camps. As early as 1901, 22 camps operated on Camano, and camps continued to run on every part of that island for the next 20 years.

These operations exploited both new and old sources of timber. Congress had set aside sections one and sixteen for the support of the public schools when it created the territory, and in the twentieth century, for the first time, numerous tracts of these school lands could be legally logged. Between 1900 and 1905, stumpage from 2,435 acres of school land was sold at auction, leaving only a small remnant of timber from the original school grant to trickle onto the market in subsequent years. The timber from lands that had been partially logged during the nineteenth century and abandoned for taxes supplemented the stumpage from the school lands. Loggers acquired these lands at tax sales for prices ranging from $.48 to $5.65 an acre and made single purchases as large as 1,600 to 1,700 acres. After they relogged it, timbermen abandoned most of this once again. The last lands logged on the islands belonged to Puget Mill. In 1913, the company valued its timber holdings in the county at $400,000. When Puget Mill logged off the last large tract of this land, 1,480 acres on north Camano, in the early 1920s, large-scale logging in the county ended. Afterward only small logging contractors, called gyppo operators, would work the woods.[2]

A new technology made this final attack of the loggers on the forests of the county far different from the bull team logging that had gone before it. During the early years of the century, steam power replaced animal power in the woods as the donkey engine supplanted the bull teams and the horses. First patented in 1882 by John Dolbeer, the donkey engine was a small steam engine set on skids and attached to a winch. Manufacturers gradually increased the amount of power the engine generated, until by the early twentieth century one engine might power four or five winches. Loggers attached cables from these winches to metal chokers that they placed on the logs, allowing the engine to reel in the attached logs. Originally loggers used the machine only for yarding, that is, gathering the logs from where they were cut to a central point so the bull teams could pull them to tidewater, but by 1900 the donkey engine had entirely replaced the bull teams in some operations. Donkey engines set up by tidewater, streams, and railroad tracks pulled in logs from up to a mile away. Loggers reported that the steam donkeys more than halved the cost of log removal.

High lead logging provided a substantial refinement in steam logging techniques. Loggers hung a block or pulley on a selected spar tree and ran the line from the donkey engine through it. Moving the log through the air instead of along the ground measurably increased both the speed and the danger of logging operations. High lead logging, a post-1910 development, affected only the last of the operations in Island County, however.[3]

Steam technology gave loggers the capability to take logs out of the woods so efficiently and so cheaply that the exhaustion of commercial forests in the county became foreseeable at a time when the county government needed tax revenues from the woods far more urgently than ever before. The County's population of 1,870 in 1900 had increased to 5,489 by 1920. Immigrants largely moved into previously unsettled areas of the islands, and they needed and demanded schools, roads, and services. The only means the county government had for generating the revenue to meet these demands was the property tax.[4]

The reliance of county and state governments on property taxes complicates any discussion of the impact of new technologies on the land. Lumbermen argued that the existing tax system forced them to use their new machines recklessly if they hoped to gain any profit from the forests. As long as the state and county annually taxed land with standing timber in proportion to its market value, loggers would have to cut the forests quickly. If timbermen let the forests stand, they would pay taxes on the same "crops" year after year, and each year's property taxes subtracted from their eventual profits on the trees. It made more sense to cut the lumber immediately and avoid years of additional taxes on it. Once they logged the land, its value would drop and so would their tax burden. But even the reduced taxes on cutover lands remained sufficient, lumbermen agreed, to make reforestation financially infeasible. In their eyes, the problem was not the new technology or their own logging practices; instead, it was a foolish tax system that made it necessary for timbermen to cut valuable forests prematurely and then prevented them from planting new trees. The government forced them to use their new technology recklessly.

The lumbermen's argument was simple and cogent, and many conservationists made the same points. Perhaps the most forceful statement of this position came in a massive report written for the United States Forest Service in the 1920s by Fred Fairchild of the Yale School of Forestry. Fairchild concluded that only through tax reform could the country ensure a lasting supply of timber and the reforestation of private lands. The arguments of Fairchild and the lumbermen became the common reform wisdom of the period, and any examination of the impact of the new technology must take it into account.[5] Since the Island County taxes did rise precipitously in the early twentieth century, the question becomes: Did the property tax prompt lumbermen to use the new steam technology so ruthlessly that they eliminated the county's last remaining stands of virgin timber by 1920?

Between 1904 and 1924 the tax load of Island County sextupled and the value of assessed property doubled, a rise that does not reflect merely an increase in real value (see Table 9). In 1908 the

TABLE 9. RISE IN TAXES, ISLAND COUNTY

Assessed Value	1904	1913	1918	1924
Land				
Improve-	$854,309	$1,242,430	$1,434,570	$1,867,045
ments	. . .	185,425	115,505	243,710
State Tax	8,052	9,112	15,838	33,626
County Tax	16,579	27,106	37,714	47,663
Road Levy	. . .	15,889	18,265	24,739
Total*	$ 24,631	$ 74,727	$ 101,028	$ 167,183

*Total includes diking, drainage, and municipality taxes not listed here.

SOURCE: Annual Reports of the Island County Auditor, 1904, 1913, 1918, 1924.

ratio of assessed value to real value was only 34.98, which meant that the county entered property on the tax rolls at only a little over one-third of its market value. In only five counties of the state was the ratio lower. By 1922, however, the county assessed land at nearly one-half its real value (46 percent); only King County, which includes Seattle, had a higher ratio.[6]

This rise in taxes (to fund the new roads, schools, and services that an expanding population demanded) forced county officials to reevaluate older tax policies regarding the forests. Before 1900 taxes on forest lands had remained minimal, but after 1900, unless officials were to place the increased tax burden solely on agricultural lands and town lots, taxes on forest and cutover lands had to rise. For half a century the forests had provided little direct support for public institutions. Now, when the county needed to turn to these lands for tax revenue, steam technology and changing markets had given lumbermen the power to rapidly reduce them to cutover wastelands. To tax the forests, lumbermen argued, would only speed the cutting and narrow the tax base of the county still further. To tax trees was to destroy them, and by this logic, social needs and conservation were simply incompatible.

The county could ill afford to ignore the lumbermen's claims. If a farmer harvested a crop and moved on, he still left behind valuable agricultural land. When a timberman harvested his crop, he left behind a waste of slash and stumps. If and when the forest returned, it would be second growth, commercially worthless for years to come. At the turn of the century, such cutover lands already made up between two-thirds and three-quarters of the real estate in the county outside of the towns. Since these lands produced nothing of economic value, there were definite limits to the tax revenue they could yield. In 1910 they provided about 50 percent of all assessed taxes, and this proved to be the maximum they could produce. Although the total assessed value of all county lands rose 70.9 percent between 1910 and 1920, the assessed value of unimproved lands rose only 55 percent. Unimproved and cutover lands thus provided a smaller proportion of county revenue in 1920 than in 1910 (see Table 10). Cutover land, unproductive and often virtually treeless, was not a productive resource. Producing neither jobs nor substantial tax revenues, it posed a major social and economic challenge for county government. In a sense, logged-off lands represented the ultimate product of lumbering.

County officials thus faced a substantial dilemma. They could not turn to cutover lands for increased tax revenues without inviting the wholesale abandonment of such lands. Yet the agricultural portion of the approximately one-third to one-quarter of their land

TABLE 10. Assessed Value of Various Types of Land, Island County

Land Category	1910	1915	1920
Timberland Acres	8,804	18,100	5,575
Avg. Value per Acre	$ 19.05	$ 22.44	$ 40.51
Total Value	$167,710	$406,240	$225,845
Unimproved Acres	99,942	90,835	98,659
Avg. Value	$ 6.37	$ 7.72	$ 9.87
Total Value	$636,320	$701,364	$974,190
Improved Land Acres	10,110	11,190	15,666
Avg. Value	$ 33.97	$ 33.27	$ 48.53
Total Value	$343,445	$372,291	$760,280

Source: Minutes and Official Proceeding of the State Board of Equalization of the State of Washington, Sessions of 1910, 1915, 1920.

base capable of productive use was already disproportionately taxed. And if they increased taxes on their remaining timberlands, lumbermen threatened to use the new steam technology to increase the pace at which they were creating worthless wastelands. In the face of such threats, officials did not rush to increase taxes on timberlands. As late as 1910, they chose to keep the bulk of the tax burden on unimproved lands and farmlands. After 1910, however, assessors did turn to forests for revenue, making the taxes on timberlands in 1915 greater than those on the farmlands. There was a logic to their actions that lumbermen denied. For them to continue disproportionate taxation of farmland at a time when the county sought a larger farming population, and when timbermen left behind only wastelands, seemed a destructive and counterproductive policy.

The full scope of the changes in the tax policies of Island County does not emerge until the gross changes in tax revenue assessment between 1910 and 1920 are broken down. When taken as a whole, the decade between 1910 and 1920 witnessed only a modest rise in timberland tax assessment (see Table 11). Both agricultural and unimproved lands had a higher percentage rise in assessed value, and by 1920 both bore a larger share of taxes than

TABLE 11. RISE IN ASSESSED VALUE, ISLAND COUNTY

Category	1910	1915	1920	Total Rise, 1910–20
Total Valuation	$1,147,475	$1,479,895	$1,960,315	. . .
Total Rise	. . .	28 %	32 %	70 %
% Timberland	14.6%	27.5%	11.5%	. . .
Rise in Value	. . .	142.0%	−46.5%	42.8%
% Unimproved	55.5%	47.4%	49.7%	55.0%
Rise in Value	. . .	10.2%	38.9%	55.0%
% Agriculture	29.9%	25.1%	38.8%	. . .
Rise in Value	. . .	8.0%	104.0%	113 %

SOURCE: Minutes and Official Proceedings of the State Board of Equalization of the State of Washington, Sessions of 1910, 1915, 1920.

timberland. This comparison is, however, distorted. It ignores the sizable shifting of taxes to the forest lands that took place between 1910 and 1915.

County officials used two techniques to increase revenues from the timberlands. Initially, they reclassified culled lands from unimproved to timberland and thus raised their assessed value. Between 1910 and 1915, a time of heavy logging, the acreage of timberland in the county actually more than doubled. The total assessed value of timberlands increased 142 percent in five years at a time when nearly all the best timber had been cut. For the same period, the total assessed value of all real property increased only 28 percent. In 1910 timberlands composed 14.6 percent of the total value of real estate in the county; by 1915 this had risen to 27.5 percent. After 1915, with little culled land left to be reclassified, officials used another technique to increase revenue: They increased the assessed value of timberlands. The average value nearly doubled in five years.[7]

These developments in Island and other lumbering counties brought angry denunciations from mill companies and speculators, who demanded revision of state and county tax laws that they regarded as archaic and punitive. They repeated the standard arguments that, by including the value of growing timber in the assessed value of forest lands, tax laws forced them to pay "taxes on the same crop year after year until the timber is removed."[8] This arrangement, they claimed, put timberland owners under pressure to cut rapidly in order to diminish the value of their land and, hence, their taxes. Landowners also contended that taxes dashed their plans to reforest by making the cost of holding land prohibitive. Taxes supposedly forced them to sell or abandon their land.

In Island County most large owners did choose to dispose of their logged-off lands. The Port Blakely Mill Company sold land from the turn of the century on. Puget Mill did not enter the land business until the 1920s, when it had completely finished logging operations in the county, but then it sold off virtually all its land, continuing its sales for the next quarter of a century. Speculators, too, put their land on the market, often pretending their cutover lands were fit for farming—but if buyers did not materialize, they simply abandoned their holdings.[9]

Mill owners contended this pattern of premature cutting and

land abandonment could be corrected if only the state would adopt a rational tax policy. In Washington such theories had been common since at least 1910, when the report of the Washington State Commission on Forest Legislation had advocated a minimal annual property tax in conjunction with a large yield tax at harvest to replace the existing tax system. Without tax reform and state forests, the commission predicted that Washington's virgin timber would be exhausted before new forests replaced the old. With tax reform, premature cutting could be avoided and cutover land could be profitably reforested. Conservationists and lumbermen continued to advocate forest tax reform for more than twenty years in Washington, but the state legislature consistently rejected their proposals. Not until 1931 was a law passed that provided for forest tax reform.[10]

As repeated legislative defeats show, the supposed relation between taxation and reforestation posited by reformers obviously did not convince everyone during this period. In 1915 Burt Kirkland, a professor of forestry at the University of Washington, published a short article on reforestation. After analyzing costs and expected profits, Kirkland concluded that capital costs, largely interest on investments, formed the real barrier to reforestation and that only those who could borrow capital at less than 5 percent could afford to reforest land and protect it from fire. In practice, this would confine reforestation to the federal government, the state government, some municipalities, and very large corporations. In other words, according to Kirkland, reforestation would not be feasible for most private landowners no matter how low taxes were.[11]

TABLE 12. TAX DELINQUEN

Taxes	1913	1915	19
$ Owed the County for Taxes	. . .	3,415	25,
Total Owed State and County	7,850	12,138	85,

SOURCE: Auditor's Report, Island County, 1913–

When examined closely, the relationship between taxation and premature cutting does not appear as simple as reformers liked to make it. Puget Mill liquidated its timber holdings at a time of rapidly rising taxes, but this does not spell a cause and effect relationship. Puget Mill Company records reveal that both the desire to produce immediate dividends for stockholders by liquidating long-held assets and the fear that increased settlement on lands adjoining Puget Mill holdings had heightened the danger of fire in company forests were as important as taxes in the decision of the company to log their last lands in Island County. It is doubtful that the virgin timber of Island County would have survived the 1920s even if taxes had not risen.[12]

The relationship between high taxes and land abandonment also does not emerge as clearly as reformers contended. In the 1880s, when taxes were minimal, the extensive tax sales demonstrated the propensity of landowners to abandon lands that did not produce immediate revenue. In 1902, a year in which unimproved land was taxed from five to ten cents per acre, the sheriff of Island County held a tax sale at which he sold over 6,351 acres, exclusive of town lots. In 1903 the county took additional land for taxes due since 1897. The taxes owed ranged from $.58 to $7.24 per tract. High taxes hardly caused such delinquency. Land abandonment was widespread in Island County long before tax rates began to rise.[13]

There are no continuous figures on lands sold for taxes in the early twentieth century in Island County, but there are records of tax delinquency (see Table 12). The amount of delinquency rose substantially between 1915 and 1920 along with the tax rates.

ND COUNTY

25	1930	1935	1939
143	25,625	38,647	38,210
208	. . .	107,474	97,180

nty Clerk's Report, 1930–39.

But this rise also coincides with the heyday of clearcut logging in the county. Thousands of acres of forest land now had no marketable timber left on them, and owners apparently had little reason to retain them. Tax delinquency rose most rapidly in the 1920s, a few years after loggers left the county. Not even the Depression would push it much higher.[14]

In all probability, tax reform would not have significantly altered this pattern of land abandonment and deforestation. In 1931 the legislature finally passed a tax reform law and, after much litigation, it took effect in 1934. It allowed landowners to apply to have their land classified for reforestation and have it assessed at $1 per acre as long as they replanted their holdings to fir and patrolled them for fire. In some counties, assessors almost immediately dropped the valuation of all unimproved lands to $1 an acre, but not in Island County. In 1934, the average valuation of unimproved land in Island County was $9.38 an acre; theoretically, therefore, the act should have had much appeal to county landowners (see Table 13). But between 1934 and 1940, not one owner of cutover lands in Island County applied for reforestation classification.[15]

TABLE 13. VALUATION OF UNIMPROVED LAND FOR TAXES
IN ISLAND COUNTY, 1930–40

Acre of Unimproved Land	1930	1934	1937	1940
Average Assessed Value	$7.63	$9.38	$9.00	$9.01

SOURCE: Minutes and Official Proceedings of the Washington State Board of Equalization, 1930, 1934, 1937, 1940.

Even with low taxes, timberland owners remained unwilling to take on the risk and expense of reforestation. The price of timber, whether $11.58 per thousand board feet in 1912 or $23.80 per thousand board feet in 1932, hardly seemed to promise an adequate return on their investment in planting and protection. Kirkland's argument seems compelling: It was capital costs and the lack of return on investment, more than taxes, that prevented private reforestation. The rates of taxation cannot logically be blamed for rapid cutting or land abandonment. The problem was not taxation; it was competition, overproduction, and the lure of quick profits. At least in Island County reforestation through tax reform was a pipe dream without a significant rise in lumber values.

In Island County, therefore, the relationship of taxes to rapid deforestation seems to have been exactly the opposite of what lumbermen claimed. Harvesting did not speed up because taxes rose; instead, taxes rose in response to the rapid logging of prime timberlands that left only worthless cutover lands behind. Faced with an expanding population in need of basic services, county officials had to tax forests while they still remained to be taxed. They did not force reckless use of the new technology. Instead, the economic system that produced it provided neither restraints nor the incentives for self-restraint that might limit its destructive use. One victim of the resultant rapid harvesting that followed would be the forest itself, but the other would be the basic public services of Island County. Steam technology thus possessed both social and ecological dimensions. Before examining the ecological consequences of steam technology, however, an additional section of Kirkland's argument should be examined. If private owners refused to reforest the cutover lands, he argued, couldn't the state have stepped in and attempted the task?

Theoretically, reforestation was financially possible for the state, but in practice Washington did as little as private landowners in replanting the timberlands. In 1923, the legislature had created a State Forest Board authorized to acquire land by gift or purchase for the purpose of reforestation. And in 1927, the legislature allowed county commissioners to turn over abandoned lands to the state for reforestation. The state was to return a percentage of the income from such land to the county government upon harvest. The commissioners of Island County never acted; as late as 1944 Island County was one of the few counties in western Washington in which no tax delinquent lands had been deeded to the state. All the sustained yield, timber conservation, and tax reform discussions of the Progressive and New Deal eras had had minimal impact on the county. No concrete steps toward timber management and conservation had been taken.[16]

In Island County, therefore, there were not only no institutional restraints on the new technology, there were also no institutional correctives for the damage it caused. And the damage was substantial. The impact of the donkey engine went well beyond increased speed and efficiency. Land cut by donkey engine crews bore the mark of the new technology. Not only did marketable fir and cedar come down, loggers also cut hemlock to cushion the fall of commercial trees. After loggers felled the trees and cut them into twenty- to thirty-foot logs weighing many tons, the donkey engine skidded them out of the woods and down skid roads. Pulling logs of this size through the woods at high speeds cut and gouged the land and leveled small trees and seedlings. Sporadically the cable pulling the log would break, and the whiplash of the broken cable as the machine reeled it in could cut both men and small trees in two. At the end of a steam logging operation, the ground would be gouged into a collection of hummocks and hollows covered with a tangled mass of rotten wood, branches, small timber, broken trees, stumps, and tops. On the average, loggers left 24,000 cubic feet of slash, or waste, on an acre of land when they finished a logging operation.[17]

The presence of large numbers of men and machines in the woods, coupled with the huge amounts of waste they created, enormously increased the chance of fire. For years after the loggers had departed, the slash, drying out each summer, remained a fire danger. And when this slash ignited a new kind of forest fire resulted. Investigators found that fires started in the slash burned at temperatures as high as 1,814 degrees F. At such temperatures fires consumed approximately twenty-five tons of organic material, 89 percent of the duff layer of the forest, for every acre burned. Slash fires thus tended to be much hotter and more destructive than fires in virgin or second-growth forests, where foliage, dead trees, and broken limbs provided most of the fuel.[18]

In Island County, the number and intensity of fires almost certainly increased in the first years of the century, although statistics on the nineteenth century are not reliable enough to say for certain. Fittingly enough, the first major fire of the twentieth century started in the Cavalero Camp on Camano Island where the first donkey engine was operating. The fire destroyed the camp and threatened several others. This general area, north central Camano, became the scene of repeated fires between 1900 and 1920, but such fires were common in all forested areas of the islands. In

August 1902, for instance, several fires erupted, including a major one on Whidbey that apparently burned for weeks in the woods and cutover lands north of Oak Harbor. In the worst years accidental fires would burn from 1,000 to 3,500 acres of land. Such fires continued long after logging operations in the county ceased, since the major portion of the land affected was not timberland, but logged-off land, brush land, and previously burned land. In 1911, out of 1,320 acres burned, only 10 contained marketable timber, and only 50 more had second growth trees. In 1919, out of 1,690 acres burned, only 35 had marketable timber and an equal number had second-growth trees. (See Tables 24 and 25.)

Accidental fires made up only part of the fires that burned in the slash loggers left behind. During these same years, farmers burned other lands under permit to clear them for agriculture. This controlled burning rarely spread to neighboring lands, but on the cutover land it had the same effect as slash burning. The number of fires started under permit varied from year to year, with a low of 22 in 1905 and a high of 147 in 1921. In terms of acreage, farmers burned from 500 to 2,000 acres annually.[19]

These fires continued the series of ecological changes begun by logging. Logging and slash fires created or maintained new expanses of open land, where the increase in berries, fireweed, and other successional species supported an increasing mammal population. Not only deer, but also mice, squirrels, chipmunks, and (later) rabbits multiplied. These animals, in turn, had significant effects on forest vegetation. The damage they did by browsing on Douglas fir seedlings and eating the new growth on young trees, for instance, became an important factor in the forest ecology.[20]

The forest adapted to these changes as best it could. The cull trees left by the bull team loggers had once been a source of seeds, but after 1900 loggers cut such trees along with the rest. Likewise, the loggers eliminated stands of virgin forest that had once seeded neighboring cutover lands. Mature forests no longer neighbored on cutover land in the twentieth century; now young forests or more cutover lands bordered recently cut lands and, consequently, newly cut land lacked a readily available seed supply. By 1916, for example, when Puget Mill began logging its land on north Camano, all the surrounding land in the area was either burned or cutover.[21]

Nevertheless, on most lands at least a first crop of young seedlings followed logging. The fires that inevitably came in the
wake of cutting often destroyed these trees that sprang from seed
stored on the forest floor. These initial fires not only eliminated
seedlings; they created conditions even less promising for the
young trees. Fire destroyed humus and thus lessened moisture retention of the soil, essential for the germination and survival of
Douglas fir seedlings, and it changed the nutrient balance of the
forest floor. It altered soil pH, and burning measurably increased
amounts of potassium, nitrogen, and calcium while decreasing
phosphorus. In the long run, this sudden abundance of nutrients,
which ordinarily would have been made available over a period of
years, probably hurt the growth of young trees. It encouraged
seedlings to develop shallow root structures and large crowns and
thus made them more vulnerable to eventual drought. Furthermore, in place of the organic layer, fires deposited a layer of black
charred debris that increased heat retention on the forest floor. On
hot summer days, the temperature of the mineral soil of the area
would rise only to 125 degrees F, but the temperature of the
burned soils would rise to 150 degrees F and higher. At such temperatures forest studies revealed 16 to 40 percent of the young
seedlings under observation died. Those seedlings that survived
had to contend with the increased animal population that thrived
on land opened up by logging, as well as with the danger of further fires.[22]

By the 1920s the results had become apparent. A 1927 Forest
Service report concluded that "whatever reproduction takes place
does so, for the most part, in spite of present methods, not as a
result of them." Systematic research by the Forest Service only
confirmed the increasing failure of natural reforestation. A 1932
survey of the county found 790 acres of land logged before 1920
that had failed to return to forest, as well as an additional 2,500
acres logged or burned around 1920 that still did not have new
growth. But total deforestation was only part of the price paid.
The study revealed that, since 1900, such reforestation as did take
place was increasingly inadequate. Seventy-eight percent of the
stands that germinated around 1900, the year when donkey engine
logging was only beginning in Island County, were well stocked.
But of those stands germinating in 1910, when donkey engine

Penn Cove in the late 1850s (drawing by J. M. Stanley, from *Pacific Railroad Surveys*)

Cultus Bay in the late 1850s (drawing by I. M. Stanley, from *Pacific Railroad Surveys*)

Grennan and Cranney's Sawmills, Utsalady, Camano Island, 1862 (drawing by C. B. Gifford)

Penn Cove, circa 1900

Whidbey Island, circa 1900

House frames from Skagit village at Snatelum Point

Club wheat field, Bash Farm, Oak Harbor, circa 1900

Barkley Mill, Lone Lake, Whidbey Island, 1912

Timothy and wheat field, Bash Farm, Oak Harbor, circa 1900

Oat field in dyked salt marsh, Bash Farm, Oak Harbor, circa 1900

Meadow, Bash Farm, Oak Harbor, circa 1900

logging dominated the woods, only 59.2 percent were well stocked, and for 1920 the percentage was only 55.4 percent. For comparison, of the stands that germinated in 1880, after bull team loggers had cut the original forest, 92.9 percent were well stocked.[23]

Even restocking is an adequate measure of the changes brought to the forest by the new technology and the new logging methods that accompanied it. In response to new conditions, the very composition of the forest changed. Broadleafs, previously a minor component of the forests, now covered almost 6,000 acres. This total remained insignificant compared with the 80,000 acres of Douglas fir, but the acreage of the deciduous trees was greater than that of predominantly hemlock, cedar, and spruce forests combined. Even in terms of cubic feet, alder ranked ahead of spruce and cedar, and only a little behind western hemlock and white fir.[24] (See Table 26.)

Alder germinates best in damp, low-lying areas. The deep scarification of the land, brought on by logging roads and skidding, allowed water to collect and favored the establishment of alder on land that had previously supported fir. Fir might still germinate among the alder, but it was now at a severe disadvantage. Alder grows much more rapidly than does fir. Even at a normal growth rate, fir does not equal alder in height until thirty or forty years of age. Fir underneath alder, however, does not attain a normal growth rate because of the shade created by the rapidly growing broadleaf. Instead, young firs are suppressed and usually die off in five to seven years. When the alder (itself a relatively short-lived tree) dies, it is succeeded not by fir but by shade-tolerant hemlock. In effect, the successional pattern of the forest had undergone a significant change. The dominant species of the area, the Douglas fir, had been locally eliminated and two trees of lesser commercial value, the red alder and the hemlock, had replaced it.[25]

Donkey engine logging exacerbated social problems in Island County. By clearly increasing the rate of deforestation it not only created environmental problems, but it also severely restricted the means officials had of coping with local social and economic problems. Yet it must be reemphasized that the new technology was not the root of Island County's problems. Donkey engine technology did not have to deprive the county of part of its tax base and destroy much of the forest. It did so because the economic and social system made it profitable for logging technology to run amuck in the first place.

The consequences of the new logging technology could be controlled when it was profitable to do so. The best example of this can be seen in the steps taken to curb forest fires. In the nineteenth century there had been laws against deliberate setting of forest fires on public lands, and even against culpable neglect in case of accidental fires, but it was only in the twentieth century that anyone made real attempts to regulate burning. In 1903 the legislature made the state land commissioners ex-officio fire wardens.[26] By 1908 the mills had formed the Washington Forest Fire Association to supplement state programs. The Association assessed 2,500,000 acres of land, owned by members, two cents an acre for protection.[27]

In Island County, at least, this program for the protection of mature timber was successful. After the passage of the 1905 law, the number of accidental and wildfires in the county shows a fairly steady decline. Although a significant amount of land still burned each year, little of it contained marketable timber. Timberland owners continued to show little desire to protect land without marketable trees, but fire prevention coupled with judicious cutting had served to protect their investments in actual timberlands. That protecting investments was not the equivalent of protecting the forest mattered little.[28] (See Figure 1.)

By any measure, the forest in Island County deteriorated rapidly

Figure 1. Accidental fires

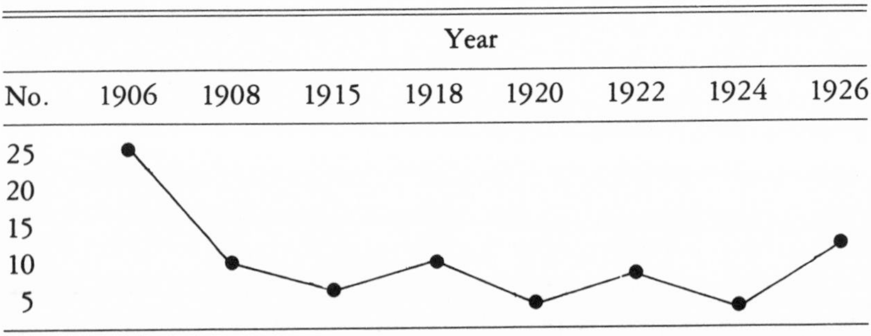

between 1900 and 1920. Donkey engine logging had hampered or eliminated reforestation, changed the composition of the forest, and made the rapid cutting and elimination of timberlands possible at a time when the development of the county created a need for timber resources to provide both jobs and taxes. Timbermen introduced the donkey engine for commercial reasons; an irony of its use was that logging methods based upon it changed conditions so fundamentally that a new forest was created, a forest far less useful to the lumbermen who had introduced the machine.

Profit and loss were the only criteria by which the men who controlled the new technology judged the changes that it caused. The men who operated the machine and the economic system they operated under, as much as the machine itself, shaped the county forests of the twentieth century. For landowners it remained more profitable to strip and scar the forest and move into fresh lands than it was to stay and replant. There was no reason that lumbering technology should not run amuck when the economic system gave it every incentive to do so, and when the political system failed to apply even the most basic restraints.

With some bitterness, a few county residents realized in the early twentieth century that they were the ones who would have to cope with acres of unproductive cutover lands when the loggers were gone. In 1903, the *Island County Times* ran an editorial denouncing corporations for destroying the forests and raising lumber prices. The writer advocated national ownership of forest land, controlled cutting, and the sale of timber at public auction. But few people in the county echoed this call, and the federal government never established a national forest.[29]

Foresters, conservationists, and government officials recognized that the reforestation question was fundamentally economic and social as well as technical. They focused most of their attention not on the donkey engine but on such larger social and economic questions as: Who bore the responsibility for reforestation and how could it be implemented? How could forest lands best be maintained and still be made to support social institutions? The actions that sprang from the attempts to answer these questions, however, were often contradictory and counterproductive.

Timbermen and reformers formulated the issue of reforestation around tax reductions for mill companies and large landowners. In a logging county faced with rising taxes, this could only seem a plan for financial disaster to the county government. Such tax plans ultimately proved unworkable and forestalled the possibility of constructive state action. Likewise, lumbermen, out of a real concern for the damage being done by uncontrolled fires, made fire itself seem a primal enemy of the forest. Because of their own economic assumptions, they failed to recognize that fire had created the forests they were lumbering; that the problem was not fire per se, but the new conditions they had created for fire. As a consequence, conservationists and the lumber industry succeeded in totally reversing the old relationship of fire and the forest. In the mature forest, where fire was a part of the existing ecology, they successfully banished forest fires. In cutover and deforested areas, where repeated fires prevented the return of healthy forests or altered the forest composition, lumbermen created ideal conditions for slash fires and largely let them burn. They protected their investment and, in the process, altered the ecology that had created and maintained the forest they were exploiting. By 1938, the National Land Planning Board would treat the county as an unforested area so far as future planning was concerned.[30]

The failure to adequately answer the questions the reformers posed does not mean that the questions themselves were at fault. Reformers were correct to see the problems as more complex than mere technological change. They recognized, rightly, that there was an economic and social organization that encouraged men to use technology recklessly, but the legal restraints they imposed remained inadequate. As primitive as donkey engine technology was, it was in a sense far more sophisticated than the economic and social system in which it operated. Loggers proved more adept at refining the machine than lawmakers did at devising means to control its use.

Hindsight, however, makes this failure look worse than it appeared to most contemporary residents of the county. Residents saw logging not merely as the destruction of the forest, but also as a preparation of the land for real settlers. Behind the loggers came the stump farmers. And the farms, and the growing population and expanding economy they represented, became the hope of many county residents for the future.

Chapter VI

POOR MEN ON POOR LANDS

The Movement onto the Logged-off Lands

The feeble efforts made during the early twentieth century to preserve the forest of western Washington in general and Island County in particular never grew into anything substantial because most people retained the old belief that the forest only represented an obstacle to farming. To remove the forest was a sign of progress, a mere prelude to the creation of farms. A pervasive unease over the destruction of the forest began to affect many Americans only when it seemed that this centuries-old pattern of destroying forests to create farms might collapse. For two hundred years the axe and the plow had come in automatic succession, the axe, like some iron prophet, preparing the way for the plow. And for much of this period the same hands had held both tools—the axeman was the plowman. But by the late nineteenth century in Wisconsin, Michigan, and Minnesota the axeman was no longer synonymous with the plowman, and there came to be a break in the rhythm of settlement, a pause in the natural progression as unnerving as if summer had hesitated in following spring. Loggers, not farmers, cut the forests, and after the forest fell the plowmen did not appear. In an odd and unnatural manner, the farmer had to be coaxed into performing his appointed task of planting the ground from which the forest was taken.

In the late nineteenth and early twentieth centuries, people in Washington expressed concern that here, too, the natural order was somehow being perverted—the necessary and accustomed succession was being broken. Many began to face the prospect that the western third of the state would consist of a desolate and unproductive waste of huge stumps and shattered trees. They recoiled from the prospect, but their solution was not to reforest but rather to encourage settlement. To understand events in Island County between 1900 and 1940, this concern, and the back-to-the-land movements it spawned, must be examined in some detail. Largely urban in inspiration, back-to-the-land movements are perceived as barely affecting the city, and as unimportant even in the countryside. Dismissed as a mere romantic or sentimental reaction to industrialization, their literary artifacts reveal intellectual trends, but scholars assume their concrete social accomplishments to have been negligible. Many of these movements, however, are more than the stillborn brainchildren of romantic intellectuals, more than mere hankerings after idealized agrarian pasts. They have often succeeded in placing thousands of families in the countryside and have had important social and ecological consequences. Furthermore, back-to-the-land movements proceeded from intellectual assumptions more complicated than mere romanticism, and their remains are more than literary. A proper understanding of back-to-the-land movements must take into account the rationale behind the movement, the experience of people who worked the land, and finally the relationship of settlement to environmental change. These three interrelated aspects of back-to-the-land settlement are clearly revealed in the movement to place settlers on the logged-off lands of western Washington, and in the actual settlement of people in Island County, during the first four decades of the twentieth century.[1]

Early twentieth century advocates of back-to-the-land movements proceeded from the assumption that the cities were overpopulated while the rural districts were correspondingly underpopulated. From this fundamental imbalance (in their eyes a development alien to American history and American institutions) flowed the myriad of social problems—unemployment, poverty, disease, moral decline—that they believe would, if unchecked, eventually destroy the nation itself. In the western United States, particularly, the scarcity of small farms and the rapid growth of cities aroused considerable concern. Regions such as Island County, with more than half of their total area left an unproductive wasteland by logging, seemed vivid signs of impending doom. As Judge Frederick Bausman, speaking of the logged-off lands, frankly told a Seattle audience in 1916, "an emergency exists."[2]

In retrospect the failure of people to settle these cutover lands and create farms without considerable urging is not mysterious. The deforested portions of western Washington consisted of neither fertile virgin land awaiting the plow nor extensive established rural districts. It was a desolate and unproductive waste of huge stumps and shattered trees. An observer sympathetic to the movement to settle the logged-off lands gave a frank description of a typical tract of cutover land in 1917:

> Stumps from two to nine feet in diameter lift their ugly heads above the brush and debris; dead snags reach up here and there to stand twisted, half uprooted and stripped of limbs. Logs, water soaked, interlace the ground, often overlapping three and four deep. A tangle of underbrush covers the ground. The surface is generally broken and is one mass of hummocks and hollows. The ground conceals a network of roots, often massive in size, and running out many yards from the parent tree.[3]

Unlike the stumps of the deciduous forests of the East, or even the pine forests of New England, Minnesota, Wisconsin, and Michigan, these conifer stumps could take a human lifetime to rot. Simply to remove the stumps, which might be up to ten feet in diameter, the new farmer had to work harder and spend more money than in any other forested area of the United States. Furthermore, although soil types varied in the cutover region, light podzolic soils composed the bulk of the upland forest area of western Washington. Infertile, leached by heavy winter rains, and easily eroded when vegetation had been removed, these soils were simply unsuited for agriculture.[4]

Boosters never recognized these obstacles. To them, the failure of either timber companies or the federal and state governments to reforest Island County and similar areas in western Washington left agricultural settlement as, seemingly, the only remaining route to renewed productivity. They did not turn to such settlement out of desperation; it was the preferred solution. Advocates of agricultural development remained unaware of the infertility of the forest soils they planned to transform into farms. The still primitive soil science of the early twentieth century could not judge fertility with any great accuracy. When boosters claimed the "land which grew the sturdy evergreen will grow anything else," few challenged them. As late as 1931, the State Director of Agriculture for Washington advised prospective settlers to choose land with plenty of big stumps because such land was certain to be fertile.[5]

Even if reforestation had seemed financially feasible, the logic of the back-to-the-land boosters would probably have forced them to reject the planting of trees on cutover lands. Reforestation ignored the fundamental social logic of the movement. Planting trees did not correct urban social ills; new forests would not drain large numbers of unemployed workers from the cities. When a booster of logged-off land settlement denounced the Forest Service for trying to "grow trees on land that should grow men," he was only underlining the logic of the whole movement.[6]

Despite anti-urban rhetoric, back-to-the-land activities arose from motives far more complicated than a mere hatred of the city and its ills. The promoters of rural settlement were not themselves farmers. Politicians, lawyers, editors, speculators, businessmen, bankers, foresters, and lumbermen organized and promoted the movement. The Everett Chamber of Commerce called the first Logged-off Conference in 1908, and the head c: the Seattle Chamber of Commerce announced his support for the settlement of the logged-off lands. George S. Long, the manager of the Weyerhaeuser timber interests in the state, helped organize the settlement movement, and lumber trade journals as well as business journals regularly featured articles on what was referred to as the problem of the logged-off lands. In 1912 the movement in the Northwest spawned its own journal, *Little Logged-off Lands.*[7]

Although many of these men, or the corporations they worked for, owned logged-off lands, the whole movement represented more than a speculation dreamed up by landowners and timber companies. Indeed, boosters condemned timber companies for not selling their land and attacked speculators for selling land at inflated prices. The interest of the supporters of settlement often went beyond immediate profit; they wanted to save the city by redeeming the countryside. The economic and social concerns that surfaced in the logged-off land movement of Washington were by no means peculiar to the Pacific Northwest. The same promotional zeal for settlement, the same excess of private and official encouragement, and the same lack of public aid that would characterize settlement of cutover lands in Washington also developed in Minnesota, Wisconsin, and Michigan in the late nineteenth and early twentieth centuries. And, in its most influential manifestation, this back-to-the-land movement focused not on the logged-off lands at all, but rather on the arid lands of the West. Under George Maxwell of California, the National Irrigation Congress (NIC) promoted an irrigation program as a tool for economic development and as a safety valve for social tensions in a manner similar to that used by the supporters of settlement on the logged-off lands. Maxwell made the NIC a pressure group far more formidable than any logged-off land association.[8]

Nowhere does the bias of the movement in favor of the city emerge more clearly than in its autarchic assumptions. For the urban booster the city demanded a productive hinterland; the rapid cutting of the forests, therefore, threatened cities like Seattle and Tacoma with ruin unless the land could be returned to productive uses. Since reforestation seemed slow and unprofitable, agriculture provided the only answer. Proponents of settlement cited figures indicating that Seattle alone consumed three million dollars worth of food monthly, but not more than 20 percent of it was produced in the Northwest. According to *Little Logged-off Lands,* residents of Washington sent twenty-six million dollars out of the state in 1910 for dairy, poultry, and pork products that logged-off farmers could have produced in Washington. Not only would these new settlers retain needed capital, they would also consume the products of the industries the capital would create. To fill the lands, boosters sought unemployed urban workers and recent foreign immigrants. In theory, such settlers would perform a double service: By leaving the city they would automatically lessen its social problems, and by settling on the logged-off lands they would feed the urban population and stimulate urban industry.[9]

It is within this economic context that the movement's anti-urban rhetoric should be understood. Propagandists trotted out all the venerable agrarian homilies, but they put them at the service of the city. They argued that the attraction of people to the soil was instinctive, that urban life was unnatural, and that moral and civic virtue sprang directly from agriculture. Advocates of stumpland farming even added a corollary: The harder the land is to bring into production, the greater is the yield of virtue. As H. W. Sparks, an official of the state college demonstration farm in Pullman, put it in 1913:

> I believe it fortunate for this favored country and good people who inhabit it that the land is expensive to prepare for cultivation in that we are practically free from that class of undesirable adventurers who have been for generations moving from one piece of virgin soil to another exhausting the accumulated fertility, giving nothing in return, whose sole motive has been exploitation.

It seemed that land full of ten-foot stumps would produce men and women far superior to those unfortunates who, stumbling upon the fat lands of America, had been seduced by easy prosperity.[10]

Most prospective settlers probably proved to be far more immune to these invocations of agrarian virtue than to the boosters' promise of sure financial success. Organizations from local chambers of commerce to the state government of Washington assured potential settlers that farming logged-off lands would surely make them comfortable and might very well make them rich.[11]

Between 1900 and 1920, a substantial number of settlers apparently believed such propaganda and did begin farming the logged-off lands west of the Cascade Mountains. Western Washington gained almost seventeen thousand farms during this period, and fifteen thousand of the farms contained less than fifty acres (see Table 14). In Island County, the population doubled between 1900 and 1910 and continued to increase during the following decade. The number of farms in the county tripled between 1900 and 1920. During the twenties, this growth was reversed in both the state and the county as the combination of rural depression and urban prosperity pulled people in off the land. Between 1920 and 1930 Island County lost population, and between 1925 and 1930 the number of farms decreased. With the Great Depression, however, the movement boomed again. The cities no longer pulled people in; they now disgorged the desperate and unemployed. In the thirties the number of farms reached their peak and the population of the county surged once more.[12]

The experience of these people on the land has been largely ignored. Who were they and what happened to them? Before 1920,

TABLE 14. INCREASE IN NUMBERS OF FARMS, WESTERN WASHINGTON, 1900–40

Census Category	1900	1910	1920	1925	1930	1940
Number of Farms	14,013	21,220	30,922	38,718	37,475	48,389
Farms under Fifty Acres	5,234	12,321	20,018	27,848	26,627	36,370
Acreage in Farms	1,724,370	1,699,183	1,908,456	1,907,828	1,906,200	2,203,049
Improved Land in Farms	348,177	495,870	679,123	646,801	715,854	824,960

Compiled from Twelfth Census, Agriculture, 1900: Vol. 5, pt. 1, 135–39; Thirteenth Census, Agriculture, 1910: Vol. 7, 840–43; Fourteenth Census, Agriculture, 1920: Vol. 6, pt. 3, 292–95; Fifteenth Census, Agriculture, 1930, Vol. 2, pt. 3, 430–33, 436–39; Sixteenth Census, Agriculture, 1940, Vol. 1, pt. 6, 548–51, 556–59; Improved land 1925–40 calculated by cropland and plowable pasture.

TABLE 15. POPULATION AND AGRICULTURAL GROWTH, ISLAND COUNTY, 1900–40

Census Category	1900	1910	1920	1925	1930	1935	1940
Population	1,870	4,704	5,489	...	5,369	...	6,098
Foreign-Born White	548	994	1,250	...	1,170	...	...
Number of Farms	254	458	763	950	877	1,063	1,044
Acreage	30,705	38,976	51,932	49,776	48,877	54,666	54,969
Average Size	121	85	68	52	56	51	53

SOURCE: Twelfth Census, 1900, Population, 1:45, 606; Twelfth Census, 1900, Agriculture, 5, pt. 1:304; Thirteenth Census, 1910, Population, 3:977, 999; Thirteenth Census, 1910, Agriculture, 7:841; Fourteenth Census, 1920, Population, 3:1082; Fourteenth Census, 1920, Agriculture, 6, pt. 3:293; Fifteenth Census, 1930, Population, 3, pt. 2:1240; Fifteenth Census, 1930, Agriculture, 2, pt. 3:431; Sixteenth Census, 1940, Population, 2, pt. 7:362; Sixteenth Census, 1940, Agriculture, 1, pt. 6:549.

the settlers who took up cutover lands seem to have been in large part the very people urban propagandists were aiming for. A survey by the United States Department of Agriculture (U.S.D.A.) estimated that the bulk of the settlers on cutover lands in the prewar years were foreign-born, ranging from 83 percent of all settlers between 1898 and 1903 to 70 percent between 1910 and 1915. Most of these settlers came from Scandinavia, especially Norway and Sweden. As late as 1921, Scandinavians constituted 55 percent of cutover farm settlers, with the great majority having acquired their lands before World War I. Between 1900 and 1920, settlement in Island County took place largely in the cutover districts of northern and southern Whidbey and, to a lesser extent, on northern Camano. On southern Whidbey two new precincts, one at Clinton and one at Holmes Harbor, were created and the population increased from 331 to 1,684 between 1900 and 1910. Southern Whidbey, which had 17.7 percent of the population of the county in 1900, had over 33 percent in 1910 (see Table 15). On northern Whidbey, the influx of people into Clover Valley and Swanton raised the Oak Harbor precinct's population from 447 in 1900 to 1,097 in 1910. From 1900 to 1920 immigrants, largely Scandinavians, composed roughly 20 percent of the population of the county, but they also composed nearly half the farmers. In Clinton, a precinct made up entirely of logged-off lands, half the farmers had been born in Scandinavia.[13]

During the 1930s, however, foreign immigration virtually ceased and two new streams of settlers, unemployed workers from the cities and refugees from the dust bowl, dominated the flight to the cutover lands. According to a survey by the Washington Agricultural Experiment Station, slightly more than half of the cutover land settlers of the 1930s came from inside the State of Washington, most of them from urban areas, and almost 50 percent migrated from outside the state, mostly from the drought-stricken regions of the northern plains. The urban workers often sought little more than a small plot to grow food while they worked elsewhere. Their farms often remained only glorified gardens, too small even to be counted by census takers. The people fleeing the northern plains, however, attempted to start more ambitious farms.[14]

The dust bowl migrants began arriving in 1932 and their

number peaked between 1934 and 1936. Driven from their homes by crop failures and drought, these uncelebrated companions of Steinbeck's Okies moved west because, as one migrant explained, "We all seem to have our eyes turned that way." Lois Phillips Hudson, whose own family finally settled on a cutover farm, wrote years later, "It didn't seem to matter where you were during those depression years. After you'd been in one spot for awhile you decided things couldn't be quite so bad anywhere else and so you moved." But most moves were not so aimless as this. Like the original settlers on the prairies, these migrants sought out relatives and old neighbors, recreating plains communities on the cutover lands. They settled where land was cheap, and there they generally stayed. Surveys found that three-quarters of the drought migrants remained in the county where they first settled. Contemporary studies of population movement found a depressing logic behind these rural migrations: The worse the land, the greater its availability and the greater the influx of immigrants.[15]

Nearly one hundred thousand acres of cutover land awaited these various waves of migration in Island County. The land ranged from the wet but fertile soils of Clover Valley to the droughty Holypus soil series of the uplands, which were hopeless as agricultural soils and liable to erode if not protected. Whidbey Island gravelly sand dominated cutover lands, covering 32 percent of the total area of the county. A Class IV soil, "suitable for tillage only part of the time or under extreme care," it was best adapted for pasture.[16]

But in 1900, and even in 1930, there was no reliable knowledge of the capabilities of these soils. There were U.S.D.A. soil surveys in 1905 and 1911, but the primitive soil science employed did little to help the stump farmer. The surveyors frankly discouraged the production of staples on logged-off lands, but they went out of their way to encourage specialty farming and dairying. According to these surveys, nearly all county soils were suitable for some kind of farming.[17]

County boosters were even more reckless. The *Island County Times* announced in 1902 that "almost the whole surface of the island is tillable when cleared." That same year the county attorney estimated the amount of tillable land at 120,000 acres. The local chamber of commerce promised farmers splendid crops, and state officials hinted at "fortunes" to be made in chicken farming. More moderate men admitted that all land could not be farmed and asked for more soil surveys. But since soil surveys were incapable of distinguishing soil capabilities with accuracy, they meant little.[18]

During the early years of settlement, 1900–20, most settlers had little farm experience to steer them through the maze of expert opinions concerning the cutover lands. By 1921, according to the United States Department of Agriculture, only 27 percent of these settlers had ever run a farm before they took up stumpland. Most had probably been rural workers—farmhands, loggers, and fishermen. Such people tended to accept the word of promoters, scientists, and government officials about the practicability of stumpland farming. By the 1930s, more than 50 percent of the immigrants had farmed previously, but usually in a totally different environment. The understandable concern of the dust bowl migrants with water, not soil, led them to overrate the cutover lands, whose lush growth seemed to promise abundant crops. Before these migrants discovered that bracken did not translate into oats, nor fireweed into potatoes, they had often fallen prey to real estate promoters or lumber companies who had sold them worthless land on contract.[19]

In the early years of the century, any skepticism settlers might have had about the potential of the land could be dissipated by pointing to the Clover Valley Dutch. Clover Valley was a mixture of lowland marsh, prairie, and forest, much of it wet alder bottom, unique on Whidbey Island. The land needed draining, but outside of the prairies and tidelands, the valley contained some of the best soil in the county. Eighteen Dutch families arrived in Clover Valley in 1895 with from $2,500 to $10,000 apiece to invest. They bought land from the Ellens Land Company and prospered from the beginning. By 1897 the new colony numbered two hundred people. Imaginative, hardworking, and well financed, the Hollanders turned to dairying and began to grow specialty crops, such as flower bulbs and seed. They made their farms the showpieces of the county. Although both their valley and the amount of capital they brought to it were unique, they seemed to offer testimony to the belief that good farms could be found on the logged-off lands.[20]

Numerous land companies promised settlers that they could attain similar success. In the 1890s, the Lake Superior and Puget Sound Land Company had begun surveying and disposing of its holdings on northern Whidbey. Almost simultaneously, the Whidby Development Corporation began selling land near Holmes Harbor on southern Whidbey. Both the Port Blakely Mill Company and the Essary Brothers sold off their land as soon as it was logged, and on Camano Nils Anderson, an independent logger, sold "garden tracts" of from five to forty acres at Mabana to twelve families from Seattle. Puget Mill was the last to dispose of its land, holding it off the market until 1920. Speculative corporations supplemented the offerings of the logging companies. On southern Whidbey the Whidby Land Company and the Glendale Improvement Company tried to attract settlers, and Jacob Anthes solicited buyers for farms around Langley. On northern Whidbey the Whidby Development Corporation offered ten thousand acres for sale in 1903. Annually, schemes for selling the logged-off lands grew up in the cutover regions as luxuriant as the bracken. As late as 1922, promoters sought to settle two hundred families on berry farms near Stanwood on Camano Island. And that same year Henry Pinney, a local real estate promoter, announced plans to form the Whidby Island Development Company and push the population in the county over sixty thousand.[21]

The state, too, had cutover land to dispose of and the government advocated promotional schemes of its own. In 1917 the state published *Vacant Logged-off Lands,* a pamphlet that offered state-owned tracts in Island County and elsewhere for sale. The county government could not afford such publications, but the Island County chamber of commerce filled the gap by publishing, in the early years of the century, a brochure entitled *Island County, Washington, A World Beater* in order to boost local settlement. The people such literature attracted would find county tax lands as well as private and state-owned lands for sale.[22]

Except for the Dutch of Clover Valley, the new settlers of both the first and second migrations onto the logged-off lands of Island County arrived with little available capital. On the surface this did not seem an insurmountable disadvantage. Land in Island County remained relatively cheap (between fifteen and twenty-five dollars an acre in 1913), unlike lands bordering the cities, and cutover lands propagandists assured settlers that they needed to buy only small farms: Twenty acres of logged-off land could supposedly support a family. The settlers bought correspondingly small farms, very often under twenty acres (see Table 16). As late as 1939, a Washington agricultural experiment station study calculated that ten to forty acres of cleared, reasonably fertile land could support a family on the cutover lands, and if the family raised poultry even less land was necessary. It was easy to ignore the crucial section of such estimates: The land must be relatively fertile and it must be cleared. Fertile land was rare, and to clear stumpland settlers required much more capital than they needed to purchase it. The cost of clearing land remained between two hundred and three hundred dollars an acre until the 1930s, when the bulldozer reduced it to about one hundred dollars.[23]

TABLE 16. FARM SIZE IN ISLAND COUNTY, 1900–40

Number of Farms	1900	1910	1920	1930	1940
Over 175 Acres	52	53	62	57	65
Under 20 Acres	13	96	194	277	335

SOURCE: Twelfth Census, 1900, Agriculture, 5, pt. 1:136; Thirteenth Census, 1910, Agriculture, 7:8:41; Fourteenth Census, 1920, Agriculture, 6, pt. 3:293; Fifteenth Census, 1930, Agriculture, 3, pt. 3:339; Sixteenth Census, 1940, Agriculture, 1, pt. 6:559.

This lack of capital and the expense involved in mechanized clearing, as much as the infertility of the soil, shaped the settlement experience. Recognizing the difficulties, promoters of settlement turned to the state for aid relatively quickly. The first meeting of the Washington Logged-off Land Association in 1908 asked for limited state aid through experimental farms and soil surveys. The Governor of Washington, however, was willing to go much further, speaking with approval of state aid for clearing and developing the cutover region. Increasingly, after 1908, promoters emphasized the formidable difficulties the new farmer faced, with Austin Griffiths frankly asserting that the task was beyond the capability of an individual farmer and his family. Boosters still held settlement to be worthwhile and necessary, but the immensity of the task was now emphasized. Boosters asserted that logged-off lands in Washington were more difficult to bring under cultivation than eastern woodlands, and the old pioneer methods would no longer suffice.[24] This assessment was realistic, but it was also tactically wise. Promoters had to justify aid from the state.

Advocates of government aid to settlers of logged-off lands did not see such assistance as a drastic departure from other patterns of new land settlement. They drew obvious parallels with existing reclamation projects on arid land and marshlands and saw assistance to cutover farmers as simply a logical extension of such projects. By 1912, *Little Logged-off Lands* had begun a concerted campaign to secure governmental assistance. After soliciting and printing proposed bills and organizing popular support, the journal claimed that only one major newspaper in the state, the *Yakima Republic* (which, with remarkable perspicuity, protested that logged-off lands were not worth the cost of clearing), opposed state aid.[25]

As a result of this campaign, state legislators in 1913 confronted a formidable array of plans to reclaim the cutover lands for farming. After a joint legislative committee consolidated the proposals, a new law, providing for agricultural development districts that were coextensive with the counties, passed both houses by lopsided majorities. Under the new law, each district would have three commissioners who would be selected by the voters. The commissioners could call special elections to vote on the property taxes that would fund reclamation. Once voters approved the necessary taxes, the commissioners could issue bonds, contract for clearing logged-off land, and sell the improved land to settlers at cost plus 5 percent. Before the law could take effect, however, each county had to vote to organize the development districts.[26]

In county after county, voters rejected the formation of the agricultural development districts. The electorate did not approve a single district. Thomas Murphine, the bill's sponsor, rather vaguely blamed "interest lackeys." Others explained that voters feared the granting of tax powers to local bodies other than the county government. Corruption and incompetence seemed to be very real dangers if all landowners were to be taxed to buy and clear land that might prove to be unproductive and difficult to sell. All subsequent attempts to revise the Murphine law to meet these objections failed. Now leary of popular disapproval, the legislature defeated another, far less ambitious project to create a state powder factory that would sell explosives to the settlers at cost for stumpage removal. The state continued to encourage settlement of logged-off lands and eagerly tried to sell the logged-off lands that it possessed, but it provided no financial aid to the settlers.[27]

The failure to secure government aid was a crippling blow to the logged-off land movement, but for a period during and after World War I, it appeared that corporate capital might provide an alternative to state aid. Between 1917 and 1925 the Puget Mill Company, one of the largest lumbering companies in western Washington, seriously considered providing assistance to settlers on its cutover lands. The company had sizable holdings in Island County, but the pilot project the company attempted took place in nearby King County. In the past, many (although not all) lumber companies had discouraged settlement on their lands. Few regions had as yet been totally logged, and companies like Puget Mill feared the effects of cutover settlement on nearby virgin timber lands. Not only would settlers in such regions demand schools and roads, thus raising property taxes that would fall most heavily on valuable virgin timber lands, but in clearing the land settlers often set fires that spread to adjoining lands and destroyed valuable standing timber.[28]

After World War I, new technologies and the rapid pace of cutting removed both those dangers by stripping all marketable timber from huge areas of western Washington. As discussed earlier, such deforested lands were valueless to the companies; indeed, they actually drained corporate resources since, although they produced nothing, taxes still had to be paid on them. The timber companies continued to reject reforestation of these lands, regarding the price of timber as too low to make private reforestation feasible. Instead, they preferred to sell off their cutover tracts for whatever they could obtain and to seek virgin timber on more isolated private holdings and on the public lands.[29]

It was the failure of standard promotional techniques to dispose of much of this land that led the Puget Mill Company to undertake an experiment in the early 1920s on seven thousand acres of stumpland it held near Seattle. Unable to sell the land as the loggers had left it, Puget Mill decided to build roads, schools, and set up a demonstration poultry farm—the Alderwood Manor Demonstration College and Farm—on the tract. It then undertook a massive advertising campaign, advertising the land in five- and ten-acre tracts, with one acre already cleared, asking two hundred dollars per acre, with only a 10 percent down payment. Puget Mill promised settlers a comfortable living from their small poultry farms, and by 1922 almost 1,500 people had settled at Alderwood Manor. Like previous cutover land farmers, few of these people had ever farmed before and, not surprisingly, few actually made their new farms work. Most ended up as commuters to Seattle, and Alderwood Manor eventually evolved into a suburb of Seattle rather than a colony of independent small farmers. In the end Puget Mill successfully disposed of its land, but the cost of doing so proved so extravagant that the Company did not undertake any further settlement projects, nor did other companies seek to imitate Alderwood Manor.[30]

The failure to secure either governmental or corporate funding made the settlement experience an individual effort more by default than design. For new settlers without capital, possessing infertile land, and faced with tremendous expenses for clearing, the chances for success on cutover farms were slight. Out of necessity, new settlers tried for almost forty years to duplicate on the cutover lands individual settlement usually associated with eighteenth and nineteenth century pioneer settlement in the eastern United States. Boosters encouraged the settlers to see opportunity instead of disaster. They told migrants that the heavy rains of western Washington, which actually leached the limited fertility of thin soils, were "just enough to make everything grow to perfection." Boosters claimed that the logging debris that made clearing so expensive was actually "fuel for all time . . . at the doors of the home." They even informed settlers that the logging debris that littered their farms actually represented profits of up to $280 an acre through the sale of wood and such by-products as turpentine, charcoal, and tar.[31]

Instead of profits, the debris yielded only years of hard work and drudgery. Farmers had to clear logging wastes before farming could begin. Confidence men promoted miracle chemicals to dissolve stumps, but most farmers followed the carefully researched techniques recommended by the Washington agricultural experiment stations. Before any attempt to remove stumps could be made, the logging debris had to be gathered into piles and burned. Only when this had been done, and the whole tract burned over to destroy the brush; could a settler attack the huge stumps. The methods of removing stumps involved variations of burning, blasting, and pulling. The cheapest and one of the most common techniques was the char-pit method, which consisted of making an intense fire in a circle around a stump stripped of its bark, then partially burying the fire to conserve and focus heat. The char-pit method demanded little equipment and had few material costs, but it was slow and tedious.[32]

Dynamite removed stumps more quickly, but it cost more, too, and it was fast only in comparison with burning. The Department of Agriculture estimated that a farmer working alone required four hundred hours of his labor, thirty-four hours of horse labor, and forty dollars worth of dynamite to clear an acre of stumpland. A far faster and more efficient technique involved using a donkey engine to pull the stumps. A trained crew could clear almost an acre a day, but the estimated cost of clearing with machines ran as high as three hundred dollars an acre.[33]

Because clearing cutover lands demanded either immense amounts of time and labor or heavy capital expenditures, only a slow and tedious accretion of improved acreage took place in the county. Farmers brought an average of 236 acres a year into production in Island County between 1901 and 1917, or about one-half acre a year per farm. Only World War I, and the subsequent demand for farm products, increased land clearing. After the war the pace of land clearing slowed. By the 1930s, the average stumpland farms in western Washington once again gained only one-half acre of cleared land a year.[34]

Most farmers turned to forms of agriculture that could be undertaken with the stumps still in place. In Island County this meant dairying, raising poultry, and growing berries. From necessity, but also on the advice of the Department of Agriculture and logged-off land propagandists, the stumpland farmer invested his limited capital in cows and chickens. Before World War I dairy farming, as measured by the number of milk cows, dominated county agriculture, reaching a peak around 1916. After the war, chicken raising boomed, and the value of poultry on county farms rose steadily until the Depression (see Table 27). By 1930, there were 319 poultry farms in the county compared with 162 dairy farms, and the assessed value of poultry had tripled in a decade. It was chicken farming and berry farming that supported agriculture in the county between the wars (see Table 28).[35]

No matter what type of farming upland cutover farmers undertook, they had to meet the challenge of competition with the farmers of the fertile prairies and lowlands. Few of them could. Their lack of capital rendered them unable to take advantage of new technologies and economies of scale. Furthermore, the basic physical limits of their land rendered production for a competitive market nearly hopeless. Nowhere did this show up earlier, or more clearly, than in dairy farming.

The major liability of dairy farmers on the logged-off lands was the infertility of their soil. The most productive soil of the cutover uplands was less fertile than the least productive soil of the lowland prairies and diked bottomlands and marshes. Because of the low fertility of upland fields, the grasses adaptable to them had lower nutritive value than those of the lowlands. Cows on logged-off farms thus required more pastureland than cows on lowland soil, and upland herds produced less butterfat per cow than lowland herds. To compensate for infertile land and inadequate pastures, upland farmers had to expend money for feed, which became the largest single expense on most stumpland farms. Even with purchased feed, however, the cows of upland farmers still produced less butterfat per hundred dollars worth of feed than did the cows of the lowland farmers. As early as 1915, a survey by the U.S.D.A. revealed that the average upland dairy farm, despite its advantages in invested capital and in both improved and total acreage over other upland farms, earned substantially less annually ($384) than did the upland poultry and fruit farms ($524). The advent of expensive new technologies, which the small cutover farmer simply could not afford, sealed the doom of small dairy herds. After World War I, dairying grew less and less significant on the cutover lands as chicken raising became the dominant activity. During the 1920s, however, many lowland farmers turned to poultry raising, and once more the superior fertility of their land and greater access to capital gave them significant advantages.

These lowland farmers could grow their own feed, invest in modern equipment, and take advantage of economies of scale. By the end of the decade, upland farmers faced a declining competitive position in egg production as well as dairying, and their position worsened during the 1930s. Experts at the Pullman agricultural experiment station estimated in 1940 that the minimum number of hens and pullets needed for a successful poultry operation was one thousand. Only fifty-three farms in the county had as many as eight hundred in 1939.[36]

What allowed cutover farming to survive and expand during the 1930s was not an improved competitive position, but the near-total collapse of farm markets. During the 1930s, egg prices in Washington averaged only 72 percent of those of the 1920s, and butterfat prices were only 52 percent of the 1920–29 average. The new settlement on cutover lands during the thirties was not commercial settlement at all. For the first time since the early years of settlement, subsistence farming became widespread in western Washington. Between 1930 and 1940 the number of self-sufficing farms west of the Cascades increased from 2,339 to 21,869 and formed the single largest category of farms in the state. In Island County itself there were 381 subsistence farms by 1940. Self-sufficing was a census category, however, not an economic reality. In practice, subsistence was synonymous with poverty, and most of these farms produced neither adequate food nor provided adequate shelter for their owners.[37]

TABLE 17. FARM INCOME, WESTERN WASHINGTON, APRIL 1938

	Old Farms			
Logged-off Farms	Small	Medium	Large	Undevelo
Number	56	57	35	47
Average Size (Acres)	39	83	131	30
Farm Earnings	$237	$447	$819	$ 75
Non-farm Earnings	$487	$272	$277	$587

Table adopted from Heisig, WAES *Bulletin 339*, Table 4, p. 24.

This near-total collapse of commercial farming on the uplands was the culmination of a long trend on the cutover lands. Few of these farms had ever yielded adequate incomes. Earnings had been low before World War I (averaging $386 in 1915), improved during the war, but then declined to $414 in 1921. The average earnings for 1921 actually disguised the bleakness of the situation following the war. A comparison of 47 farms run by the same operators in 1915 and 1921 revealed an actual decline in average net earnings from $395 in 1915 to $290 in 1921. In 1921, 20 percent of the 150 cutover farms surveyed operated at a loss.[38]

By 1939, according to a Washington agricultural experiment station study, only the largest (average size, 131 acres) and most atypical cutover farms, with an average earning of $819, came close to the estimated $901 necessary for a decent rural standard of living. Other cutover farms, the vast majority, came nowhere near this figure. The abandoned farms settled during the thirties and still undeveloped produced an average income of $75 per year. In order to survive, most stump farmers had to work off the farm. The proportion of farmers working off the farm in the cutover counties of western Washington varied between 40 and 60 percent. Non-farm work was not casual labor. In both 1934 and 1939, 44 percent of the farmers in Island County had off-farm jobs. Off-farm employment averaged 143 days per farmer in 1940, and among farmowners (as distinct from renters and sharecroppers) the average was even higher, 152 days. According to the agricul-

RCH 1939 SAMPLE

	New Farms	
ll	Medium	Large
8	14	. . .
6	68	. . .
8	$771	. . .
7	$145	. . .

tural experiment station survey of 1938–39, most cutover farmers in Washington earned more by working off the farm than by working on it (see Table 17).[39]

During virtually every period of settlement between 1900 and 1940, therefore, the logged-off lands produced relatively little income, and most owners hovered near poverty. To study only income, however, distorts the picture somewhat. The settler's real opportunity for security lay not in what he produced, but in rising land values. In isolated rural regions, unimproved logged-off land prices remained low (between $5 and $25 an acre) throughout the period, but near the coastal cities they averaged nearly $100 an acre by 1910–15. Such land, bought for less than $20 an acre before 1903 and then improved and cultivated, would be worth an average of $227 between 1910 and 1915. If a cutover farmer had been lucky or farsighted enough to acquire land near an urban area while prices remained low, he could indeed reap a profit. Between 1915 and 1921, gains from rising land values represented, on paper, an income far larger than what cutover farmers received for their crops. Economists calculating the return at 7 percent had cutover farmers gaining $809 annually by 1921. Such gains compensated somewhat for a decline in farm incomes that increasingly forced settlers to work off the farm, but unless translated into cash by mortgage or sale they did little to improve living conditions. These gains were not distributed evenly; they largely benefited older settlers who had bought land when it was cheap; the success of later settlers, who paid more for their land, is not so clear. The rise in the population of Island County pushed the prices of improved lands upward, although not to urban levels, and early settlers registered substantial gains between 1900 and 1910 (see Table 18). Land values leveled off by 1920, however, and after 1925 rural real estate values in the cutover region dropped steadily for fifteen years. By 1935, the average value of an acre of farmland in Island County had dropped 33 percent from its 1925 high. Despite investments by farmers of time, money, and labor, their lands did not appreciate. As the cutover lands declined in value, the last financial rationale of cutover settlement disappeared.[40]

The failure of settlers to achieve adequate economic or financial security after they returned to the land is only a partial measure of

TABLE 18. AVERAGE VALUE OF FARMLAND AND BUILDINGS PER ACRE, ISLAND COUNTY

	1900	1910	1920	1925	1930	1935	1940	1945
Value	$21	$73	$96	$107	$105	$72	$82	$123

SOURCE: Thomas Pressly and William Schofield, *Farm Real Estate Values in the U.S. by Counties, 1859–1959* (Seattle, 1965), p. 67.

the new social price paid for settling the cutover lands. Boosters of settlement had admitted the human cost of logged-off land settlement during their agitation for government aid. One such booster, George Long, conceded that "isolation from markets, lack of roads, lack of neighbors, and lack of school facilities" often made farming logged-off lands a life of "dreary existence . . . without any practical rewards." To spend years in hard, lonely labor without any practical gain while one's family lived in isolation and poverty and one's children grew up with inadequate education represents not only an individual but also a social failure. Such a social failure is, however, largely immeasurable statistically. Before 1930 the individual farmers and their families paid the price themselves. Only in the 1930s, with New Deal relief measures, did society compensate, in part, for the failure of the farms and assign a dollar value to social suffering.[41]

During the 1930s, public relief came to provide a substantial portion of the income of people on the logged-off lands. Of the cutover farmers surveyed by Washington agricultural experiment station personnel in 1938–39, 35 percent had received either direct aid or work relief. A much higher proportion (54 percent) of those families who had started their logged-off farms during the 1930s than cutover farmers in general (35 percent) were on relief at some time during the survey period. A similar survey of drought migrants found that approximately 50 percent had obtained public assistance after arriving in the state. In Island County, where county commissioners protected the public purse with Republican zeal, relief was hard to obtain. Cutover farmers in the county probably received less aid than logged-off settlers in general, not from lack of need, but because of the exigencies of local politics. Even with relief, farm families lacked adequate diets and often lived in houses that were little more than shacks. Many families found their farms produced little but tragedy.[42]

The social cost of these farms went well beyond the relief payments and personal suffering. Because of the scattered nature of much cutover land settlement, the cost of providing essential public services, such as roads and schools, was often far higher than in more prosperous regions. There are no available figures for Island County, but in another cutover county the cost of educating grade school children from isolated cutover farms was three times as expensive as educating the other children of the county. The growing social costs of cutover settlement were not lost on officials and businessmen in Island County. Initially, during the early 1930s, county leaders welcomed renewed settlement of the cutover land, but by 1934 when the federal government inquired about settling dust bowl migrants, the county chamber of commerce had changed its position. Members announced that they did not want any "dole seekers." In their minds, stump farmers had become drains upon the county, not the assets they had once been.[43]

The settlers now transmuted from hardy pioneers to "dole seekers," were not, however, the only ones who had suffered. The land they had tried to make into farms and homes had suffered, too. Ultimately, the social cost of settlement cannot be separated from the environmental cost. When farmers had burned to clear slash, the same kind of soil depletion took place as when loggers burned slash. Even before they planted, they had often destroyed 90 percent of the organic material in the soil.[44]

Their farming practices only compounded this initial damage. Most farming depends on the eradication of native vegetation from fields and pastures, but cutover farmers found this to be impossible. Because of the stumps and roots that remained even after slash was burned, they could not use the plow to destroy the native plants that quickly returned. This problem was most critical in dairying, where the native invaders could not support cows. Some experts recommended that farmers immediately seed potential pastureland with a timothy–clover mixture after the slash had been burned. On sections of the uplands, however, the water retention of the soil was so poor that the domesticated grasses would be dead by summer. And elsewhere, even when the plants survived, farmers found that the pastures could not maintain a dairy herd the year round. Most of the grasses recommended for the uplands had relatively short life spans, and all of them suffered under heavy grazing. Within a very few years, unpalatable native plants reinvaded the fields. When this happened, the experts recommended that farmers pull up the stumps, plow the land, and reseed. For most settlers, however, this remained financially impossible. Out of necessity they resorted to a type of farming similar to the slash and burn techniques of the tropics. In western Washington, however, farmers did not follow the tropical pattern of abandonment of fields to the forests after a few years of farming. Instead, they continued burning at regular intervals to kill the invading vegetation. By burning, farmers only changed the normal vegetation succession into a relentless reinvasion of bracken fern. Bracken, with its dense underground network of rhizomes and the death of its topgrowth in the late summer (before fall burnings), survived the fires and spread as other plants were eliminated. The more often burning occurred, the higher the proportion of bracken in the fields. Since bracken was poor feed after its first growth, this meant fewer and fewer animals could be grazed each successive year. Repeated burning ultimately not only destroyed the ecological basis of the farmer's livelihood, but also blocked natural reforestation after he abandoned his farm. Conifer seedlings simply could not establish themselves among dense patches of bracken.[45]

If partial clearing followed by burning disrupted and degraded natural succession, full removal of stumps on the uplands and plowing of the fields brought other dangers. When plowed or overgrazed, steeper uplands tended to erode, and under the winter rains their meager topsoil washed down the slopes toward Puget Sound. A National Resources Board Survey of the 1930s found moderate sheet erosion (25 to 75 percent of the surface soil removed; infrequent gullies) over much of the cutover region in the western counties. Forest trees returning to the degraded landscape of the cutover land would not be commercially valuable fir (usually the natural invader of cleared forest land, but alder.[46] Alder, the prime deciduous invader of severely disturbed land, found its niche in the gullies and uneven surfaces the farmer left behind. It succeeded where the farmer had failed. With the abandonment of the stump farms, the amount of alder in a cutover area such as

Island, Kitsap, and San Juan counties, where logging had largely ceased, increased from 11,000,000 to 408,000,000 board feet. Farming had not only failed, it had also helped to finish the ruin of the land for commercial logging.[47]

Recognition of this dual social and environmental disaster on the logged-off lands first emerged during the 1930s. The dust bowl had done the most to sharpen a national awareness of the relationship between poor land and poor men, between ecological disaster and social disaster, but the insight was eventually applied to the logged-off lands as well. In a series of studies, the National Resources Board, the Washington Agricultural Experiment Station, the Resettlement Administration, and the Washington State Planning Commission recommended detailed land use surveys to locate land suitable for agriculture and advised reforestation of all remaining lands. These agencies also suggested that the people on the worst lands be resettled, and they advised rural zoning to prevent further settlement and misuse of the cutover areas.[48]

It was this awareness of the fundamental connection between human suffering and inefficient use of resources in such areas as the logged-off land districts that brought the Resettlement Administration into existence. In its rhetoric, if not in its actions, the Resettlement Administration in the Pacific Northwest sought a more sensible resource policy. "Human tragedy, like a wheeling vulture, followed closely the devastation of the forests," the Portland Resettlement Administration office declared in 1936, and the agency announced plans to help "stranded" settlers off the land. The Resettlement Administration realized that some stump farms could support families (indeed, they were actively seeking to put dust bowl refugees on such land), but they also realized that most cutover farms should be replanted to forest.[49]

In practice these agencies accomplished little. The Resettlement Administration, along with the Federal Emergency Relief Administration and the Soil Conservation Service, had the authority to purchase marginal lands and to help the farmers on that land to relocate. Yet the agency often did little but issue press releases. The Resettlement Administration did not retire a single acre of marginal land in the Pacific Northwest, and it resettled only 173 farm families in western Washhington.

Attempts to prevent people from making what was by now

agreed to be the disastrous mistake of settling marginal cutover lands were no more successful. In 1936, the Washington State Planning Council made land classification one of its leading priorities and recommended rural zoning. Farmers' committees, organized by county, classified lands and the Resettlement Administration conducted a few detailed surveys, but in Island County this amounted only to a classification of land by farmers in 1939. None of these measures had any teeth. There was no rural zoning and no way to keep people from settling the cutover lands. In 1936 the state legislature authorized the creation of county planning commissions, but these too had little real power. As late as 1937, the Rural Rehabilitation Divison recommended that prospective settlers consult the county commissioners before settling on the islands. How the county commissioners were to know what lands were suitable for farming without detailed surveys was not explained.[50]

Those people already on the cutover lands received little more assistance. Most cutover lands simply were not worth enough to qualify as collateral for the standard Farm Credit Administration loans. Some loans went to cutover farmers through the Rural Rehabilitation Division of the Farm Security Administration, but only a small number of families on the best logged-off lands received these loans. Most aid to the families came through relief agencies, and the Works Progress Administration programs became essential to many farm families. Not until 1941, when a pilot project began in Lewis County, did a concerted and coordinated attempt to deal with the problems of the logged-off lands get under way. This was followed in 1942 by regional recommendations from the Pacific Northwest Regional Planning Commission. Such efforts came too late. By 1941, war industries had begun to draw people in off the land, and in Island County military bases took over substantial amounts of farmland. The decline in the number of farms in Island County was particularly drastic, falling from 1,044 to 681 between 1940 and 1945.[51]

There was, however, another far more successful, farming advance onto new lands during this period. The bulk of farm acreage permanently added to county farms between 1915 and 1940 came from diking and draining, not slashing and burning. The total area of marshland and tideland involved in reclamation projects was far less than the cutover lands settled by stump farmers, but most of it would remain in farms long after farmers had abandoned the stumplands.

The soils of the tidelands and marshes of Davis Slough, Useless Bay, Dugualla Bay, Crescent Harbor, and Clover Valley were much more suited for agriculture than the upland soils of north and south Whidbey, where most of the stumpland farmers had settled. And not only were these soils relatively fertile, the state was willing to aid in their draining and diking. By 1895, the legislature had passed the laws that enabled the formation of diking and drainage districts. This legislation allowed landowners to organize into districts and elect commissioners who were empowered to issue bonds, build dikes, drain lands, and assess the landowners who benefited. Here was government aid for bringing relatively fertile soils into cultivation, everything logged-off land propagandists would later dream of, yet for more than twenty years few in the county took advantage of these laws.[52]

Timbermen remained too influential. They opposed any draining that would deprive them of the bays and slough where they floated and stored their logs. In 1913 farmers organized the first diking district, but it was quickly abandoned. Not until 1914 did they finally organize a diking district on Deep Lagoon in Useless Bay and bring it into operation despite local protests. Five diking and four drainage districts would be formed over the next few years, and seven of the nine remained in operation.[53]

These districts assaulted the last substantially unaltered area of the pre-white environment of Island County. The marshes and tidelands still harbored the same vegetation and the nesting grounds of the huge flocks of waterfowl that had been important to the Salish. The assault on the tidelands centered on Whidbey. Farmers diked sections of Dugualla Bay on north Whidbey and of Maxwellton Beach and Useless Bay on south Whidbey. On Camano they organized a diking district for Elgers Bay, but little came of it. In all, they drained and diked 846 acres on Useless Bay, 530 acres on Dugualla, and 300 acres at Maxwellton Beach between 1915 and 1937. Not all districts succeeded; the original Useless Bay district and the Maxwellton Beach district prospered, but the others were failures. The Dugualla Bay district was never even farmed, and most of its land was foreclosed during the Depression after all attempts to meet its debts failed. The second Useless Bay district drained only 386 out of a proposed 800 acres, and that at a cost of almost one hundred dollars an acre. Both districts would eventually recover, but not until the 1940s. Successful or unsuccessful, however, their dikes destroyed the tideland nesting grounds of waterfowl. By the thirties, although many birds still remained, the massive flocks the older settlers remembered had vanished.

The drainage districts of the marshlands of Clover Valley, Crescent Harbor, and Oak Harbor were more successful: 2,576 acres were drained and all the districts remained in healthy financial condition. During the 1930s, drainage projects expanded to Crockett's Lake and the Davis Slough areas of north Camano. In all, between 1930 and 1937, farmers reclaimed roughly 2,090 acres of land by diking and another 3,456 acres by draining. Of these, they successfully brought 3,342 acres into cultivation. Here, too, the major price paid was a decline in waterfowl.[54]

Between stump farming and diking, about 25,000 acres, or approximately 20 percent of the land in the county, had been significantly altered. The differences between the development of the tidelands and the logged-off lands are significant and instructive. On the tidelands men and women had exploited fertile soils, backed by adequate capital raised through taxes. The environmental losses were great, but they were balanced by social gains—a solid and prosperous farming community. On the stumplands, men and women, often without any agricultural experience, had moved onto infertile soils, highly vulnerable to degradation, without sufficient capital. They came with government and other encouragement, but with no government aid. On the logged-off lands environmental disaster had yielded social disaster.

For all its progressive concerns, the back-to-the-land movement was finally reactionary in its rationale and destructive in its application. It was designed to salvage the city for the middle class. Its backers would diffuse urban discontent by removing the poor to the countryside where they would provide food, exports, and markets for the urban economy. Middle-class city dwellers encouraged settlement on the logged-off lands, although they themselves rarely settled on farms, hoping to see workers and immigrants transformed into an amalgam of the rural virtue they still believed in and the urban entrepreneurship that many of them practiced.

It is, of course, difficult to establish that this agitation actually caused the settlement of the logged-off lands. Certainly, by the 1930s, the Great Depression and drought on the plains had more to do with settlement of logged-off lands than did propaganda. But, at the very least, simultaneous with this urban agitation, men and women moved onto the stumplands where infertile soils were highly vulnerable to degradation. They came with much encouragement, but without capital and without aid. And on the logged-off lands social and environmental disaster mingled and became one. For nearly forty years this migration continued until, finally, the suffering, the failure, and the environmental destruction were so overwhelming that they could no longer be ignored. Social disaster and environmental disaster in tandem made the often subtle relationships between human society and the natural environment seem graphic; the two catastrophes had become so entwined as to be inseparable. By the 1930s refugees from the dust bowl fled unwittingly into another environmental disaster, the logged-off lands, and again paid a heavy price.

Few of the members of the two major groups who composed the migration onto the cutover lands—Scandinavian immigrants and dust bowl refugees—ever established successful farms. Those Scandinavian settlers who came at the turn of the century probably did gain some security from rising land values. These people, however, appear to have been relatively few. The dust bowl refugees fared even worse. Their land not only produced little, its values did not rise until years after they had left it. In the end, both groups found themselves trapped in a vicious economic and ecological circle that scarred both themselves and their land.

On the logged-off lands a whole series of assumptions failed. Belief that growth was good for its own sake; that agriculture was the highest use to which land could be put; that merely living on the land, any land, and working it brought prosperity, virtue, and serenity; and that given hard work, almost any land had some kind of agricultural potential had only resulted in personal suffering and environmental damage. There was finally, it seemed, a price to be paid for the human arrogance involved in thinking nature to be infinitely malleable. But the cost, as usual, fell on those who could bear it the least—the poor, the migrants, the immigrants, and the unemployed—and not on those who had urged settlement.

Chapter VII

THE URBAN SHADOW

*The Impact of Promoters and Tourists
on the Rural Landscape*

By the twentieth century, the geographic isolation of Island County from the mainland had become more figurative than real. Only a few miles away, urban areas had begun to spread along the eastern shores of Puget Sound. The Alaskan gold rush had sparked Seattle's rise into a major city, but Tacoma also grew steadily, if less spectacularly, and directly across from Whidbey and Camano islands the mill town of Everett replaced the forests along Port Gardner Bay. Island County remained predominantly rural—a countryside of farms, logging camps, and small villages—but it was now ringed by major population centers. This urban shadow gave rural life on the islands an ambiguous quality. City dwellers intruded more and more into the lives of the people of the county. Residents could hardly ignore the smoking mills of Everett a few miles to the east, the urban center of Seattle thirty miles from south Whidbey, or the steady stream of urban visitors who soon crossed to the islands.

The accessibility of the county from surrounding urban areas increased constantly during the century. A new ferry began service across Deception Pass in 1913, supplementing the regular steamers from Seattle to Coupeville and Oak Harbor. And in 1913, too, a new bridge to Stanwood linked Camano directly to the mainland. South Whidbey remained relatively isolated, dependent on often irregular steamers, until the mid-1920s, when a regular ferry run from Mukilteo on the mainland to Columbia Beach on Whidbey Island was established. This ferry quickly became a major route to

Whidbey from the Seattle-Everett-Tacoma area. The last major ferry connection for the island, a summer ferry from Keystone, south of Ebeys Prairie, to Port Townsend on the Olympic Peninsula, began to operate about the same time.

But many county residents wanted even more direct access to and from the mainland. Initially in 1908, and then repeatedly thereafter, local officials and businessmen supported proposals for a bridge that would span Deception Pass. During the 1920s the legislature actually appropriated funds for construction, but the governor vetoed the bill. Finally, in the 1930s, using State Emergency Relief Administration funds with a matching grant from the Works Progress Administration and with labor from the Civilian Conservation Corps, construction was begun. When it was completed in 1935, boosters hailed the bridge as the dawn of a new era for Whidbey, "making Whidby Island's scenic beauty . . . easily accessible to all."[1]

The automobile, combined with the proximity of the county to urban areas, allowed city populations in search of recreation (in that word beloved by travel agents) to "discover" Island County. In ferry line brochures Whidbey Island became Romantic Whidbey Island and was promoted as a place for a "delightful outing." By the 1920s, automobile owners could participate in special Sunday automobile tours of Whidbey, and Seattle newspaper columns devoted to car touring told readers that "scenery that challenges comparison anywhere is the reward of the motorist" who journeyed to Island County. City dwellers came for a day, a week, or longer and, as they built or rented "a place on Whidbey," cabins and cottages began to dot the woods and shore.[2]

Enthusiasm for this influx of summer visitors seemed more prevalent in the small villages of the county than in the countryside. Coupeville held an annual Water Festival, and Oak Harbor had its Holland Days. For some townspeople, at least, visitors from the cities became a partial replacement for an older ambition that had failed to reach fruition: the growth of large cities in the county itself.[3]

Since 1853, when R. H. Landsdale built the first store at his town site on Coveland, promoters had attempted to create cities on the islands. They were not satisfied with visions of a rural future for the county, and the plats of the cities they hoped to create still lie virtually untouched in the county courthouse. On these plats the county bristled with towns and cities, roads and industries. In the fevered mind of the most ardent county booster of the time, Lester Still, the county attorney, there seemed to be no reason that Whidbey should not contain more people than Sicily.

During two booms, the first in the late 1860s and the second during the early 1890s, the reality of farms, marshes, and forests momentarily vanished. On paper, at least, townsite promoters transformed Whidbey Island into a metropolis. The first of these booms climaxed in 1871, following the large Northern Pacific purchases in the county. For a brief time residents of Coupeville enjoyed dreams of urban grandeur. They built hotels and prepared to grow rich off their town lots and other land. But another one of Jay Cooke's speculative land companies had bought the site of Tacoma, and the Northern Pacific built its line to Tacoma and Commencement Bay, not to Coupeville and Penn Cove.[4]

The second boom began in 1889 and collapsed in 1891. Again promoters proposed making the county, which had no railroads and no deep-water harbor, the terminus of a transcontinental railroad, this time the Great Northern. In this new scheme a canal would be cut across Ebeys Prairie to attach the Strait of Juan de Fuca to the town site of San de Fuca near the head of Penn Cove. This idea was particularly compelling since it permitted not only the San de Fuca town site at one end of the imaginary canal, but the twin town sites of Brooklyn and Chicago at the other end.

By 1891 the railroad and canal routes were actually surveyed and building began in the towns. By year's end San de Fuca, Brooklyn, and Chicago not only possessed grandiose names and ambitions, but also actual residents living in houses and hotels. Soon there was an Admiralty Addition to Chicago, followed within a few months by the Dyer's and Monroe Additions. Speculators filed for two additions to San de Fuca, and in the surrounding area other town sites blossomed—St. Louis, Juanita, and Glenwood. The promoters of Glenwood even supplemented their imaginary city with an equally imaginary suburb, Glenwood Heights. But by the fall of 1891 the platted cities of Whidbey were in shambles. The whole scheme turned out to be as shaky as the new three-story hotel in the town site of Chicago, which suddenly collapsed in the spring of 1891. By 1899 an army surgeon, out shooting ducks near Crocketts Lake, would find weeds growing in the abandoned houses of Chicago.[5]

Until 1940 few areas of Island County would even qualify as villages. The populations of Coupeville, Oak Harbor, and Langley all hovered between 250 and 350 people, and Freeland, the socialist settlement on south Whidbey, was even smaller. When residents of Coupeville tried to incorporate their village in the early twentieth century, they suffered the indignity of having their request rejected by the county commissioners on the grounds that the proposed boundaries took in too much good farmland.[6]

Although no cities (or even large towns) emerged, some residents found solace in the claim that the countryside that remained attracted far more city people to the county than the town sites ever had. The beauty of the county had, of course, long been recognized both by those who lived on the islands and by visitors. George Vancouver had praised the vistas, and John Muir had written that Whidbey was the "garden of Washington Territory." But in the twentieth century residents of Seattle, Tacoma, and Everett helped boosters to discover that scenery had real economic value. In 1901 Frank Pratt, a La Conner attorney, wrote Almira Enos, heir to the Ebey farms, about buying land. Almira Enos' longtime tenant, Ed Jenne, had assured Pratt that Ebeys Prairie was fertile, but Pratt wasn't interested in fertility. He wanted the land for the splendid view it commanded of Admiralty Inlet and the Olympic Mountains.[7]

Frank Pratt and others like him taught county residents that the islands were scenic, and that scenery was a commodity that could be bought and sold. Scenery depended on the interaction of the observer and the landscape; it was not inherent in an area. In part scenery was beauty, but this was only one element; in any given area, accessibility and the facilities to provide for basic creature comforts were equally important ingredients. Valleys deep in the Cascades, for instance, might be beautiful, but because they were inaccessible, they were not "scenic." The comfort of the observer was essential for scenery. If he was wet, cold, hungry, exhausted from the journey, and worried about where to spend the night, the beauty of the landscape would not be catalyzed into scenery. The visitor needed hotels, restaurants, and good roads; these were as essential a part of scenery as the Olympic Mountains towering over Puget Sound, and these elements made scenery profitable.

Almira Enos did not sell her land to Frank Pratt, but by 1900 the possibilities of the islands for scenery and recreation had become apparent to local promoters. The *Island County Times* formally announced in 1901 that Whidbey Island was becoming a tourist area. Lester Still, never a man for half measures, proclaimed Whidbey's destiny as the "great summer home and watering place of the Northwest as well as the Mississippi Valley." Seattle businessmen proposed building a resort on Whidbey near Ebeys Prairie. They never built the resort, but within a few years promoters did construct Sunlight Beach on Useless Bay, "an ideal community for camping purposes" and Lester Still opened Still's Park on Penn Cove, "ideal for summer home purposes."[8]

Providing for the needs of summer visitors became a significant part of the county's economy, and land use was increasingly influenced by the demands of urban people for recreation and relaxation. For many county residents scenery and recreation became new elements in the old strategy of economic development. They emerged as new ways of promoting growth. As the *Island County Times* wrote in 1927 on the opening of the Keystone Ferry, "Everything that tends to bring more people through here is of greatest advantage to us." Once lured by the beauties of the county, it was presumed that the economic opportunities they discovered might convince many visitors to stay.[9]

The needs and desires of urban visitors to the county were quite various. Some wanted only a pleasant Sunday drive, a weekend visit at one of the inns on Whidbey, or a trip to the beach or forest. Others desired summer homes or a rural retreat. A third, and perhaps the most influential group were the urban sportsmen: the hunters and fishermen who came for deer, quail, pheasant, and salmon. Although the last two groups sometimes overlapped, each of these three urban elements had an influence on resource use, and thus an impact on the landscape of the islands.

By the 1920s the casual visitor from Seattle, Tacoma, or Everett almost invariably traveled by car. Good roads were essential to attracting these people to the islands, and consequently the summer vacationer and the good roads movement proved mutually supportive. The demands of these vacationers for easy and comfortable access to Whidbey became one of the most common arguments for more and better roads. By 1935 there were 325 miles of paved roads in the county. And along the roads these visitors found auto parks, beach cabins, and resorts eager to cater to them. On summer weekends in the 1920s or 1930s, between 2,000 and 4,000 cars per day crossed over the Stanwood bridge to Camano. The dependence of island merchants on these people became so great that when confronted with economic collapse during the Depression, the *Island County Times* almost reflexively editorialized that what the county needed was a hundred more auto camps and beach resorts. Years later the paper continued to demand better roads in order to attract more tourists.[10]

This desire to attract visitors led to the creation of Deception Pass State Park on northern Whidbey in 1922. The land bordering Deception Pass had been a military reservation since 1866, but the reserve, which contained some of the last stands of virgin timber on the island, had never been used by the army. The whole tract was regarded as poor farmland, "not worth much for grazing," and following World War I the Island County Farm Bureau led a campaign to have the area made into a park. The arguments of the park's supporters (and in the newspapers, at least, the park had virtually no opposition) emphasized that a state park would attract visitors who would increase local business revenues and who might stay to become permanent residents. Almost as an afterthought, it was added that county residents might enjoy the park too.[11]

The owners of summer homes on the islands, although fewer in number than the clientele of auto camps and resorts, probably commanded greater individual financial resources. These people bought the sites that commanded the views Frank Pratt had craved, and developers did not forget their needs in the allocation of the county's resources. There were numerous summer homes on the islands by the 1920s, and the desire for even more led to demands like that of the *Island County Times,* in 1938, that more roads be built along the shorelines in order to open them up for further summer home development. By the end of the 1930s, catering to summer visitors and summer residents had become a big enough business to rank with logging and agriculture in the economic hierarchy of the county. Boosters frankly sought to capitalize on "the natural wonders nature has bestowed upon us" and state Senator Pearl Wanamaker, from Coupeville, introduced legislation to provide state aid for attracting tourists.[12]

Unfortunately, nature's wonders in the county had been taking a battering for nearly three-quarters of a century and quite a few of them badly needed some rehabilitation. Now, for the first time, dollar value could be attached to land that grew flowers, not wheat; land that supported deer, not cows; and water that yielded fish not for the market but for the visiting fisherman. These things brought vacationers, and vacationers brought money. By the 1930s there were campaigns to save elements of the island environment that seemed on the point of vanishing.

During the 1920s and 1930s, the *Island County Times* campaigned to preserve the natural vegetation of the prairies and forests. In 1921, the paper editorialized that the very abundance of the forest in the county had led to its abuse, and that "some appeared to be obsessed with the idea that the right thing to do is to get rid of every tree and shrub no matter where it grows." Successively, the *Times* participated editorially in movements to save the wild rhododendrons of the county, to plant madrona trees (*Arbutus menziesii* Pursh) along the shoreline drives, and to prevent the disappearance of the lady's slipper (*Cypripedium montanum* Dougl.), the beautiful wild orchid that grew in the forests. When, in the 1930s, one of the last virgin groves of Douglas fir was threatened with destruction, a successful public protest preserved the trees.[13]

Meeting the needs of the sportsmen, the third group of urban visitors, did not prove as easy or as uncontroversial as building roads and resorts and protecting wild flowers. The game on Whidbey and Camano had attracted outside hunters since the 1850s, but only in the twentieth century did the improved accessibility of the islands bring hunters in economically significant numbers. Here, as elsewhere, farmers objected to urban sportsmen. The attitude of farmers toward deer and ducks, two of the most abundant game animals on the islands, had always been ambivalent. They yielded some meat, but farmers often regarded them as little more than crop pests. But to many farmers, game animals appeared benevolent in comparison with their new urban predators. Each fall hunters broke fences, trampled fields, killed domestic animals, and sporadically slaughtered each other in pursuit of game animals in the fields and woods of the county.

In the early twentieth century, hunting was unregulated enough and intense enough to make real inroads into the game population of the islands. There were legal hunting seasons, but these went unenforced. Soldiers at Fort Casey near Ebeys Prairie amused themselves year round by killing eagles, seals, and ducks. And in the fall of 1902, hunters from Seattle, taking up to forty quail and pheasant apiece, killed so many game birds that late October hunting dog trials ended up a total failure from lack of quail. Hunters contended that overhunting and abuse of game laws were not entirely the work of city men, that county residents participated, too, but the farmers reacted by attempting to ban all hunting on their lands. Banning hunters would have been a heavy blow to the infant resort industry, which proudly advertised abundant game. On the other hand, if overhunting continued, there would be neither game nor hunters.

In the fall of 1904, the county commissioners reacted by appointing a game warden at thirty dollars a month. One warden could hardly have been expected to eliminate out-of-season hunting and overhunting, but he may have curbed it. More significantly, to keep the game population up to the numbers required to attract hunters, the county game warden began stocking game birds and fish, as well as providing feed when necessary.[14]

But the farmers were not appeased so easily. In 1915 after a hunting season that featured, besides the usual trampled fields and broken fences, four serious accidents—including one death— farmers tried to have the county declared a game refuge and have hunting banned. They failed, but their hostility toward hunters and their quarry never disappeared. In 1934, farmers in the Clover Valley and San de Fuca regions began posting "no hunting" signs on their farms, and the movement spread to Ebeys Prairie. State officials argued that since the government paid for raising game birds, farmers were commercializing a publicly maintained resource, and the farmers were forced to back down. For the farmers the situation remained doubly frustrating: Not only did the hunters damage their property in pursuit of game, but also, for most of the year, hunting laws did not allow the farmers to shoot the deer that browsed in their grain fields, nor the game birds that ate in the poultry yards.[15]

This widespread hunting for sport, not for food, introduced a new element into the ecology of the islands. On one hand, it gave wildlife an economic value it had never before enjoyed, since game attracted urban hunters, but on the other hand it put many animal populations under intense pressure. Deer were so well adapted to the environments that agriculture and logging had created that they thrived, despite local hunting laws that allowed for a long hunting season and even the killing of does. Other animals, however, suffered from overhunting. California quail (*Lophortyx californica*) and pheasant (*Phasianus colchicus*) had been introduced into the Puget Sound area in the nineteenth century, but under heavy hunting they needed annual restocking to maintain their populations. Bears (*Euaretes americanus*), having barely survived for years, were exterminated in the county. The waterfowl population also declined, but probably more from the loss of marshland than from overhunting.[16]

Most non-game animals were immune to the consequences of hunting for sport. Hunters largely ignored raccoons (*Procyon lotor*), weasels (*Mustela frenata* and *Mustela erminea*), and skunks (*Mephitis mephitis*). In the early 1930s the Eastern cottontail rabbit (*Sylvilagus floridanus*), an animal that proved impervious to overhunting, joined these other small mammals in the county. The Eastern cottontail became the most successful and destructive animal invader of the islands since the pig. Within a few years of its introduction, it had proliferated into a major agricultural pest. In 1940, the county commissioners passed a resolution urging the game department to remove all restrictions on the hunting of the rabbit. The game department relaxed the regulations, and sportsmen and farmers organized special night hunts to destroy the cottontails, but all attempts to eliminate the rabbit population failed. After World War II, the number of rabbits in the county finally stabilized at between 300,000 and 400,000 animals.[17]

Of the non-game animals only predators, especially predatory birds, suffered from hunting. Sportsmen condemned predatory birds for killing game birds, and hunters even joined farmers in waging a campaign against crows (*Corvus brachyrhynchos hesperis*) because they killed young birds and damaged crops. By March

1936, the campaign against predatory birds and animals had reached a high enough pitch for sportsmen to declare a special predatory animal day in western Washington and to organize hunts devoted solely to the killing of predators. In Island County itself, by 1937, sportsmen's organizations and game farms offered private bounties of twenty cents on each hawk (largely *Buteo* sp. and *Falco* sp.) or owl (*Otus* sp.) brought in. But the major casualty of the war on predators occurred long before this campaign reached its zenith. Sometime after the turn of the century, hunting and increasing settlement made the once abundant bald eagle (*Haliaectus leucocephalus washingtonii*) only an occasional visitor in the county's skies.[18]

Sportsmen had clearly won their conflict with farmers over resource use by the mid-1930s, but by that time they were locked in an even more basic and far-reaching contest with commercial fishermen over the allocation of salmon. By 1931, commercial fishermen on Whidbey had conceded that the great runs of salmon (which passed up the Saratoga Passage on their way to the spawning grounds of the Snohomish, Skagit, and Stillaguamish rivers) were declining. Fishermen blamed the pulp mills and logging operators for polluting the rivers and destroying the spawning beds, but others, especially sport fishermen, blamed the commercial fishermen for overfishing. By the early 1930s a movement to outlaw fish traps entirely was gaining strength. These fish traps, largely owned by Anacortes cannery operators, had lined Whidbey for thirty years. They were an important aspect of the county's economy.[19]

By the 1930s, however, sport fishing was also an important year-round industry on the islands. The first resort catering exclusively to sport fishermen opened on southeastern Whidbey in 1928, and numerous others followed. By 1938 the resorts had spread to the west coast of Whidbey. If salmon decreased in numbers, so would the patrons of these resorts. The debate that developed over the movement to outlaw fish traps centered on conservation, but in Island County at least it was also a contest between two different economic interests—sport fishermen and resort owners on one hand, and commercial fishermen and cannery operators on the other. In 1934 sportsmen succeeded in placing Initiative 77, a proposal to ban fish traps and fish wheels, on the ballot.

On Whidbey sportsmen's organizations backed the measure enthusiastically and participated in public debates with commercial fishermen. The initiative passed statewide, and in Island County it carried by a vote of 1,238 to 1,117. Although very close, the vote demonstrated the hold the recreation industry had on the county and revealed the ability of sportsmen and their allies to assert their priority in resource allocation.[20]

The vocal and well-organized sportsmen's clubs of the county participated in several other conservation battles during the 1930s that eventually reserved shellfish on the islands for non-commercial users. By the late 1930s heavy, and largely unrestricted, exploitation had severely depleted clam and oyster beds on the islands. In 1938, the North Whidbey Sportsmen Club and the Holmes Harbor Rod and Gun Club mustered support for House Bill 276, which would have put an end to unrestricted clam digging. The bill died in committee. In 1939, state Senator Pearl Wanamaker introduced another bill, which would have closed depleted beds to commercial diggers. It passed the Senate but died in the House. The best sportsmen could do in the 1930s was to use the provisions of the state game code, passed by initiative in 1932, to obtain a twenty-pound limit on clams and have it enforced.[21]

Not until 1941 did pressure for sportsmen and conservationists in western Washington result in the Fisheries Department receiving authority to close clam and oyster beds for preservation. In the past, the department could regulate fisheries but did not have the power to close them, nor did it have the power to distinguish between commercial fishermen and sport fishermen in enforcement of the laws.[22]

The impact of the urban visitors on the islands was far-reaching, but it is probably a mistake to read into the changes they brought in land use changes in the attitudes of residents and visitors toward the natural world. Appreciation of the lady's slipper or the rhododendron or the desire to preserve game animals and shellfish only indicated that another element had been added to the continuing commercial exploitation of natural resources. It is hard to picture drunken city dwellers shooting cows, deer, and each other on fall afternoons (and to farmers, at least, hunting often seemed little more than this) as representing a significantly new attitude toward the natural world.

The vacationer, the hunter, the city dweller in general still approached the natural world as if he sought to furnish the islands much as he would his living room, including what he liked, discarding what he didn't. Shellfish, lady's slippers, rhododendrons, pheasant, and quail would remain; hawks, owls, and crows would be destroyed. That there might be ecological relationships between species that rendered this approach simplistic simply did not occur to him.

Although the impact of city dwellers on the county environment was, in part, beneficent, they eventually rendered the ecology of the islands even more unstable than it had been before their arrival. They did save elements of the old Salish ecology that might otherwise have disappeared from the county. Salmon and deer, as well as quail and pheasant, assumed important functions in the life of many of the human residents of the islands; they did not follow bears, elk, and wolves into local extinction. These fish, birds, and animals, however, were now part of a new ecology based on American attitudes and technologies. Except perhaps for deer, they were almost as dependent on humans as were cows and corn. The old ecosystem of the Salish had been destroyed; it had been replaced by another human-created and human-managed environment. The game and fishery agents imitated, in the forests and lakes, the farmer in his fields; they planted trout, pheasant, and quail much like farmers planted wheat and potatoes, and in the summer and fall each were harvested. If fish and game agents did not stock trout and salmon, they would disappear. If they did not raise quail and pheasant on game farms, these birds would be gone in a season.

Human values and human decisions had consciously preserved, and in some cases introduced these animals, but other human values and human decisions continued to threaten them. The construction of summer homes, military bases, and towns destroyed the habitat of local wildlife. Even with human aid, most native wildlife seemed precarious visitors in a world where they had once seemed permanent fixtures. The only fauna that seemed to thrive in the county, totally impervious to human wishes and designs, were the rabbit and man's old traveling companion, the rat. Only the invaders were secure on the islands; the natives had just obtained a reprieve.

Urban migrants and visitors increased their pressure on the country's environment following World War II. In the late 1960s, a new Boeing aircraft plant at Mukilteo, just across from south Whidbey, led to demands for a bridge to the island. Only when Boeing's sales and employment slumped badly were the plans dropped. If built, such a bridge would have reduced south Whidbey to little more than a suburb of Seattle and Everett. But even without the bridge, the county's growing population strained resources people once took for granted. New housing developments meant new wells, and in a county surrounded by water, drinking water became a dwindling resource in some communities as the wells lowered the water table and salt water began to intrude. In such an altered world, even the oldest white-dominated landscape on the islands, the prairie farms, seemed to be a precarious remnant of a vanished order. Between 1964 and 1969, the number of farms in the county fell from 441 to 240, and only 80 of these actually remained productive enterprises. In the 1970s the prairie farms seem about to become victims of the very changes that the men and women who settled them 120 years before had begun.[23]

CONCLUSION

In 1864 George Perkins Marsh, in his book *Man and Nature*, asserted that not only did nature shape human society, but that humans, in significant and far-reaching ways, had also shaped nature. Marsh argued on a grand scale; he dealt with the despoliation of continents and the fall of empires in order to demonstrate that men had altered natural systems and that these alterations had had consequences for their societies. A century after Marsh's book was published, people no longer have to go back to the fall of Rome to find evidence of the profound impact of human beings upon the natural world. Only the least attentive residents of the United States in the past decade could have escaped the daily barrage of information about the impact of technology on the environment that has altered the meaning of the word "ecology" and has made it a part of common speech. After reports on DDT and the announcements, apparently premature, of the death of Lake Erie, even Marsh might seem bland and passé.

To conclude, then, that men and women have shaped the environment of Island County should startle no one. But the history of man upon this land is obscured as much as illuminated by this kind of generalization. In a way, such a conclusion merely reverses the old neo-Darwinist assumption of an all-powerful nature and inserts a new assumption of a nearly omnipotent, if often insensitive mankind. The actual history of environmental change and its consequences in Island County has been more complex.

Humans have influenced the environment of the islands in two related, but significantly different, ways. One Marsh recognized a century ago: Human technology has altered the operation of natural systems so that new environments have been created and the face of the earth has been changed. Men have plowed land, drained marshes, and cut forests. As Marsh realized, the eventual consequences of this kind of human manipulation are very often far from what was originally intended. In Island County, the moisture retention of some soils decreased until they were unable to produce crops, while other soils eroded or declined in fertility. In the forests, donkey engines, new mills, and railroads created a set of conditions that led to a new forest with an increased proportion of hemlock and deciduous trees and with less well-stocked stands. These changes were not anticipated by the residents, but they resulted, nonetheless, from conscious human manipulation.

Marsh, however, did not deal with another kind of change in which humans have been the dominant agents and, often, conscious initiators, but that in other cases has also been the almost inevitable result of their movement across the face of the earth. When human beings moved among ecosystems that had been isolated for centuries, they transferred plants, animals, and diseases peculiar to each into the others. Some of the plants and animals introduced into Island County, such as wheat, cattle, and pigs, were purposeful; others, such as rats and Canadian thistle, were not. For the Indians and the environment they maintained, mere contact with Europeans, because of diseases to which the Salish had no resistance, resulted in change no matter what subsequent actions the whites took.

The real complexity of environmental change on these islands resulted from the simultaneous and interdependent operation of both technological manipulation and ecological invasion. Each type of impact influenced and magnified the consequences of the other. Before the arrival of the Europeans, there had been technological manipulation of the environment by the Salish to increase such desired plant species as bracken, nettles, and camas, but there had been only limited introductions of new species. When Indians altered the floral composition of the prairies, for instance, one element of the island ecology (bracken) succeeded others (wild grasses). But when whites altered the prairies, they also introduced new elements, either intentionally or unintentionally. Wheat and thistle did not have some kind of inherent biological superiority that allowed them to displace native plants. Rather, their advantage came from their adaptation to the kinds of changes, largely cleared or disturbed lands, that resulted from European land use.

The environmental changes that grew out of the dual impact of men upon the land cannot, however, be easily separated from the underlying cultural, social, and economic causes that influenced human land use. If the ways in which humans used the land very often shaped the natural environment, then the factors that influenced this land use become crucial in understanding environmental change.

There is no doubt that the Salish viewed the natural world far differently than did the Europeans. The Indians populated it with spirits and powers that often gave natural events a double significance by imposing upon them a second, spiritual level of meaning. But too often this quite valid observation has led to the unwarranted conclusion that since the Indians did not impose a yawning intellectual chasm between themselves and the rest of the natural world, they therefore behaved like so many bison, trees, or butterflies following the mystical comands of nature. This kind of deduction goes against what seems convincing evidence that the Salish did not hesitate to alter natural systems when it was to their advantage to do so. Their views of nature were undoubtedly relevant to their use of the natural world, but how their cultural outlook influenced their land use is a matter for investigation, not simple deduction. Since Indian land use did not eliminate species or entire habitats, the Salish themselves may not have seen any contradiction (nor, inherently, does there seem to be one) between their metaphysical and religious views and their economic uses of the natural world.

The American view of nature on the islands revolved chiefly, but not solely, around judgments of its economic usefulness. Americans tended to encourage what they regarded as economically valuable plants and animals and to discourage or be indifferent about the others. But within the context of a changing economy and society, what was regarded as economically valuable could shift with great rapidity. For most nineteenth century farmers, natural vegetation remained an obstacle to be removed and, for most lumbermen, the forest was only a resource to be cut.

In the twentieth century, however, demands for recreation have given rhododendrons, lady's slippers, deer, virgin groves of Douglas fir, and scenic vistas real monetary value because of their ability to attract urban visitors and sportsmen. The attempt to preserve these tokens of the natural world does not seem the outgrowth of any significant new attitude toward nature. The same basic standard, economic value, still governed the attempts at preservation. Remnants of the older natural systems had attained greater value as they grew more scarce and as urban dwellers gained the time and the means to enjoy them.

From 1859 to 1940, changes in the economy and in technology had repercussions on natural systems. The alteration of the forest environment by the donkey engine has been the most notable example, but market agriculture and the type of farming it produced on the prairies has also been significant. Nevertheless, economics do not provide a full explanation of what happened to the land in Island County.

The movement onto the logged-off lands, for example, goes much deeper than hope of profit. Desire for economic gain alone could not have sustained forty years of consistently unsuccessful farming. The logged-off land movement derived at least part of its strength from a set of cultural attitudes that, apparently, were still widely subscribed to in the early twentieth century—that farming was the best way of life; that any land, given hard work, could be made productive; that farming inculcated virtue; and that farmers were the backbone of the republic. The failure and tragedy that came out of the movement is a reminder not only that human land use has been shaped by factors other than economics, but also that these factors, merely because their motive is not profit, are not somehow inherently superior. In this case they proved as disastrous as greed to the land and its inhabitants.

Human manipulation of the natural world has inevitably had consequences for human society as well as for the environment. Some of these consequences have been exactly what the manipulators intended and men have regarded them as beneficial. For the Salish the prairies produced bracken, camas, and nettle; for the whites they produced wheat, oats, and potatoes. In both cases people were fed. When, however, environmental change went awry, when diseases decimated the Salish, when the prairie fields produced thistles and velvet grass, when the species composition of the forest changed, and when the salmon runs declined and threatened to fail, there were other repercussions that adversely affected human society on the islands. The destruction of the forest and the failure of reforestation, for example, meant not only a loss of jobs, but also the elimination of an essential part of the tax base of the county at a time when tax revenues were needed to support schools and roads for an increasing population. Likewise, the destruction of the large, infertile uplands by stump farmers burdened the county with a class of rural poor whose only faults were bad advice, poor land, and bad farming. The land was ruined and so were human lives.

From an examination of Island County, change in the natural environment appears to be an inevitable consequence of human land use. The problem is, however, not the elimination of human impact, but an understanding of its extent and the limitation of its undesirable consequences. There can be successful alterations in natural systems. The Salish changed the landscape and created an environment that remained stable and maintained the culture that created it over a long period of time without any weakening of its productive capacity. Not all white changes proved so successful. The alterations that Americans have made in the islands have been more far-reaching than those of the Indians. Historically the farmer, the lumberman, and the fisherman have proved more adept at refining technologies and increasing the scope and rate of environmental change than the larger society has been in gauging the consequences of the technologies and in creating institutional means to control them. In the short run, the result has often been profit for a few and jobs for more, but eventually the actual residents of the area have been left with depleted resources, an altered and often impoverished ecology, and the necessity to renew the search for new ways to exploit the land and support human institutions. In Island County, after 120 years of white settlement, agriculture, fishing, and lumbering have all declined, and the resources upon which they were based have been depleted. The county survives largely as an urban and military colony, the physical site of air bases, vacation homes, beaches, and parks. In many ways it is still a pleasant place, but there is, of course, no guarantee that the scenery residents and visitors have discovered will survive exploitation any longer than did the other resources already depleted.

APPENDIX A

Population—Methods and Estimates

The Indian population of Island County is difficult to estimate. In the only thorough study of Puget Sound's Salish population, Herbert Taylor has selected 1780, before the catastrophic epidemics reached the sound, as the area's population peak. At that date he gives an estimated population of about 10,300 for the tribes from the Skohomish on Hood Canal to the Swinomish north of Whidbey. This is roughly twice James Mooney's early estimate of 6,000. This population, however, was far from evenly distributed. Alan Bryan has identified north Whidbey and north Camano as the major population centers of Puget Sound.

In 1792, Joseph Whidbey of the Vancouver expedition thought the lands bordering Saratoga Passage were the most populous areas in the region. He estimated a population of 600 for western Camano and eastern Whidbey, but he apparently did not include the Penn Cove villagers, then fishing at Deception Pass, in this count. The elimination of the Penn Cove population, the area's undoubted center, is quite significant. In 1842, Joseph Perry Sanford of the Wilkes expedition estimated the Penn Cove population at from 400 to 500. By then, according to Taylor, there had been a significant population drop all over the sound, a decline he estimates at around 50 percent. These two estimates, adjusted for the known population decline, seem to indicate a population of from 1,300 to 1,500, not including the Snohomish village on Cultus Bay and the Kikialos villages east of Utsalady. If 100 persons are allowed for each of these (a very conservative estimate, since there were 50 people at Cultus Bay as late as the 1870s), then the total population numbered from 1,500 to 1,700. This figure only uses the explorers estimates, which have usually proven to be quite low.

The 1,500 to 1,700 population figure can safely be taken as a minimum figure. The U.S. Court of Claims in 1932 (after extensive testimony) awarded the Whidbey Skagits damages on the basis of 47 permanent houses with 248 family compartments. At the rate of 6 persons per family, which is Colin Tweddell's minimal estimate for the Whidbey and mainland Snohomish, this gives a population of 1,488 for the Skagit alone. Tweddell himself has estimated the total Snohomish population at "into the thousands," which, if only a quarter lived on the islands, would give a minimum population of at least 300. Since Joseph Whidbey of the Vancouver expedition saw 200 at the Sandy Point village, and this village was apparently smaller than the village at Cultus Bay, 400 would seem a more accurate minimum estimate for the Snohomish on Whidbey. Likewise, Osmundson has estimated the maximum Kikialos population at 500, which would give an upper range of about 2,400 for the islands as a whole.

These population estimates ignore the early figures given by settlers and Indian agents because they vary so widely and are so imprecise that they are virtually useless. The only exception is the head count taken by R. C. Fay in 1856 when the Skagit, Snohomish, and Kikialos were confined to reservations during the 1855–56 Indian war. This count yielded 1,266 for all three tribes and almost certainly did not include all of the upriver Snohomish and Skagit. This figure, given the preponderance of saltwater over upriver Indians, and Taylor's estimate of a 50 percent decline since 1780, fits quite nicely with the 1,500–2,400 estimate of maximum population.

If the Salish population of what would be Island County lay within these 1,500–2,400 limits, then the county's population density in 1780 would be between 7.2 and 11.1 persons per square mile.*

*Herbert C. Taylor, "Aboriginal Populations of the Lower Northwest Coast," *PNQ* 54:4 (October 1963), 160, 162–63; Bryan, *Survey*, 20–23, 82–83, map, Appendix, figures 1 and 2; Tweddell, *Snohomish*, 100, 154–56; Joseph Perry Sanford, *Journal*, June 15–16, 1841; Vancouver, *Voyages*, 2:162, 168; U.S. Congress, 34th Congress, 3rd Session, House Ex. Doc. 76 (Serial #906), 9; Osmundson, "Camano," 35; U.S. Archives, W.S., R. C. Fay to Stevens, May 24, 1856; *Duwamish et al.*, 2:833. The population estimates I have derived here could easily have been higher, since if I had used Tweddell's larger estimate of 8 per family group almost 500 more Skagit would have been added, and an increase of 200 Snohomish might also have been justified, yielding a maximum figure of c. 3,000.

APPENDIX B

TABLE 19. Original Productivity of Townsend Loam Soil, 1860

To	Farms	Improved Acres	Wheat (Bu.)	Oats (Bu.)	Potatoes (Bu.)	Livestock Value
Townsend Loam Soils T32N, R1E	29	781	2,820	11,090	14,740	$15,180
Ebeys Loam Soils T31N, R1E	25	716	3,120	5,260	5,230	$11,400

SOURCE: Manuscript Census, Agriculture, 1860.

TABLE 20. Percentage of Island County Farmers Growing Over, 1860

Farmers	100 Bushels of Wheat	100 Bushels of Oats	250 Bushels of Potatoes
County as a Whole	34.3%	31.9%	34.2%
Farmers Born in Mid-Atlantic States and Va.	46.6%	47.4%	. . .
Farmers Born in N.Y. and Pennsylvania	. . .	. . .	29.2%

SOURCE: Manuscript Census, Agriculture, 1860. Manuscript Census, Population, 1860.

NOTE: Figures are given only for crops produced in large amounts in region of birth.

TABLE 21. MAJOR OWNERS OF TIMBERLAND, ISLAND COUNTY, 1871

Name	Acreage	Representative of
J. W. Sprague	17,420.25	Lake Superior & Puget Sound Land Co.
Benjamin Hackney	3,753.57	Speculator
Benjamin Goldsmith	2,622.41	Speculator
Pope & Talbot	2,616.4	Puget Mill
Grennan & Cranney	2,143.61	Grennan & Cranney
Marshall Blinn	1,173.74	Washington Mill Co.
John Collins	940.08	Speculator
Henry Maryott	881.03	Farmer (Speculator)
Nicolas Code	800.75	Speculator
Amos & Phinney	708.70	Port Ludlow Mill Co.
William Renton	603.13	Port Blakely Mill Co.

SOURCE: Summary of Island County Land Holdings, 1871, Auditor's Office, Island County Courthouse.

TABLE 22. EMPLOYMENT IN LUMBER INDUSTRY, ISLAND COUNTY, 1896

Employed In	Men Employed	Avg. No. Days	Avg. Hours	Mo. Pay	Total Pay
Mills	30	150	10	$35	$ 5,250
Camps	115	240	10	$35	32,200
Total	145				$37,450

SOURCE: *First Annual Report, Bureau of Statistics, Agriculture and Immigration,* Olympia (1896), 135–36.

TABLE 23. SCHOOL LANDS, ISLAND COUNTY, FIRE DAMAGE BY SECTIONS

Fire Damage	South Whidbey	North Whidbey	Central Whidbey
Yes	3	2	0
No	3	5	4
Uncertain	2	1	1

SOURCE: School Lands of Island County, Report of Appraisers, Dec. 11, 1890, Auditor's Office, Island County Courthouse.

TABLE 24. ACREAGE BURNED BY ACCIDENTAL FIRE, SAMPLE YEARS

	1908	1911	1915	1917	1919	1921	1923	1925
Acreage	115	1,320	3,000	66	1,690	38	557	2,890

SOURCE: Reports of the State Fire Warden to the Washington State Forest Commissioners Board.

TABLE 25. ACREAGE BURNED BY ACCIDENTAL FIRE,
ISLAND COUNTY

	1925	1926	1929	1930	1934	1935	1939	1940
Acres	2,890	2,592	3,534	760	379	1,189	47	24
Acres with merchantable timber	80	85	55	86	0	3	0	0

SOURCE: Reports of the Division of Forestry to the Dept. of Conservation and Development.

TABLE 26. RESTOCKING OF FOREST LAND IN ISLAND COUNTY
BY ACREAGE, 1932

Age Class	Degree of Stocking	DFS[d]	WHS[e]	DF2[f]	Total	Percent
	G[a]	12,660	40	. . .	12,700	55.4
10	M[b]	7,555	275	. . .	7,830	34.0
	P[c]	2,390	. . .	. . .	2,390	10.6
					22,920	
	G	6,190	80	745	7,015	59.4
20	M	2,670	. . .	2,120	4,790	40.6
	P	. . .	. . .	. . .	. . .	
					18,805	
	G	100	. . .	1,490	1,590	78.1
30	M	. . .	. . .	445	445	21.9
	P	. . .	. . .	. . .	. . .	. . .
					2,035	

[a] G—good—growth dense enough to cover 70 to 100 percent of area as measured by stocked quadrant method.

[b] M—medium—growth dense enough to cover 40 to 70 percent of area as measured by stocked quadrant method.

[c] P—poor—growth dense enough to cover 10 to 40 percent of area as measured by stocked quadrant method.

[d] DFS—Douglas fir seedlings and saplings.

[e] WHS—Western hemlock seedlings and saplings.

[f] DF2—Douglas fir second growth.

SOURCE: U.S.D.A. Forest Service, "Forest Statistics of Western Washington Counties: Forest Statistics of Island County, Washington," Table 4, Pacific Northwest Experiment Station, Portland, March 1934 (mimeographed).

TABLE 27. ACREAGE, DAIRYING, AND POULTRY
IN ISLAND COUNTY

Year	Improved Acreage	No. of Milk Cows	No. of Sheep	Dollar Value Poultry (in Thousands)
1901	8,032	. . .	2,576	. . .
1902	8,236	. . .	2,821	. . .
1903	. . .	. . .	. . .	. . .
1904	8,606	. . .	3,118	. . .
1905	8,497	. . .	2,734	. . .
1906	8,882	1,668	2,131	$ 3,232
1907	9,030	1,706	1,773	4,185
1908	9,317	1,787	2,201	5,575
1909	9,473	1,932	2,267	5,337
1910	10,110	1,668	2,139	3,979
1911	10,127	1,778	2,114	5,531
1912	10,880	1,830	2,128	6,525
1913	10,950	1,838	1,669	5,740
1914	10,990	2,486	1,489	8,265
1915	11,190	2,647	1,497	7,885
1916	11,300	2,732	1,417	7,320
1917	11,583	2,091	1,428	7,310
1918	14,093	1,885	1,661	7,740
1919	14,204	1,534	1,874	6,577
1920	15,666	1,828	2,664	19,128
1921	15,634	2,232	1,904	15,083
1922	15,826	1,916	1,722	14,173
1923	15,936	2,068	1,607	19,275
1924	16,130	2,052	2,150	22,975
1925	16,727	1,858	1,831	19,005
1926	16,902	1,892	1,911	24,170
1927	16,923	1,716	2,516	31,467
1928	16,480	1,698	2,135	31,247
1929	16,480	1,794	2,360	33,578
1930	16,500	1,883	2,093	33,975
1931	16,352	1,676	2,020	18,510
1932	16,766	1,857	1,653	11,405
1933	17,082	1,366	1,368	13,580
1934	17,131	1,708	1,240	4,480
1935	17,131	1,811	1,140	10,855
1936	18,686	1,657	874	8,155
1937	18,700	1,872	780	11,295
1938	18,800	2,031	790	12,890
1939	18,800	1,901	916	12,045
1940	18,850	1,824	861	8,245

SOURCE: *Minutes and Official Proceedings of the State Board of Equalization of the State of Washington,* 1901–40.

TABLE 28. AGRICULTURAL PRODUCTION,
ISLAND COUNTY, 1920–40

Census Category	1920	1930	1940
Value of Dairy Products	$325,925	$ 294,640	$246,735
Poultry Products	$190,981	$1,614,755	$593,061
Hay and Forage (tons)	13,861	11,036	10,813
Small Fruits (quarts)	88,225	1,056,421	. . .
Dairy Farms	. . .	162	234
Poultry Farms	. . .	319	236
Self-Sufficing Farms	. . .	34	381

SOURCE: Fourteenth Census, Agriculture, 6, pt. 3:297, 301; Fifteenth Census, Agriculture, 6, pt. 3:297, 301; 3, pt. 3:320; Sixteenth Census, Agriculture, 1, pt. 6:561, 565, 571; 2, pt. 3:237.

NOTES

Introduction

1. Whidbey is the original spelling of the name of the island. It was corrupted to Whidby by the first American settlers. Both spellings are still in use. Throughout the study, United States Geological Survey spelling of place names is followed, even though some of them, such as Penn Cove instead of Penns Cove, differ from local usage. Frederick Buerstatte, "The Geography of Whidby Island," 1–2, 6–15; United States Department of Agriculture, Soil Conservation Service, *Soil Survey: Island County, Washington,* Series 1949, no. 6, August 1958, pp. 3–9 (hereafter cited as U.S.D.A., *Soil Survey*).

2. This is not to say that such works as Roderick Nash's *Wilderness and the American Mind* or Samuel Hays's *Conservation and the Gospel of Efficiency* are not substantial achievements. But the very success of such works has enabled them to overshadow earlier attempts to study the relation of man and the environment. James Malin, *Winter Wheat in the Golden Belt of Kansas* and *The Grassland of North America: Prolegomena to Its History* are the two best examples of this neglected aspect of environmental history. Alfred Crosby's recent *The Columbian Exchange* may indicate a resurgence in this kind of study.

3. Ellen Semple, *American History and Its Geographic Conditions;* Ellsworth Huntington, *The Red Man's Continent;* Walter Prescott Webb, *The Great Plains;* George Perkins Marsh, *Man and Nature.* For examples of recent studies in other fields see F. R. Fosberg (ed.), *Man's Place in the Island Ecosystem;* Andrew H. Clark, *The Invasion of New Zealand by People, Plants, and Animals: The South Island;* Roy Rappaport, *Pigs for the Ancestors;* William L. Thomas (ed.), *Man's Role in Changing the Face of the Earth;* Frank Fraser Darling, *The West Highland Survey: An Essay in Human Ecology;* and Helje Kjekshus, *Ecology Control and Economic Development in East African History.*

4. Darling, *West Highland Survey,* p. 53. See also Frank Fraser Darling, "The Ecological Approach to the Social Sciences" in *The Subversive Science: Essays Toward an Ecology of Man,* edited by Paul Shepard and Daniel McKinley, pp. 316–27; Frank Fraser Darling and Raymond F. Dasmann, "The Ecosystem View of Human Society" in *The Ecology of Man: An Ecosystem Approach,* edited by Robert L. Smith, pp. 40–45.

5. D. J. Easterbrook, "Late Pleistocene Glaciation of Whidby Island, Washington" p. 198; D. J. Easterbrook, "Pleistocene Stratigraphy of Island County," pp. 21–32; Henry Hansen, "Postglacial Forest Succession and Climate in the Puget Sound Region," p. 35; J. Harlen Bretz, *Glaciation of the Puget Sound Region,* pp. 17–22, 106–63, 199; U.S.D.A., *Soil Survey,* pp. 3–4, 13, 15, 18, 25.

6. Henry Paul Hansen, *Postglacial Forest Succession, Climate and Chronology in the Pacific Northwest,* pp. 57–58, 71–73, 78–81; Hansen, "Postglacial Forest Succession and Climate in the Puget Sound Region," pp. 34–35.

7. Hansen, *Postglacial Forest Succession, Climate and Chronology,* pp. 57–58, 71–72, 80–81; Thornton Munger, "The Cycle from Douglas Fir to Hemlock," pp. 451–59; J. V. Hoffman, "The Establishment of a Douglas Fir Forest," pp. 49–54; George Neville Jones, *A Botanical Survey of the Olympic Peninsula, Washington,* p. 32.

8. For early descriptions of Island County forests see: E. Holbrook to Mother, Jan. 26, 1854, in Works Progress Administration, *Told by the Pioneers: Tales of Frontier Life Told by Those Who Remember the Days of the Territory and Early Statehood of Washington* (3 volumes, Olympia, 1937), 2:153; *Washington Standard,* April 17, 1875, p. 2; Immigrant Aid Society of North-Western Washington, *Northwestern Washington: Its Soil, Climate, and General Resources,* p. 38; C. F. Newcombe (ed.), *Menzies Journal of Vancouver's Voyage—April to October 1792,* pp. 49–50; James Swan, *Scenes in Washington Territory,* Pacific Northwest Collection, University of Washington, no. 9. These descriptions are usually general, providing few details. For general works on the area's forests, see Buerstatte, "The Geography of Whidby Island" and United States Department of Agriculture, Jerry Franklin and C. T. Dyrness, *The Natural Vegetation of Oregon and Washington,* (hereafter cited as U.S.D.A., Franklin & Dyrness, *Natural Vegetation*).

9. A. W. Kuchler, "The Broadleaf Deciduous Forests of the Pacific Northwest," pp. 122–47.

10. B. Robert Butler, *The Old Cordilleran Culture in the Pacific Northwest,* p. 51.

11. Roy Carlson, "Chronology and Culture Change in the San Juan Islands," p. 583; Alan Lyle Bryan, *An Archaeological Survey of North*

Puget Sound, pp. 28, 33–34; Arden King, "Archaeology of the San Juan Islands, A Preliminary Report on the Cattle Point Site" in *Indians of the Urban Northwest,* edited by Marian Smith, pp. 136, 145.

12. Bryan, *Archaeological Survey,* pp. 28–34; King, "Archaeology of the San Juan Islands," pp. 136–37; Carlson, "Chronology and Culture Change," p. 584; John Lyle Mattson, "A Contribution to Skagit Prehistory," pp. 36–49.

13. Bryan, *Archaeological Survey,* pp. 33–34, 81–82; Carlson, "Chronology and Culture Change," pp. 562, 583–84; A. L. Kroeber, *The Cultural and Natural Areas of Native North America,* pp. 28–29; Marian Smith, "The Cultural Development of the Northwest Coast," pp. 272–79.

14. Carlson, "Chronology and Culture Change," pp. 562, 585; Philip Drucker, *Indians of the Northwest Coast,* pp. 20, 23; Morris Swadesh, "The Linguistic Approach to Salish Prehistory," in *Indians of the Urban Northwest,* edited by Marian Smith, p. 166.

Chapter I. Shaping the Face of the Land

1. Marian Smith, *The Puyallup-Nisqually,* pp. 28–32.

2. Smith, *Puyallup-Nisqually,* pp. 58–59; June Collins, *Valley of the Spirits,* read in proofs; Hermann Haeberlin, "The Mythology of Puget Sound," *Journal of American Folklore,* 37:378–79, 383–84, 391; Ella C. Clark, *Indian Legends of the Pacific Northwest,* pp. 199–201; James Swan, *The Northwest Coast, or Three Years' Residence in Washington Territory,* p. 316; Claude Levi-Strauss, *The Savage Mind,* pp. 3–10. Levi-Strauss makes the general point of the exact knowledge of plant life typical of many hunting and gathering peoples.

3. *Olympia Pioneer and Democrat,* April 9, 1853; Victor J. Farrar (ed.), "Diary of Colonel and Mrs. I. N. Ebey," *Washington Historical Quarterly,* 8:139; Paul Kane, *Wanderings of an Artist,* pp. 157–58.

4. Hermann Haeberlin and Erna Gunther, *The Indians of Puget Sound,* pp. 136–37.

5. Herbert C. Taylor, "Aboriginal Populations of the Lower Northwest Coast," *Pacific Northwest Quarterly,* 54:160–63, provides a basic population estimate. Bryan, *Archaeological Survey of Northern Puget Sound,* pp. 12–13, provides basic data on village sites. I have modified these sources with information from: Colin Tweddell, "A Historical and Ethnological Study of the Snohomish Indian People," Expert Testimony before the Indian Claims Commission, Docket 125, pp. 25–26, 32, 100, 128–29, 154–56; John Osmundson, "Man and His Natural Envi-

ronment on Camano Island, Washington," pp. 20–22, 35; George Vancouver, *A Voyage of Discovery to the North Pacific*, 2:168; United States Archives, Records of the United States Exploring Expedition under the Command of Charles Wilkes, 1838–42, Joseph Perry Sanford, *Journal*, June 15–16, 1842 (microfilm); *Duwamish et al. vs. U.S.*, Docket No. F-275, 2:833; Hermann Haeberlin and Erna Gunther, *The Indians of Puget Sound*, pp. 15–17. For an explanation of how I arrived at population figures, see Appendix A.

    6. Erna Gunther, *Ethnobotany of Western Washington*, pp. 13–50.

    7. This account of the Salish diet and food cycle is a composite of information found in Tweddell, *Snohomish*, p. 53; Haeberlin and Gunther, *The Indians of Puget Sound*, pp. 20–21, 26; June Collins, "John Fornsby: The Personal Document of a Coast Salish Indian," in *Indians of the Urban Northwest*, pp. 294–95, 302; George Gibbs, *On the Indians of Western Washington and Northwest Oregon*, p. 193; *Duwamish et al. vs. U.S.*, 1:314–15; Bryan, *Archaeological Survey of Northern Puget Sound*, Appendix, pp. 1–11; Gunther, *Ethnobotany of Western Washington*, passim; Loye Miller, "Some Indian Midden Birds from the Puget Sound Region," *Wilson Bulletin* 72:392–94.

    8. June Collins, "John Fornsby," p. 302.

    9. United States Archives, Washington Superintendency of Indian Affairs, Letters from Employees Assigned to Local Agencies, Jan. 1, 1856–Nov. 1858 (Roll 10) R. C. Fay to M. T. Simmons, Jan. 1856, Jan. 1, 1857, Dec. 31, 1857, March 31, 1858, Fay to I. I. Stevens, March 9, 1856, July 29, 1856, Oct. 7, 1856, Nov. 30, 1856, Jan. 1, 1857; U.S. Department of the Interior, *Report of the Commissioner of Indian Affairs Accompanying the Annual Report of the Secretary of Interior for the Year 1857*, pp. 336–37; U.S. Department of the Interior, *Report of the Commissioner of Indian Affairs . . . for the Year 1858*, pp. 238–40; R. C. Fay, Journal, May 23, June 1, 6, 12, 20, 28, August 7, 15, 16, September 11, 15, 1856, R. C. Fay Collection, Washington State Library, Olympia; George Gibbs, *On the Indians of Western Washington*, p. 194; U.S. Congress, House, "Indian Affairs in the Territories of Oregon and Washington," House Executive Document 39 (Serial 955), p. 14; Richard White, "The Treaty at Medicine Creek," pp. 109–13.

    10. U.S. Archives, Washington Superintendency of Indian Affairs, Letters from Agents Assigned to the Puget Sound District, Starling to I. I. Stevens, Dec. 10, 1853; U.S. Congress, House, *Letters Addressed to the Commissioner of Indian Affairs* (Serial 741), Stevens to Manypenny, Dec. 26, 1853, p. 11.

    11. Haeberlin and Gunther, *Indians of Puget Sound*, p. 20; Loye

Miller, "Some Indian Midden Birds from the Puget Sound Region," *Wilson Bulletin* 72:392–394.

12. Bruce Proudfoot, "Man's Occupance of the Soil," in *Man and His Habitat*, ed. by R. H. Buchanan *et al.*, p. 12.

13. *Ibid.;* Gunther, *Ethnobotany*, p. 28; *Duwamish et al. vs. U.S.*, 1:314–15; Swan, *Northwest Coast*, p. 77.

14. U.S. Congress, Senate, *Reports of Explorations and Surveys*, "Report Upon the Botany of the Route," by J. G. Cooper, Volume 12, Book 2, p. 23, hereafter cited as Railroad Report; Farrar (ed.), "Ebey Diary," *Washington Historical Quarterly*, 7:311, hereafter *Washington Historical Quarterly* cited as *WHQ;* Bryan, *Archaeological Survey of Northern Puget Sound*, Appendix, p. 4.

15. Railroad Report, "Botany of the Route," by J. G. Cooper, 12, 2:22–23; W. S. Ebey, Diary, July 1, 1858, July 5, 1858, Ebey Collection, University of Washington Library, hereafter cited as Ebey Collection; Walter Crockett to H. Black, Oct. 15, 1853, University of Washington Library; Francis Kautz (ed.), "Extracts from the Diary of A. V. Kautz," *Washington Historian*, 1:184; Carl Sauer, *Land and Life*, pp. 180–81.

16. Gunther, *Ethnobotany*, pp. 14–15; F. Fraser Darling, *The West Highland Survey*, p. 172; Jones, *A Botanical Survey of the Olympic Peninsula*, pp. 36–37; U.S.D.A., Forest Service, Franklin and Dyrness, *Natural Vegetation*, p. 89.

17. Farrar (ed.), "Ebey Diary," *WHQ*, 8:134; U.S. Congress, Senate Executive Document 1, 33rd Congress, 2nd Session (Serial 746), p. 455; Railroad Report, "Indian Tribes of Washington Territory," by George Gibbs, 1:432–33; Sauer, *Land and Life*, p. 180; *Duwamish et al. vs. U.S.*, 1:314–15, 319–20; Gunther, *Ethnobotany*, p. 25; Collins, *Valley of the Spirits*, p. 55.

18. *Duwamish et al. vs. U.S.*, 1:319; Walter Crockett to H. Black, Oct. 15, 1853, University of Washington Library; Farrar (ed.), "Ebey Diary," *WHQ*, 8:134.

19. J. G. Swan, Diary, Nov. 21, 1863, Swan Collection, University of Washington Library. For more information on the use of timber by the Salish see: Gunther, *Ethnobotany*, pp. 16–20, 26–27, 39–40, 42–43; Haeberlin and Gunther, *Indians of Puget Sound*, pp. 15, 32, 34; Osmundson, "Camano," p. 41. The reaction of Charles Wilkes to the timber of the Puget Sound region is typical: Charles Wilkes, *Narrative of the U.S. Exploring Expedition During the Years 1838–1842*, 4:481.

20. Gunther, *Ethnobotany*, p. 41. Gunther apparently rules out the possibility here that the Salish procured fireweed by burning.

21. The ecology and successional patterns of the forest of the Pacific Northwest can be pursued in: Thornton Munger, "The Cycle from Douglas Fir to Hemlock," *Ecology*, 21:451–59; J. V. Hoffman, "The Establishment of a Douglas Fir Forest," *Ecology*, 1:49–54; Jones, *Botanical Survey*, p. 32; U.S.D.A., Forest Service, Franklin and Dyrness, *Natural Vegetation*, pp. 82–84.

22. U.S. Department of the Interior, Bureau of Land Management, Portland, Oregon, *Field Notes of the United States Surveyor*, Book 1, pp. 312, 333, 576, 585, 596, 603; Book 10, pp. 486, 523, 534, 540, 562, 582; Book 11, p. 686; Book 12, pp. 422, 426, 445, 456, 525, 526, 542, 588.

23. For natural succession and plant growth following burns see: U.S.D.A., Forest Service, Franklin and Dyrness, *Natural Vegetation*, pp. 82–84.

24. U.S.D.A., U.S. Forest Service, Pacific Northwest Forest and Range Experiment Station, Miron L. Heinselman, "The Natural Role of Fire in Northern Conifer Forests," in *Fire in the Northern Environment—A Symposium*, ed. by C. W. Slaughter, Richard J. Barney, and G. M. Hansen, pp. 64–67.

25. *Ibid.;* Vancouver, *Voyages*, 2:167; Walter Crockett to H. Black, Oct. 15, 1853, University of Washington Library; Bryan, *Archaeological Survey of Northern Puget Sound*, p. 47, Appendix, pp. 7–11; U.S. Archives Wilkes Expedition, Perry, Journal, June 15, 1841.

26. The population of the county was 4,704 in 1910. It had only been 1,807 in 1900, *Thirteenth Census of the United States*, 1:977; June Collins, "John Fornsby," pp. 294–95, 302.

27. Erwin Ackernecht, *The History and Geography of the Most Important Diseases*, p. 63; Crosby, *Columbian Exchange*, pp. 35–63.

28. Vancouver, *Voyages*, 2:69, 91, 111–12.

29. For the ravages of disease among the Salish see: U.S. Congress, Senate, Senate Executive Document 1, pp. 447–48, 453; Herbert Taylor, "The 'Intermittent Fever' Epidemic of the 1830s," *Ethnohistory* 9:160–78; Taylor, "Aboriginal Populations," p. 162; Wilkes, *Narrative of the U.S. Exploring Expedition*, 4:482; Collins, *Valley of the Spirits;* U.S. Archives, Washington Superintendency, Letters from Agents Assigned to the Puget Sound District, Starling to Stevens, Dec. 4, 1853, and Letters from Employees Assigned to local Agencies, Fay to Simmons, Dec. 31, 1857; U.S. Dept. of the Interior, *Report of the Commissioner of Indian Affairs . . . 1855*, p. 454; *Report of the Commissioner of Indian Affairs . . . 1857*, p. 136; *Report of the Commissioner of Indian Affairs . . . 1858*, p. 240; Railroad Report, "Indian Tribes of Western Washington," by George Gibbs, 1:428, 432; R. C. Fay, Journal, Oct.

25, 1857, R. C. Fay Collection, Washington State Library, Olympia; William F. Tolmie, "History of Puget Sound and the Northwest Coast of America," unpublished manuscript, Bancroft Collection, University of California, Berkeley (microfilm, University of Washington), pp. 29–30; Walter Crockett to Dr. Black, Oct. 15, 1853, University of Washington Library; *Pioneer and Democrat*, Oct. 21, 1854; Gibbs, *Indian Tribes*, pp. 207–209; U.S. Congress, House Executive Document 39 (Serial 955), p. 14; Robert Boyd, "Another Look at the 'Fever and Ague' of Western Oregon," *Ethnohistory*, 22:135–54, makes a convincing case for "intermittent fever" being malaria.

30. Ackerknecht, *Most Important Diseases*, pp. 102–105; Aleš Hrdlička, "Tuberculosis Among Certain Indian Tribes of the United States," Bureau of American Ethnology, Bulletin 42:4, 15.

31. F. N. Blanchet, *The Catholic Church in Oregon During the Past Forty Years*, p. 107.

32. Smith, *Puyallup-Nisqually*, pp. 58–59, 68; Collins, *Valley of the Spirits*, pp. 213–14.

33. Bryan, *An Archaeological Survey of Northern Puget Sound*, Appendix 8, pp. 4–7, 11; Hubert Howe Bancroft, *History of Washington, Idaho, and Montana*, 31:11–12 (hereafter cited as *Works*); Collins, "John Fornsby," p. 310; George O. Wilson, Diary, April 23, 1851, p. 83, University of Washington Library.

34. White, "Treaty at Medicine Creek," pp. 8–10; Collins, *Valley of the Spirits*, p. 38; Gibbs, *Indian Tribes*, p. 196; Clarence Bagley (ed.), "The Nisqually Journal," *WHQ* 6:190, 268.

For a more detailed discussion of the impact of the fur trade upon Indian attitudes, see Calvin Martin, "The European Impact on the Culture of a Northeastern Algonquian Tribe: An Ecological Interpretation," *William and Mary Quarterly*, 31:3–26, and Calvin Martin, *Keepers of the Game*.

35. June Collins, "Growth of Class Distinctions and Political Authority Among the Skagit Indians During the Contact Period," *American Anthropologist*, 52:3.

36. Vancouver, *Voyages*, 2:162; Gunther, *Indian Life on the Northwest Coast of North America*, p. 72; Haeberlin and Gunther, *Indians of Puget Sound*, p. 30.

37. Bryan, *Archaeological Survey of Northern Puget Sound*, Appendix B, pp. 4–7.

38. For origin and travels of the potato, see Carl O. Sauer, "Agricultural Origins and Dispersals," *Bowman Memorial Lectures*, pp. 51–52.

39. Blanchet, *Catholic Church*, p. 110; Wayne Suttles, "The Early Diffusion of the Potato Among the Coast Salish," *Southwestern Journal of*

Anthropology, 7:3; Great Britain, Admiralty Accountant General's Department Log Book, Joseph Baker, Log of the Discovery, May 19, 1792, University of Washington Library.

40. Blanchet, *Catholic Church,* p. 110; Wilkes, *Narrative of the U.S. Exploring Expedition,* 4:481; Charles Wilson, Diary, Feb. 21, 25, 1851, p. 73; Railroad Report, "Indian Tribes of Western Washington," by George Gibbs, 1:432.

41. Farrar (ed.), "Ebey Diary," 8:45, 8:134; *Duwamish et al. vs. U.S.,* 1:251, 324; 2:833; U.S. Archives, Washington Superintendency, Misc. Letters, J. S. Smith to I. I. Stevens, Feb. 15, 1855; U.S. Department of the Interior, *Report of the Commissioner of Indian Affairs . . . 1858,* 229–30.

Chapter II. The Garden and the Wilderness

1. Walter Crockett to Dr. Black, Oct. 15, 1853, University of Washington Library (hereafter cited as Crockett Letter).

2. It is well to remember that the division of the natural world into useful and useless is a cultural trait that European civilizations do not share with all other cultures. Marston Bates has written that the question, "What good is it?" is "left over from the Middle Ages; from a small cozy universe in which everything had a purpose in relation to man." Marston Bates, *The Forest and the Sea,* p. 4.

3. Jones, *Botanical Survey,* p. 15.

4. Farrar (ed.), "Ebey Diary," *WHQ* 7:240–42.

5. Settlers have been derived from claim information found on Donation Claim Map, Auditor's Office, Island County Courthouse. Statistics in this chapter have been compiled from the manuscript census of agriculture and population in Island County in 1860. The information has been keypunched and the tabulation done by computer. The census will be cited as Manuscript Census, Population, 1860 or Manuscript Census, Agriculture, 1860.

6. For earlier attempts at settlement, see Bancroft, *Works,* 31:11–12. For the progress of settlement, see *Pioneer & Democrat,* January 1, 1853, February 5, 1853, October 29, 1853, December 17, 1853 (hereafter cited as *P & D*). U.S. Department of Commerce, Bureau of the Census, *Eighth Census of the United States, 1860, Population,* p. 582 (hereafter cited as *Eighth Census, 1860*).

7. E. Holbrook to Mother, January 26, 1854, Works Progress Administration, *Told by the Pioneers,* 2:153; George Wilson, Diary, April 23, 1851, p. 4, University of Washington Library; *Railroad Report,* 12, 1:260, 2:20; Ezra Meeker, *Pioneer Reminiscences of Puget Sound,* p. 73.

8. Oregon Land Donation Act, 9 Statutes, p. 496 (1850); Act of Feb. 14, 1853; Act of Feb. 14, 1853, ch. 69, 10 Stat., p. 158; Act of July 17, 1854, ch. 84, 10 Stat., p. 305.

9. Claim information from Donation Claim Map, Auditor's Office, Island County and U.S. Surveyor, *Field Notes*, Book 10:9, 523–24, 534.

10. *Record of the Board of County Commissioners, Island County, Washington*, Auditor's Office, Island County Washington, 1:1, 2, 6, 7; 2:12, 14, 21, 30, 33 (hereafter cited as CC).

11. CC, 2:21, 30, 33; 3:7; Swan, "Scenes in Washington Territory," No. 9. "Mss. of Mrs. Julia Hancock," Washington Pioneer Project, Island County, No. 2, Washington State Library, Olympia; Jimmie Jean Cook, *A Particular Friend, Penn's Cove*, p. 37; *P & D*, March 21, 1856, April 26, 1856, Oct. 24, 1856, Dec. 12, 1856.

12. Manuscript Census, Agriculture, 1860. The abbreviated form, T32N, R1E is read as Township 32 North, Range 1 East. San de Fuca would not be founded for forty years, but it is the best place name with which to identify the township.

13. "Inventory of Isaac Ebey's Estate," Oct. 31, 1857, Probate File, Island County Courthouse. In the Manuscript Census, Agriculture, 1860, only two farmers owned tools valued any higher than Ebey's.

14. Swan, *Northwest Coast*, p. 316.

15. Geographers have devoted more attention to the significance of the fence than have historians. See, for example, John Fraser Hart and Eugene Mather, "The American Fence," *Landscape* 6:4–9; Wilbur Zelinsky, "Walls and Fences," *Landscape* 8:16.

16. A brief biographical sketch of Swan is contained in Norman Clark's introduction to Swan's *Northwest Coast*, pp. iv–xxiii.

17. Swan, "Scenes in Washington Territory," No. 9.

18. James Swan to S. F. Baird, Feb. 8, 1879, James Swan Collection, University of Washington Library (hereafter cited as Swan Collection). James Swan, "Scenes in Washington Territory," No. 9; James Swan in *Washington Standard*, Feb. 3, 1861.

19. *Port Townsend Register*, April 11, 1860; Farrar (ed.), "Ebey Diary," *WHQ* 8:126; George Albert Kellog, *A History of Whidbey's Island*, p. 43; Samuel Hancock, "Reminiscences," Clarence Bagley Collection, University of Washington Library.

20. Crockett Letter; I. N. Ebey to W. S. Ebey, April 20, 1853, Ebey Collection; Nathaniel Hill, Diary, Dec. 20, 1852, Sept. 3, 1853, copy in Island County Historical Society, Coupeville. There is a significant correlation (.508) between ownership of oxen and improved land on the 1860 agricultural census for the county.

21. Crockett Letter; W. S. Ebey, Diary, July 5, 1858, June 19,

1860, Ebey Collection. From correspondence between farmers trying to sell hay and the mill companies who were often the major purchasers, it appears that the amount of fern in the hay was often the main factor in determining the value of the crop. See M. B. Clark to Washington Mill Co., Sept. 5, 1871; George Misner to Washington Mill Co., n.d.; Eason Ebey to Marshall Blinn, August 15, 1868, Washington Mill Company Collection, University of Washington Library.

22. William Albrecht, "Physical, Chemical, and Biochemical Changes in the Soil Community," in *Man's Role in Changing the Face of the Earth*, ed. by William L. Thomas, Jr., 2:648–51; U.S.D.A., *Soil Survey, Island County*, 39–40, p. 195.

23. Nathaniel Hill, Letter, Nov. 4, 1852, copy in Island County Historical Society, Coupeville. Three farmers harvested corn in 1860, but the top yield was only sixty bushels (Manuscript Census, Agriculture, 1860).

24. Manuscript Census, Agriculture, 1860; Manuscript Census, Population, 1860.

25. Farrar (ed.), "Ebey Diary," *WHQ* 8:134; *P & D*, Feb. 26, 1858.

26. *P & D*, Feb. 18, 1854; W. S. Ebey, Diary, Aug. 8, 1859, Aug. 27, 1860, Ebey Collection; Manuscript Census, Agriculture, 1860.

27. Manuscript Census, Agriculture, 1860.

28. I. N. Ebey to W. S. Ebey, April 20, 1853, Ebey Collection; Crockett Letter; Hill, Diary, Jan. 1854 (sic); Farrar (ed.), "Ebey Diary" *WHQ* 8 (April, 1917), 136.

29. Hill, Diary, Feb. 10, 1854; W. S. Ebey, Diary, Aug. 26, 1856, Oct. 6, 1857, Feb. 3, 1858, April 20, 1858, April 23, 1858, Oct. 31, 1858, Nov. 18, 1858, Aug. 19, 1859, Aug. 25, 1859, Aug. 30, 1859, Nov. 17, 1859, Ebey Collection; Crockett Letter; Manuscript Census, Agriculture, 1860.

30. Railroad Report, 12:2:20; *Island County, Washington: A World Beater* (n.p., n.d.), p. 4.

31. Edgar Anderson, "Man As a Maker of New Plants and Plant Communities," in *Man's Role*, ed. by Thomas, 2:763–67; Marston Bates, "Man As an Agent in the Spread of Organisms," in *Man's Role*, ed. by Thomas, 2:794.

32. H. Guthrie-Smith, *Tutira: The Story of a New Zealand Sheep Station*, passim.

33. Bates, "Man As an Agent," p. 791; Granville Haller, Diary, April 3, 1865, Granville Haller Papers, University of Washington Library.

34. Invading plants were primarily identified by using the "Botanical Report" of the Railroad Report, 12,2:55–71 and cross-checking the

species listed in C. Leo Hitchcock *et al.*, *Vascular Plants of the Pacific Northwest*. In addition, Helen Gilkey, *Weeds of the Pacific Northwest*, was used for aid in identification of invaders (see, specifically, pp. 61, 69, 77, 83, 393, 423). In the case of dock, I am assuming that the plant was *Rumex acetosella* L., now a very common weed of the area.

35. W. S. Ebey, Diary, June 20, 1857, Ebey Collection.

36. Farrar (ed.), "Ebey Diary," *WHQ* 7:309–10, 318, 8:135, 147; I. N. Ebey to W. S. Ebey, May 20, 1853, Ebey Collection; Railroad Report, "Indian Tribes" by Gibbs, 1:433.

37. Farrar (ed.), "Ebey Diary," *WHQ* 8:133; B. P. Barstow Estate, Exhibit A4, filed April 16, 1855 by G. H. Kingsbury, Probate File, Island County; Hill, Diary, Jan. 1854.

38. Kellog, *A History of Whidbey's Island*, p. 20; W. S. Ebey, Diary, Dec. 4, 1856, Ebey Collection; *CC*, 2:39.

39. W. S. Ebey, Diary, May 29, 1855, Ebey Collection; Railroad Report, "Indian Tribes," by Gibbs, 1:433.

40. W. S. Ebey, Diary, June 4, 1858, June 5, 1858, Aug. 25, 1857, Nov. 3, 1858, Sept. 19, 1859, March 6, 1859, June 2, 1859, Dec. 26, 1859, Ebey Collection; George Beam, Diary, Aug. 10, 1859, Aug. 20, 1859, Sept. 26, 1859, Nov. 7, 1859, Ebey Collection; Carl Engle, untitled reminiscences, WPA, Washington Pioneer Project Files, No. 2, Washington State Library.

41. For a general account of the cattle business in the Puget Sound region, see: J. Orin Oliphant, *On the Cattle Ranges of the Oregon Country*, pp. 131–34, and J. Orin Oliphant, "The Cattle Trade on Puget Sound, 1858–1890," *Agricultural History*, 7:129–49. For specific references to the cattle business on Whidbey Island, see: "Testimony of W. S. Ebey," Oct. 5, 1855, I. N. Ebey Probate File, Island County, Courthouse; *Port Townsend Register*, Jan. 18, April 18, April 25, 1860, Jan. 2, April 10, April 24, May 22, 1861; W. S. Ebey to George Beam, Nov. 12, 1856, George Orth to W. S. Ebey, Nov. 25, 1862, Henry Roeder to W. S. Ebey, March 29, 1861, D. Jones to W. S. Ebey, Feb. 4, 1861, Ebey Collection. The W. S. Ebey diary also contains a wealth of information about the business. See W. S. Ebey, Diary, June 19, 1855, Nov. 21–22, 1855, Feb. 12–13, 1855, July 22, 29, 1855, Ebey Collection.

42. Native vegetation was identified by using the "Botanical Report" of the *Railroad Report* and cross-checking the species with Hitchcock, *Vascular Plants*, and Gilkey, *Weeds* (see fn. 34). The Railroad Report credits plants specifically to Whidbey and credits other plants with being widespread in habitats common on Whidbey. I have listed both categories as being present on the island. The Crockett letter specifically mentions a native clover on the island prairies.

43. W. S. Ebey, Diary, Feb. 7, 1861, Sept. 18, 1861, Ebey Collection; William Robertson to William Wallace, n.d., Island County Historical Society, Coupeville.

44. Manuscript Census, Agriculture, 1860; Cook, *A Particular Friend*, p. 59.

45. For habitat and habits of the Roosevelt Elk, see Olaus Murie, *The Elk of North America*, especially p. 257. For changes in Salish hunting patterns, see Bryan, *Archaeological Survey of Northern Puget Sound*, Appendix B, pp. 4–7, 11.

46. The exotics listed here have been identified by the method listed in fn. 34. For an excellent account of the way ecological invasions take place, see Charles Elton, *The Ecology of Invasions by Animals and Plants.* John T. Curtis, "Modification of Mid-Latitude Grassland and Forest by Man," in *Man's Role*, ed. by Thomas, 2:729–30; Rexford Daubenmire, *Plant Communities*, pp. 174–75. *Festuca meagalura* is mistakenly identified in the Railroad Report as *Fecua Myurus.* For the spread of sorrel see Railroad Report, 12,2:68.

47. W. S. Ebey, Diary, Feb. 11, 1863, Ebey Collection; Manuscript Census, Agriculture, 1860.

48. Manuscript Census, Agriculture, 1860. The actual Pearson Correlation between oat growers and livestock raisers is .4085.

49. Hill, Diary, March 24, 1853. On market hunting, see: *Port Townsend Northwest*, March 29, 1862; Albert Kellog, "Personal Reminiscences of Whidby Island," 1925, University of Washington Library.

50. Kellog, *History of Whidbey's Island*, p. 89. For an example of destruction by deer, see W. S. Ebey, Diary, Sept. 3, 1857, Ebey Collection.

51. Flora Engle, "Pioneer Privations and Pleasures" in W.P.A., *As Told by the Pioneers*, p. 119. While salmon are rarely mentioned in the Ebey, Hill, Crockett, or Beam papers and diaries on west Whidbey, a few miles away, in Coupeville, Louise Swift wrote in 1863 that she was "sick of salmon." See Louise Swift to Mother, Aug. 3, 1863, Dec. 7, 1863, Swift Collection, University of Washington Library.

52. Eugene Odom, "The Strategy of Ecosystem Development," in the *Ecology of Man*, ed. by Robert L. Smith, p. 28.

Chapter III. A Search for Stability

1. Darling, *The West Highland Survey*, p. 53.

2. *Puget Sound Argus*, April 28, 1887, April 22, 1879.

3. Manuscript Census, Agriculture, 1860, 1870, 1880. These data

resemble those of two other counties settled in the 1850s—Trempealeau County, Wisconsin, and Hamilton Township, Hamilton County, Iowa. Merle Curti and Alan Bogue in their respective studies reported only on actual farm operators. If any member of the family continued to reside on the farm, I considered the farm still being operated by the original settlers. For instance, if a widow or a son ran the farm, I counted the farm as continuing to be run by the same residents as the previous census, but Bogue and Curti did not. This distorts the comparison slightly. See: Merle Curti, *The Making of an American Community,* p. 142; Alan Bogue, *From Prairie to Corn Belt.*

4. Manuscript Census, Agriculture, 1860, 1870. On Ebeys Prairie the nine farmers were Jacob Ebey, Isaac Ebey, T. S. Davis, John Crockett, Grove Terry, H. Crockett, S. B. Crockett, Walter Crockett, and Charles Crockett. In the San de Fuca twonship they were I. B. Powers, R. H. Lansdale, D. Shaw, R. H. Holbrook, S. D. Howe, Jacob Smith, Thomas Hastie, E. Hathaway, and J. Condra.

5. Manuscript Census, Agriculture, 1870, 1880.

6. Immigration Aid Society of North-western Washington, *Northwestern Washington* p. 39; *P. S. Argus,* Feb. 22, 1884, Feb. 28, 1884, Dec. 20, 1888; Eason Ebey to Abraham Enos, March 8, 1879, Almira Enos to Abraham Enos, Feb. 10, 1881, Ebey Collection. U.S.D.A. *Department Bulletin 1236,* "Farming the Logged-off Uplands in Western Washington" by E. R. Johnson and E. D. Strait, p. 2.

7. G. O. Haller, Diary, June 17, 1886, through Oct. 16, 1886, May 23, 1887, Haller Collection; *Washington Standard,* June 7, 1889; U.S.D.A., *Misc. Special Report 7,* "Tide Marshes of the United States" by D. M. Nesbit, pp. 76, 98–99. There are two sets of figures offered for Whidbey and Camano: 6,000 acres of tideland and marshland on Whidbey and 1,000 acres of tide marsh on Camano.

8. Manuscript Census, Agriculture, 1870, 1880.

9. Manuscript Census, Agriculture, 1870, 1880. In 1880, sharecroppers produced an average of $1,367 worth of goods on 95 improved acres. Owners who arrived in the 1850s produced an average of $1,061 worth of goods on 148 improved acres.

10. U.S. Land Office, Seattle, *Abstract of Land Office Receipts and Patents.* For the background of Sprague's purchase for Lake Superior and Puget Sound Land Company, a land company owned by stockholders in the Northern Pacific, see Henrietta Larson, *Jay Cooke, Private Banker* p. 369. *List of Lands Sold by Sheriff, Island County, Washington Territory for Delinquent Taxes, 1883 and List of Lands Struck Off to the County of Island, Washington Territory for Delinquent Taxes of 1883, Penalties, etc.,* Auditor's Office, Island County, Courthouse; A. H. H. Stuart in *Washington Stan-*

dard, April 16, 1875; *Puget Sound Argus,* Feb. 22, 1884, Feb. 28, 1884.

11. Washington, *Code of Washington Territory,* secs. 2928–2940; Washington, "An Act to Amend Section 2934 of Chapter 226 Laws of Washington Territory . . . ," *Session Laws,* pp. 92–93 (1885–86).

12. Manuscript Census, Agriculture, 1870, 1880.

13. Eason Ebey to Almira Enos, June 4, 1876, Ebey Collection; G. O. Haller to Marshall Blinn, October 19, 1866, Washington Mill Company Collection.

14. Manuscript Census, Agriculture, 1870; Michael Olsen, "The Beginnings of Agriculture in Western Oregon and Western Washington" (unpublished Ph.D. dissertation), pp. 120–24.

15. Manuscript Census, Agriculture, 1860, 1870; Samuel Wilkeson, *Notes on Puget Sound* (n.p., n.d.), pp. 31–32.

16. Manuscript Census, Agriculture, 1870, 1880; G. O. Haller, Diary, July 23, 1886, Nov. 18–19, 1864, April 10, 1865, Haller Collection; *Puget Sound Argus,* Dec. 31, 1880; *Washington Standard,* April 17, 1875; *U.S.D.A. Soil Survey* of Island County Washington by E. P. Carr and A. W. Mangum, pp. 1045.

17. Eleventh Census, Agriculture, 5:271.

18. Tenth Census, Agriculture, 3:210, 322–23; Eleventh Census, 1890, Agriculture, 5:289, 486, 498, 535.

19. Washington Bureau of Statistics, Agriculture & Immigration, *First Annual Report,* pp. 134–35; Olsen, "Agriculture," p. 207.

20. *P. S. Argus,* May 24, 1877, March 6, 1879, April 10, 1879, Dec. 11, 1879, March 1, 1878, July 13, 1883, Sept. 13, 1883.

21. Manuscript Census, Population, 1880; Kellog, *History of Whidbey's Island,* p. 95; Twelfth Census, Population, 1:570; Twelfth Census, 1900, Agriculture, 5:137. I have counted all "colored" tenant farmers in the county as Chinese since there were virtually no Blacks in the county nor Japanese. I have found no evidence of full-time Indian farming at this date.

22. U.S.D.A., *Soil Survey,* by Carr and Mangum, pp. 1,038–48, 1,050; Kellog, *History of Whidbey's Island,* p. 95.

23. Kellog, *History of Whidbey's Island,* p. 95; *Island County Times,* Aug. 28, 1891.

24. Kellog, *History of Whidbey's Island,* p. 95; *Island County Times,* June 22, 1900, Aug. 31, 1900, Sept. 28, 1900, Jan. 18, 1900; Fourteenth Census, 1920, Population, 3:1,085.

25. *Puget Sound Argus,* Feb. 27, 1875, Dec. 28, 1877.

26. G. O. Haller, Diary, July 23, 1884, Haller Collection.

27. *Puget Sound Argus,* Sept. 10, 1880, July 14, 1882, Sept. 6,

1883; Washington, *Code of Washington* (1883), Secs. 2,238–39; Helen M. Gilkey, *Weeds of the Pacific Northwest*, p. 391.

28. *Island County Times*, March 15, 1901; Liberty Hyde Bailey, *Cyclopedia of American Agriculture*, 2:447; Haller, Diary, Dec. 28, 1882, July 22, 1884, Haller Collection.

29. *Puget Sound Argus*, May 24, 1878.

30. Washington, State Board of Horticulture, *First Biennial Report*, p. 183, 186; *Island County Times*, March 15, 1901, Sept. 30, 1901; Hitchcock *et al.*, *Vascular Plants*, 1:6; Almira Enos to Abraham Enos, Feb. 10, 1881, Ebey Collection—I am presuming the sorrel mentioned here is *Rumex acetosella*, an introduction from Europe; Hitchcock *et al.*, *Vascular Plants*, 2:171; *Puget Sound Argus*, Feb. 22, 1878, May 12, 1882, March 29, 1898.

31. Jacob Ebey to Almira Enos, Dec. 29, 1888, Feb. 2, 1889, Almira Enos to Abraham Enos, Feb. 10, 1881, Ebey Collection; G. O. Haller, Diary, July 22, 1884, July 23, 1884, July 23, 1885, Haller Collection; Ellison and Eason Ebey to R. C. Fay, June 4, 1867, on file in Misc. Papers, Auditor's Office, Island County Courthouse.

32. Twelfth Census, 1900 Agriculture, 5:170, 304; *Puget Sound Argus*, Feb. 27, 1875; U.S.D.A., *Soil Survey* by Carr and Mangum, p. 1049.

33. *Puget Sound Argus*, Feb. 27, 1875; *Island County Times*, March 15, 1901; Jacob Ebey to Almira Enos, Dec. 29, 1888, Ebey Collection.

34. Tenth Census, 1880, Population, 1:377.

35. Manuscript Census, Population, 1880.

36. *Ibid.*

37. A. H. H. Stuart, *Washington Territory: Its Soil, Climate, Productions and General Resources*, p. 33; Kellog, *History of Whidbey's Island*, p. 89.

38. *Record and Index of Fishing Locations*, Auditor's Office, Island County Courthouse; Island County, Records of the Board of County Commissioners, (*CC*), 6:114.

39. Cf. Richard Hofstadter, *Age of Reform;* Henry Nash Smith, *Virgin Land*.

Chapter IV. The Ox and the Axe

1. U.S.D.A., Franklin and Dyrness, Forest Service, *General Technical Report PNW-8, The Natural Vegetation of Washington and Oregon*, pp. 53–56; U.S. Department of the Interior, U.S. Surveyor, *Field Notes*, 12:411, 456, 475, 488, 525, 542; 1:576, 585, 596, 603; 10:486, 523–24, 562; 11:686; 14:482.

2. U.S.D.A., Franklin and Dyrness, *The Natural Vegetation of Washington and Oregon*, pp. 48, 54; Victor Shelford, *The Ecology of North America*, pp. 211–13; U.S.D.A., Soil Survey, p. 5. Biomass is best defined as the weight of living matter per unit (here hectare) of measurement.

3. U.S. Department of the Interior, U.S. Surveyor, *Field Notes*, 10:562; 12:456; "Field Notes on Claim of John Kineth," April 7, 1857, Island County Historical Society.

4. Francis Kautz (ed.), "Extracts from Diary of A. V. Kautz," *Washington Historian* 1:184; Kellog, "Reminiscences," p. 16; Wilson, Diary, April 23, 1851, p. 83, PNW Collection; W. S. Ebey, Diary, Sept. 28, 1860, Ebey Collection.

5. Reprinted in *Whidbey News*, December 20, 1973.

6. W. S. Ebey, Diary, June 5, 1857, Ebey Collection; U.S. Department of the Interior, U.S. Surveyor, *Field Notes*, 12:445, 525.

7. Paul Wallace Gates, *The History of Public Land Law Development*, p. 14; Frederick Yonce, "Public Land Disposal in Washington" (unpublished Ph.D. dissertation), pp. 235–36; John Ise, *The United States Forest Policy*, pp. 19–61.

8. Richard Lillard, *The Great Forest*, pp. 156 ff.; Gates, *Land Law*, p. 417.

9. Iva L. Buchanan, "Lumbering and Logging in the Puget Sound Region in Territorial Days," *Pacific Northwest Quarterly*, p. 43; cf. Yonce, "Public Land Disposal."

10. Edwin Coman and Helen M. Gibbs, *Time, Tide and Timber*, pp. 33–34; Thomas Cox, *Mills and Markets: A History of the Pacific Coast Lumber Industry to 1900*, p. 59; Frederick Yonce, "Lumbering and the Public Timberlands in Washington: The Era of Disposal," *Journal of Forest History*, 22:6.

11. Farrar (ed.), "Ebey Diary," *WHQ* 7:134, 146–47; Cook, *A Particular Friend*, p. 37; Gilbert Pincher and Julia Hancock statements, Washington Pioneer Project Manuscripts, Island County, 2, Washington State Library, Olympia; Nathaniel Hill, Diary, Jan. 1854; *P & D*, April 22, 1854, June 3, 1854.

12. Bancroft, *Works*, 31:337; Jones, *Botanical Survey of the Olympic Peninsula*, p. 32.

13. James Dugan, *The Great Iron Ship*, p. 34; *P & D*, Dec. 12, 1856, March 21, 1856, April 26, 1856; Coman and Gibbs, *Time, Tide and Timber*, p. 110; *Port Townsend Register*, March 20, 1861; James Swan, Diary, June 5, 1860, Swan Collection; John Izett, "Whidby Island History," (letter to editor) *Washington Historian* 1:199–200; Bancroft, *Works*, 31:337; *Port Townsend Northwest*, Oct. 16, 1862; Clinton Snow-

den, *The History of Washington: The Rise and Progress of an American State,* 5:129.

14. Snowden, *History of Washington,* 5:129; Manuscript Census, Population, 1860; U.S. Congress, House, *Topographical Memoir of Captain T. J. Cram,* House Executive Document 114 (Serial 1014), p. 66; Port Townsend Northwest, March 7, 1861; *P&D,* Dec. 14, 1860; Cook, *A Particular Friend,* p. 40; *Whidby Islander,* Aug. 22, 1962.

15. Yonce, "Public Land Disposal," pp. 235–36; Buchanan, "Lumbering," pp. 43–44.

16. Yonce, "Public Land Disposal," p. 242; Buchanan, "Lumbering," p. 45; U.S. Congress, House, *Report of the Secretary of Interior,* 47th Congress, 1st Session, House Executive Document 1, Part 5 (Serial 2017), p. 377.

17. Richard C. Berner, "The Port Blakely Mill Company, 1876–1889," *PNQ,* 57:159; Coman and Gibbs, *Time, Tide and Timber,* pp. 110–12; Yonce, "Lumbering and the Public," p. 8.

18. Gates, *History of Public Land Law Development,* p. 25; Roy Robbins, *Our Landed Heritage,* p. 288; Coman and Gibbs, *Time, Tide and Timber,* p. 113; Buchanan, "Lumbering," pp. 46–47.

19. The records of Bagley's sale of the University Land Grant are very confusing. Charles Gates, *The First Century at the University of Washington,* pp. 9–14, gives an account of Bagley's transactions. Gates put Puget Mill purchases at only 6,500 acres, but it appears that he did not include sales to agents of the company in this. *The Island County Book of Deeds,* Auditor's Office, Island County Courthouse, gives the higher figure I have used. The *Book of Deeds,* 3:79–81, listed purchases of 1,250 acres by the Puget Mill Company in Island County from the University Grant. *The Washington University Land Sales, Record Book,* Manuscript Collection, Daniel Bagley Collection, University of Washington Library, pp. 5–7, 12, 14, 16, 35–37, however, makes no mention of this, and I have not included them in the totals. The purchases probably were made, nevertheless, and they boost substantially the figures I have given above. See also Coman and Gibbs, *Time, Tide and Timber,* pp. 111–12.

20. U.S. Land Office, Seattle, Records, copy of Land Claims in Auditor's Office, Island County Courthouse; Coman and Gibbs, *Time, Tide and Timber,* p. 112; *P & D,* June 2, 1855, Feb. 4, 1866, May 10, 1873; Bancroft, *Works,* 31:364; *Book of Deeds,* 4:295.

21. U.S. Land Office Records, Island County; *A Volume of Memoirs and Genealogy of Representative Citizens of the City of Seattle and the County of King, Washington,* pp. 17–19; *Daily Pacific Tribune,* August 3, 1871, in Meany Pioneer File, Pacific Northwest Collection, University of Washington Library; Coman and Gibbs, *Time, Tide and Timber,* p. 112; *Book*

of Deeds, 4:293–94; H. K. Hines, *An·Illustrated History of the State of Washington,* p. 676. The purchases made by the Attridges are listed among the land owned by Arthur Phinney at his death in 1878, *Puget Sound Argus,* November 14, 1878 (hereafter cited as *P. S. Argus*).

22. "Abstract of Lands Entered in Island County" (internal evidence, 1872), Auditor's Office, Island County Courthouse. It is not clear whether purchases made from the University Land Grant are included in this summary of land holdings in the county. If they are not, and they do not appear to be, the total acreage claimed would be close to 92,000 acres.

23. *Book of Deeds,* 4:42, 537, 563, 629; 7:249; Land Ledger, 1892, Port Blakely Mill Company Collection, Business Records, University of Washington Library, pp. 4–5 (hereafter collection cited as Port Blakely Collection). There is no list of Puget Mill Company lands until nearly the twentieth century, and these lists vary considerably even though there is no evidence of the company either buying or selling much land at the time. In 1908 the company listed its holdings at 10,731 acres of timberland in Island County, the highest amount it ever admitted to owning. The total given in 1913 was substantially the same—"The Lands of the Puget Mill Company, 1908," p. 7, and "Recapitulation of Revised Valuation as of March 1, 1913, Based on Cruise," both in Ames Collection, Puget Mill Company, Lands, University of Washington Library.

24. Some large speculators retained their lands, but many sold them or let them go for taxes. Among major speculators were a Washington Territorial governor, Edward Saloman (640 acres), who later left office under suspicion of attempted bribery; a mayor of Portland, Benjamin Goldsmith (2,622.41 acres); a mayor of Seattle, John Collins (940.8 acres); and the chancellor of the University of Washington, Asa Mercer. Louis Magrini, *Meet the Governors,* p. 25; *Seattle Times,* Jan. 10, 1942; H. K. Hines, *Illustrated History of the State of Oregon,* p. 1,034; Herbert Bancroft, *Chronicles of the Builders,* 8:146–57; *Seattle Intelligencer,* Nov. 25, 1872, Meany Pioneer File, PNW Collection; Snowden, *History of Washington,* 3:134; "Abstract of Lands Entered in Island County."

25. Much of the land held by parent companies, such as Pope & Talbot and Amos & Phinney, or by mill managers, such as Marshall Blinn, was already in the hands of the mill companies by 1871, but the county land records often did not show such transfers until years after they had taken place.

26. Berner, "Port Blakely Mill Company," pp. 158–61; Cox, *Mills and Markets,* p. 126; Coman and Gibbs, *Time, Tide and Timber,* p. 159. For examples of farmers' dependence on markets provided by the mills,

see: Wm. Sinclair to Marshall Blim (sic), June 8, 1861; J. E. Whitworth to Capt. Blinn, May 7, 1862, May 9, 1862, Washington Mill Company Collection, Washington Mill Scrapbook, p. 39. Manuscript Collection, University of Washington; E. B. Ebey to Capt. Blinn, Oct. 22, 1864; S. B. Crockett to Marshall Blinn, March 11, 1865; Harmon Hill to Marshall Blinn, March 16, 1865; M. B. Clark to Washington Mill Company, Sept. 5, 1871; G. O. Haller to Richard Holyhoke, Aug. 10, 1879, Washington Mill Company Collection (hereafter cited as *WMC* Collection).

27. *Whidby Record*, March 20, 1969; U.S. Surveyor, *Field Notes*, 11:297, 23:228; McNaught and Leary to WMC, March 6, 1877, WMC Collection; Land Cruisers Reports, 8:34–35, Nov. 19, 1889, Pope and Talbot Collection, Puget Mill Company, Manuscript Collection, University of Washington; "Transcript of Sale for Taxes," Auditor's Office, Island County Courthouse, p. 41; "Sold for Taxes," Auditor's Office, Island County Courthouse, pp. 2–5. In determining land ownership for lumbermen, I have taken the lumbermen mentioned in the county mortgage and lien records and looked in the *Book of Deeds* to determine whether they owned land. Timber Reports, 1889, Ames Collection, PMC; Lands of PMC, 1908, Ames Collection, PMC. I have used the timber reports of 1899 to determine the amount of logging done on PMC lands. The acreage involved came from the 1909 report. Land Ledger, 1892, pp. 4–5 and "Lands of the Port Blakely Mill Co. for Assessment in Island County, April 1900," in Port Blakely Mill Co. Collection, Business Records. Of the 6,951 acres of Puget Mill Company land that can be accounted for with reasonable accuracy, only 1,362.5 acres had been logged during the nineteenth century, and most of this had been logged only partially.

28. It is hard to trace logging camps until the late 1870s, when the Mechanics Lien Law gave employees first claim on their employer's assets when they went unpaid. Since loggers neglected, with monotonous regularity, to pay their men, liens give a good indication of areas being logged. *Lien Books*, Auditor's Office, Island County Courthouse, Volumes 1 and 2, passim; Manuscript Census, Population, 1870; Manuscript Census, Population, 1880; Osmundson, "Camano," pp. 59–60. Osmundson underestimates the amount of logging taking place on Camano in the nineteenth century. *Land Cruisers' Reports, 1889,* 8:18–19, 34–35, 38–39, 42–43, 46–57, 5:2–3, and 3:46–47, 10:31, 35, 39, 41, 43; *Land Cruisers' Reports, 1891,* 18:38–39, Pope and Talbot, PMC; *Personal Mortgage Book A,* pp. 22, Auditor's Office, Island County Courthouse.

29. Stewart Holbrook, *Green Commonwealth*, pp. 32–35, gives a good

description of bull team logging. Cox, *Mills and Markets,* p. 227; Osmundson, "Camano," pp. 60–61, 75–76; Coman and Gibbs, *Time, Tide and Timber,* pp. 113–14; Buchanan, "Lumbering," p. 52; Manuscript Census, Population, 1870; Manuscript Census, Population, 1880. Secretary of State, State of Washington, *First Annual Report of Bureau of Statistics, Agriculture, and Immigration,* p. 540 (hereafter cited as Bureau of Statistics, Agriculture and Immigration, Report). "Scale Books," Ames Collection, PMC. See, for example, C. P. Eaton's Boom of Sept. 17, 1891 from Holmes Harbor and the mixed boom coming out of Utsalady on Nov. 13, 1891. By 1891, a boom out of Utsalady would probably contain logs from the Skagit River area as well as from Island County.

30. *The Forests of the United States,* Tenth Census, p. 574; Holbrook, *Green Commonwealth,* p. 33; Coman and Gibbs, *Time, Tide and Timber,* p. 441; Cox, *Mills and Markets,* p. 229; "Scale Books," scale of booms received from Island County Sept. 8, 1891 through Dec. 3, 1891. Not all the Utsalady booms included here were composed of logs cut in Island County (Ames Collection, PMC).

31. U.S.D.A., *Technical Bulletin 286,* "Decay and Other Losses in Douglas Fir in Western Oregon and Washington," by J. S. Boyce, pp. 3, 11–25; "Cruise of Puget Mill Company Timber in Island County, Washington, by Chas. F. Phillips, Oct. 31, 1913," pp. 18, 20–22, Pope and Talbot, PMC.

32. *The Forests of the United States,* Tenth Census, p. 574; Austin Cary, "The Cary Report on Douglas Fir Lumber Production," *West Coast Lumberman,* 42:58. Coman and Gibbs, *Time, Tide and Timber,* pp. 113–14.

33. U.S. Surveyor, *Field Notes,* 11:297.

34. "List of Indemnity School Sections, November 1870," Auditor's Office, Island County Courthouse; Washington, "Organic Law," *Laws of Washington* (1887–88), sec. 1947; Washington State, "An Act to Provide for the Leasing of School Lands," *Laws of Washington* (1869–71), pp. 401–402. The intention of these laws seems to have been circumvented several times. A member of the Island County Board of Commissioners was actually paid to remove timber, and on another occasion a local lumberman leased timberland that by 1890, after his lease expired, contained only second-growth timber. *CC,* 3:491, 399; "Report of Appraisers, Dec. 11, 1890," School Lands, Auditor's Office, Island County Courthouse; WMC to John Lloyd, May 26, 1883, WMC Collection.

35. The comments made by appraisers are not always clear with regard to fire damage. They often merely noted dead timber, and I have listed this as fire damage. They also noted young fir on many sections, necessarily a product of either logging or fires, yet they list the land as neither logged nor burnt. I have listed such sections as uncertain with

regard to fire damage. Southern Whidbey is defined here as the area south of Greenbank, central Whidbey is the area between Greenbank and Oak Harbor, and northern Whidbey is everything north of Oak Harbor. I have counted sections in the same manner as the appraisers, who often grouped a small indemnity lot in an adjoining section with a section holding the bulk of the school land. "Report of Appraisers, Dec. 11, 1890," School Lands, Auditor's Office, Island County Courthouse.

36. Coman and Gibbs, *Time, Tide and Timber*, p. 114; *Land Cruisers' Reports*, 8:18–19, 34–35, 39, 43, 47, and 10:31, 39, 41, 43; Pope and Talbot, PMC.

37. U.S.D.A., Forest Service, "Forest Statistics of Western Washington Counties: Forest Statistics of Island County Washington," Table 4 (mimeographed) Pacific Northwest Experiment Station, Portland, March, 1934; U.S.D.A., *Department Bulletin 1493*, "Timber Growing Practices in the Douglas Fir Region," by Thornton Munger, pp. 14–15.

38. There were reports of increased erosion because of logging on Puget Sound uplands as early as the late nineteenth century. Except for the silting of the mill pond at Utsalady, however, it is difficult to find any evidence of this on Whidbey or Camano. U.S.D.A., Soil Conservation Service, Erosion History Data, Research Compilation File, 1897–1928 (microfilm), "Denuded Lands of Washington" from *Wood and Iron*, reprinted in *Forest Leaves*, 7:n.p.; Coman and Gibbs, *Time, Tide and Timber*, p. 179; "Remarks on PMC Timber in Island County," by Charles Phillips, Oct. 31, 1913, Pope and Talbot, PMC; S. A. Graham to PMC, Feb. 14, 1914, Timber Cruises, Pope and Talbot, PMC; *P. S. Argus*, March 24, 1876, May 13, 1877, Oct. 3, 1878, March 20, 1879, March 8, 1883, Feb. 22, 1884, June 20, 1889.

39. George Beam to W. S. Ebey, Aug. 30, 1863, Ebey Collection; G. O. Haller to Marshall Blinn, Oct. 19, 1866, WMC Collection.

Chapter V. The Creation of a New Forest

1. Both the total amount of land logged and the amount of board feet of timber obtained are estimates. According to the Forest Service survey of 1932, about 50,000 acres of land either produced new growth or were deforested between 1900 and 1930. I have presumed most of this land was logged or relogged land. In addition, 27,000 acres of improved land was added to farms in this period. Much of this was cutover land. Out of these 77,000 acres, I have estimated 60,000–70,000 acres as the amount logged. U.S.D.A., "Forest Statistics of Island County, Washington" (mimeographed), PNW Experiment Station, March 1934.

The amount of timber logged is also an estimate. Contemporary estimates varied wildly. I have used an industry estimate of two billion board feet made for the state and modified it downward by using information from the Puget Mill cruises of their lands to compute the mean number of board feet per acre at 15,000. This is a low estimate, but much of this land had been culled for its best timber in the nineteenth century. See: Washington State, *Biennial Report of the Bureau of Statistics, Agriculture and Immigration*, p. 112; *Bureau of Statistics, Agriculture and Immigration* (hereafter cited as BSAI). Washington State, BSAI, *A Review of the Resources and Industries of Washington*, Statistical Appendix, p. 29; "Cruise of PMC Co. Timber in Island County," by Chas. Phillips, Oct. 31, 1913; S. A. Graham to PMC, Feb. 14, 1914, "Timber Cruise by Lafe Heath, 1916," all in Pope and Talbot, PMC, Timber Cruises; Victor Beckman, "Survey of the Lumber Industry of Western Washington" (unpublished manuscript), Pacific Northwest Collection, pp. 3–5; Jacob Anthes, "History of Langley, Washington" (unpublished manuscript), Pacific Northwest Collection. For a lower estimate of timber, see: U.S. Dept. of the Interior, U.S. Geological Survey, *Forests of the United States*, by Henry Gannet, p. 31.

For more on Puget Mill lands, see: PMC to Essary Brothers, Oct. 27, 1900, and Ames to George Pope, Sept. 7, 1909, Ames Collection, PMC.

2. *Island County Times*, Sept. 14, Sept. 28, 1900, Dec. 20, 1901, March 22, 1901, April 9, 1901, Feb. 13, 1903, Feb. 20, 1903, May 22, 1903, Nov. 27, 1903; Osmundson, "Camano," pp. 77–80; Washington State, Commissioner of Public Lands, *Twelfth Biennial Report*, p. 40; "Cruise of PMC Timber in Island County," hereafter cited as Phillips' Cruise; S. A. Graham to PMC, July 9, 1917, "Timber Cruise by Lafe Heath, 1916" (with map), "Recapitulation of Revised Valuation as of March 1, 1913, Based on Cruise of PMC Lands," "Cruise of Lafe Heath, February and March, 1916," "Comparison of Cruises of S. A. Graham, Feb. 1914 and Feb. 1919, T32N, R2E," S. A. Graham to PMC, Feb. 26, 1919, all in Pope and Talbot, PMC, Timber Cruises; Ames to Pope, Oct. 11, 1909, Ames Collection, PMC; *Island County Times*, Sept. 5, 1902, Sept. 12, 1902, Oct. 10, 1902, Feb. 20, 1903, June 19, 1903 (*Island County Times* hereafter cited as *I.C. Times*).

3. Holbrook, *Green Commonwealth*, p. 114; Peter Rutledge and Richard Tooker, "Steam Power for Loggers: Two Views of the Dolbeer Donkey," *Forest History* 14:20–24; Ralph Andrews, *This Was Logging*, pp. 64–65; Austin Cary, "Cary Report," pp. 51–52; Osmundson, "Camano," p. 76; Stewart Holbrook, *The American Lumberjack*, pp. 161–62; Thomas Cox, *Mills and Markets*, pp. 231–32.

4. Fourteenth Census, Population, 1920, 1:655.

5. For a study of the problem of cutover lands in Wisconsin, see: Vernon Carstensen, *Farms or Forests: Evolution of a State Land Policy for Wisconsin, 1850–1932*. For the reformers' position, see: U.S.D.A., *Misc. Publication 218*, "Forest Taxation in the United States," by Fred Fairchild. For the lumberman's position, see: J. T. S. Lyle, *State Taxation and the Lumber Industry* (n.p., 1921), passim, but especially pp. 10–16, and E. T. Allen, *Practical Forestry in the Pacific Northwest*, pp. 18–21.

6. Washington, BSAI, *A Review of the Resources and Industries of Washington*, p. 102; Washington State, BSAI, *Washington: Description and Statistical Information*, p. 17; Washington State, *Minutes and Official Proceedings of the State Board of Equalization of the State of Washington*, Sessions of 1910, 1915, 1920.

7. *Ibid.*

8. Quoted in Coman and Gibbs, *Time, Tide and Timber*, p. 228.

9. For Port Blakely's sales, see: *Book of Deeds*, 20:336–37, 394, 505, 42:444, 43:49, 114. For PMC sales, see: *Book of Deeds*, Volumes 34–43. There are numerous small sales beginning in 1922 and continuing into the post-World War II period. The PMC did not always sell directly. In 1930, for instance, it sold 1,147 acres to a subsidiary, the Tyee Land Company, for $10. *Book of Deeds*, 45:515. For abandonment, see: *I. C. Times*, Dec. 5, 1902.

10. For information on the legislative struggle in Washington, see: Winkenwerder to Ames, Aug. 19, 1924, Ames Collection, PMC; Ralph W. Hidy, Frank Hill, Allan Nevins, *Timber and Men; the Weyerhaeuser Story*, pp. 383–84; Coman and Gibbs, *Time, Tide and Timber*, pp. 227–30; "Report of the Washington State Commission on Forest Regulation," April 28, 1910 (typewritten copy of original), Pacific Northwest Collection, pp. 34–43a, 47, 49–68.

11. Burt Kirkland, *The Cost of Growing Timber in the Pacific Northwest*.

12. "Report of Lafe Heath on PMC Lands in T31N, R2E," 1916, Pope and Talbot, PMC, Timber Cruises. In a 1910 survey, only a little more than a third of the respondents said taxes led to early cutting, although a number of the landowners who answered said it might force them to cut in the future. "Report of Washington State Commission on Forest Legislation," p. 55.

Edward Ames of the PMC contended that the PMC had paid about $114 an acre worth of taxes on land the company had bought in the 1860s. How he arrived at this figure he did not disclose, but such an estimate for Island County would be preposterous. Most timberland brought about 10 cents an acre in annual taxes until 1900. If the land was acquired in 1865, this meant it cost Puget Mill about $3.50 an acre during the entire nineteenth century. By 1920, the best timberland in the most heavily taxed sections of Island County was taxed $3.60 a year, but by then most PMC land had been logged. If such land had been taxed at $3.60 a year for five years and at $1.80 for fifteen years (generous figures), then the total tax expenditure would only have been $48.60 an acre for the twentieth century. The total taxes would be $52.10, a figure well below both Ames's estimate and the going price of timberland in Island County in 1920. See Coman and Gibbs, *Time, Tide and Timber,* p. 228; J. B. Libbey to PBMC, Dec. 22, 1882, J. Henne to PBMC, Feb. 10, 1894, Thomas Cranney to PBMC, Dec. 6, 1901, Port Blakely Mill Company Collection; "Memorandum Showing Values and Taxes for 1900," in *Letterbook,* Ames Collection, PMC, Land Letters, p. 418.

13. *I. C. Times,* Dec. 5, 1902; Auditor's Report in *I. C. Times,* Feb. 6, 1903.

14. If tax delinquency comes only from the inability to meet taxes on unproductive land, it seems probable that the amount of delinquency should have increased substantially during the 1930s. Yet it did not. Part of the reason it did not were the lower taxes of the Depression. The tax load of the county fell from $168,190.56 in 1925 to $94,457.32 in 1935 and $84,071.88 in 1939. But this decline was compensated for by the diminished financial resources of landowners during the period. Furthermore, the 1939 figure for delinquent taxes quoted in the text included thirteen years of back taxes in the final total, but the 1925 figure included only six years—making the tax delinquency of 1939 inflated by the older reckoning. Island County Auditor, *Annual Statement of Finances,* 1913–1925, in the Pacific Northwest Collection; Island County Clerk, "Annual Reports," 1930–1936, 1938–1940, in the Pacific Northwest Collection.

15. Hidy, *Timber and Man,* p. 498; Washington State, "Taxation of Reforestation Lands," *Session Laws 1931,* Chap. 40; Washington State, Department of Conservation and Development, *Biennial Reports of the Forestry Division to the Department of Conservation and Development* (see thirty-first through thirty-sixth annual reports for land classifications). For assessor's decision to reclassify all lands at $1, see: *Thirty-Second Annual Report,* p. 3. The Forest Taxation Act never had the results expected. See Washington State, Senate, "Report of Forest Tax Committee Pursuant to Senate Concurrent Resolution 30," Senator Martin Durkan, Chairman, 1971.

16. Washington State, "An Act Relating to . . . Reforestation . . . for State Forests," *Session Laws, 1923,* Chap. 154; Washington State,

Forest Advisory Committee, *A Long Range Forest Program for the State of Washington*, pp. 9–12; Washington State, "An Act . . . for the Acquiring . . . of Lands for State Forests," *Session Laws*, 1927, Chap. 228; Hidy, *Timber and Men*, pp. 274, 528.

17. U.S.D.A., Forest Service, *Forest Research Note 21*, "Highlights of Douglas Fir Natural Regeneration," by Leo Isaac, Pacific Northwest Experiment Station, pp. 1–2; U.S.D.A., *Misc. Publication 389*, "Forest Resources of the Douglas Fir Region," by H. J. Andrews and R. W. Cowlin, pp. 74, 86; U.S.D.A., *Department Bulletin 1493*, "Timber Growing and Logging Practices in the Douglas Fir Region," 13–15. Allen Hodgson, "Logging Waste in the Douglas Fir Region," Joint Publication of *Pacific Pulp and Paper Industry, and West Coast Lumberman*, pp. 9, 15; Leo Isaac, "Forest Soil of the Douglas Fir Region," *Ecology* 18:265.

18. Isaac, "Forest Soil," p. 277; U.S.D.A., *Misc. Pub. 389*, pp. 49–50; U.S.D.A., *Dept. Bulletin 1493*, p. 13; Washington State, *Report of the State Fire Warden for 1907 and 1908 to the State Board of Fire Commissioners*, p. 23.

19. *I. C. Times*, Aug. 30, 1901, Aug. 15, 1902, Aug. 22, 1902; John and Jake Cappa to Almira Enos, Oct. 21, 1902, Ebey Collection. All the fire statistics have been compiled from the *Reports of the State Fire Warden to the Washington State Forest Commissioners Board* (1905–1920) and the *Reports of the Division of Forestry to the Department of Conservation and Development* (1920–1940).

20. Washington State, Washington State Game Department, *Biological Bulletin 13*, "The Blacktailed Deer of Western Washington," by Ellsworth Brown, pp. 97–100; U.S.D.A., Forest Service, *Research Paper PNW-6*, "Protecting Forest Trees and Their Seed from Wild Mammals," PNW Forest and Range Experiment Station, pp. 1, 5, 65; U.S.D.A., *Technical Bulletin 706*, "Wild Animal Damage," by A. W. Moore, pp. 5–18.

21. Estimate of Timber on PMC Land by Lafe Heath," Feb. and March 1916, Pope and Talbot, PMC, Timber Cruises.

22. Isaac, "Forest Soil," pp. 265, 271, 275–76; R. C. Austin and D. H. Baisinger, "Some Effects of Burning on Forest Soils of Western Oregon and Washington," *Journal of Forestry* 53:276; J. V. Hoffman, "Natural Reproduction from Seed Stored in the Forest Floor," *Journal of Agricultural Research* 11:12, 22, 25; U.S.D.A., Forest Service, *Forest Research Note 102*, "The Effects of Slash Burning on Soil pH," by Robert Tarrant, pp. 1–3.

Slash fire, as used here, means broadcast burning of slash, not burning of piled slash. By 1917 foresters realized that pile burning was less destructive, but since it was far more expensive it was never widely used. Even broadcast burning can be controlled to keep temperatures down and thus reduce its impact, but this was rarely done in the 1900 to 1930 period. Probably most slash fires of this period were accidental and uncontrolled. See Hoffman, "Natural Reproduction," p. 25; J. R. Roeser, "A Study of Douglas Fir Reproduction under Various Cutting Methods," *Journal of Agricultural Research* 28:1,237; Leo Isaac, "Fire: A Tool Not a Blanket Rule in Douglas Fir Ecology," *Tall Timber Fire Ecology Conference* 2:8–9; U.S.D.A., *Technical Bulletin 706*, pp. 49–50. See also U.S.D.A., Forest Service, *General Technical Report PNW-24*, "Regeneration and Growth of Coastal Douglas Fir," by Richard Miller *et al.*, pp. 3–1 through 3–30.

23. U.S.D.A., *Dept. Bulletin 1493*, pp. 9–14; Hoffman, "Natural Reproduction," p. 25; all statistics taken from U.S.D.A., Forest Service, "Forest Statistics of Island County," Table 4.

24. U.S.D.A., Forest Service, "Forest Statistics of Island County," Tables 3, 5, 6.

25. Michael Newton *et al.*, "Role of Red Alder in Western Oregon Forest Succession"; Richard L. Williamson, "Productivity of Red Alder in Western Oregon and Washington"; Jerry Franklin, "Comparison of Vegetation in Adjacent Alder, Conifer, and Mixed Alder-Conifer Communities"; all in Northwest Scientific Association, *Biology of Alder*, Proceedings of a Symposium held at Pullman, 1967 pp. 42, 78–82, 287.

26. *I. C. Times*, April 20, 1903; Washington, *Code of Washington* (1896), Secs. 6185–6187; Washington, "An Act to Protect from Fire," *Session Laws, 1903*, Chap. 114.

27. Hidy, *Men and Timber*, pp. 242–43; Washington, "An Act to Provide for the Preservation of Forests," *Session Laws, 1905*, Chap. 164; Washington, "An Act Relating to the Forests of the State," *Session Laws, 1917*, Chap. 107; Washington State, *Report of the State Fire Warden for 1905*, p. 18; Report of the State Fire Warden for 1906, pp. 5–6; Hidy, *Men and Timber*, pp. 243–44.

28. "Phillips' Cruise," Pope and Talbot, PMC, Timber Cruises. During only four years between 1911 and 1920 was there destruction by fire of merchantable timber in Island County. Three hundred thousand board feet of timber were destroyed by fire both in 1911 and 1915. Fifty thousand board feet were destroyed in 1919 and 3,700,000 board feet were burned in 1920. Although four and a half million board feet is a sizable amount of timber, it is still relatively insignificant in terms of the billion or so board feet standing in the county during the period. Statistics taken from *Reports of the State Fire Warden, 1911–1920*.

29. *I. C. Times*, September 9, 1903.

30. U. S. National Resources Committee, PNW Regional Planning Commission, *Forest Resources of the Pacific Northwest,* p.22.

Chapter VI. Poor Men on Poor Lands

1. Samuel Hays, *Conservation and the Gospel of Efficiency,* and James Pennick, Jr., "The Progressives and the Environment: Three Themes from the First Conservation Movement," in *The Progressive Era,* edited by Lewis Gould, pp. 118–32, treat back-to-the-land movements as something more than romanticism.
2. For Bausman quote, see "Asset or Liability? The Problem of Logged-off Lands," *Better Business,* p. 247.
3. N. B. Coffman, "The Problem of Bringing Logged-off Lands under Cultivation," in Secretary of State, Washington, *Vacant Logged-off Lands of the State of Washington,* p. 123.
4. For early soil surveys and boosters' evaluations, see: U.S.D.A., *Field Operations of the Bureau of Soils* (1905), pp. 1034, 1041–51; U.S.D.A. Bureau of Soils, *Field Operations of the Bureau of Soils, 1910: Soil Survey Western Puget Sound Basin, Washington,* pp. 12, 30–32, 41–42, 51–57, 71–74; *Island County, Washington, A World Beater,* pp. 7–14, 22–31.
5. Washington Bureau of Statistics, Agriculture and Immigration, *The Logged-off Lands of Western Washington,* pp. 19–31. Introduction of Joel Shoemaker, "Wonderful Opportunities in Logged-off Lands," *Pacific Northwest Commerce* 5:16; Washington Logged-off Land Association (hereafter cited as WLLA), *Proceedings,* pp. 11, 28–29; G. S. Long, "Washington's Logged-off Land Problems Discussed," *Pacific Lumber Trade Journal* 17:42; U.S.D.A. *Farmer's Bulletin 462,* p. 7; G. S. Long, quoted in "Comprehensive Plans for Colonizing Logged-off Lands in Washington," *Timberman* 14:34–35; *Seattle Post Intelligencer,* Sept. 3, 1931, p. 1.
6. WLLA, *Proceedings,* pp. 28–29; H. J. Andrews and R. W. Cowlin, "Forest Resources of the Douglas Fir Region," *U.S.D.A. Miscellaneous Publication 389* (1940), pp. 1, 74–80, Burt Kirkland, *The Cost of Growing Timber in the Pacific Northwest,* passim.
7. Washington State, Secretary of State, *Vacant Logged-off Lands of the State of Washington,* pp. 119–27; WLLA, *Proceedings; Timberman* 14: 34–35; Washington's Logged-off Land Problems Discussed," 41–43.
8. For other back-to-the-land movements, see: James Pennick, Jr., "The Progressives and the Environment: Three Themes from the First Conservation Movement," p. 117; Samuel Hays, *Conservation and the*

Gospel of Efficiency, pp. 9–11; Vernon Carstensen, *Farms or Forests: Evolution of a State Land Policy for Northern Wisconsin, 1850–1932*, pp. 53–74; Arlan Helgeson, *Farms in the Cutover*, pp. 1–83; Agnes M. Larson, *The White Pine Industry in Minnesota*, pp. 405–407.

9. For a sample of autarchic assumptions, see: Howard Hanson, "State Aid in Land Clearing," *LLL* 1:7; "Washington Needs More Farmers," *Pacific Northwest Commerce*, 5:1; "Washington's Logged-off Land Problems Discussed," *Pacific Lumber Trade Journal* 17:41–43; *LLL* 1:1; *Tacoma Ledger* editorial quoted in Arthur Coulter, "Washington Legislation for Logged-off Lands," *LLL* 1:9; WLLA, *Proceedings*, p. 54. For attacks on timber companies and speculators, see "The Timber Land Baron and the Remedy," *LLL* 1:4–5; *LLL* 2:10–13. George Long, "Address on Utilization of Arable Logged-off Lands," *The Timberman* (June, 1911), pp. 26–27.

Back-to-the-land movements remained distinct from such contemporary endeavors as the Country Life Movement, whose goal was the revitalization of existing rural communities and whose leader, Liberty Hyde Bailey, was skeptical of the back-to-the-land movement in all its manifestations. Liberty Hyde Bailey, *The Country Life Movement*, pp. 1–3.

10. Logged-off Paradise," *LLL* 1:22; *LLL* 2:3; A. R. Hathaway, "The Call of the Land," *LLL* 1:14. Quote from H. W. Sparks in *Island County Times*, Feb. 14, 1913.

11. Hathaway, "The Call of the Land," *LLL* 1:14; *LLL* 1:23; *LLL* 2:3; Joel Shoemaker, "Let the State Clear the Logged-off Lands," *LLL* 1:33–34; *Island County, Washington, A World Beater*, pp. 7–14, 22–31; Washington, BSAI, *The Logged-off Lands of Western Washington*, pp. 12–32.

12. Pacific Northwest Regional Planning Commission, National Resources Planning Board, *Migrations and the Development of Economic Opportunity in the Pacific Northwest*, pp. 7, 75. Carl Reuss, "Back to the Country—The Rurban Trend in Washington Population," WAES *Bulletin 426*, pp. 20–21. One survey revealed 51 percent of new cutover settlers during the 1930s settled on unimproved lands, and 22 percent settled on abandoned farms. Campbell Murphy, "Farmers on Cutover Timber Lands in Western Washington State" (unpublished M.A. Thesis), p. 22; Fifteenth Census, 1930, Agriculture, 12, Part 3, pp. 430–33; Twelfth Census, 1900, Population, 1, p. 403; Thirteenth Census, 1910, Population, 3, p. 977; Fourteenth Census, 1920, Agriculture, 6, Part 3, p. 292.

13. U.S.D.A., Dept. Bulletin 1236, pp. 19–20; Hoover, "Rural Settlement," p. 44; Twelfth Census, 1900, p. Population, 1, p. 403;

Fourteenth Census, 1920, Population, 3, p. 1093. In 1920 there were 517 Scandinavians and 285 Dutch in the county out of a total immigrant population of 1,250. In 1910 there were 210 immigrant farmers and 225 native-born farmers; in 1920 these figures were 364 and 392. Thirteenth Census, 1910, Agriculture 7, p. 841; Thirteenth Census, 1910, Population, 3, p. 977, 998; Fourteenth Census, 1920, Agriculture, 6, Part 3, pp. 292, 293. I have used the *Register of Voters, Clinton, 1924–1926,* Auditor's Office, Island County Courthouse, to obtain the figures for Clinton. I chose Clinton because it is the only precinct that includes no prairie or diked lands.

14. National Resources Planning Board, *Development of Resources and of Economic Opportunity in the Pacific Northwest,* p. 5; Carl Heisig, "Settlement Experience and Opportunities on Cutover Lands of Western Washington," WAES *Bulletin 399,* pp. 14–15.

15. WAES *Bulletin 399,* pp. 14–15, 92; Carl F. Reuss, "Social Characteristics of Parttime Farmers in Washington," WAES *Bulletin 380,* p. 19; Richard Wakefield and Paul Landis, "The Drought Farmer Adjusts to the West," WAES *Bulletin 378,* pp. 12, 18, 27. Lois Phillips Hudson, *Reapers of the Dust,* p. 95; Carter Goodrich *et al., Migration and Planes of Living,* pp. 6, 51; Carter Goodrich *et al., Migration and Economic Opportunity: The Report of the Study of Population Redistribution,* p. 191; *I. C. Times,* Jan. 2, 1931.

16. U.S.D.A., *Soil Survey* (Series, 1949), plates 1 and 2, pp. 20, 33, 37.

17. U.S.D.A., *Soil Survey* (1905), pp.. 1,034, 1,041–1,051; U.S.D.A., Bureau of Soils, *Reconnaissance Soil Survey of the Eastern Part of the Puget Sound Basin* (1911), pp. 30–32, 41–42, 51–57.

18. *I. C. Times,* April 11, 1902; Lester Still, "Whidby Island," *The Coast* 4:78; *Island County, Washington, A World Beater,* pp. 7–14, 22–31; Washington, BSAI, *The Logged-off Lands of Western Washington,* pp. 19–32; George Long, "Address on the Utilization of Arable Logged-off Lands," *The Timberman* (June 1911), pp. 26–27.

19. WAES *Bulletin 378,* p. 20; WAES, *Bulletin 399,* pp. 15–16; Hoover, "Rural Settlement," p. 44, found that 85 percent of the settlers at Alderwood Manor had never farmed before, and U.S.D.A., *Department Bulletin 1236,* "Farming the Logged-off Uplands in Western Washington," by E. R. Johnson and E. D. Strait, found that 73 percent of the logged-off farmers surveyed had never farmed before.

20. U.S.D.A., *Soil Survey* (1949), plates 1 and 2. Upper Clover Valley contains Coveland and Bellingham loam soils, while the lower valley contains Semiahoo mucks. All of these need draining. Burton Anderson, "Scandinavian and Dutch Rural Settlements in the Stillaguamish

and Nooksack Valleys of Western Washington" (unpublished Ph.D. dissertation), pp. 45–46; Kellog, *History of Whidbey's Island*, pp. 95. Buerstatte, "Geography of Whidby Island," pp. 49–51; *Island County, Washington, A World Beater*, pp. 35–39; *I. C. Times*, May 16, 1913, May 3, 1918.

21. *I. C. Times*, March 17, 1891, March 27, 1903, March 31, 1922, May 26, 1922; Osmundson, "Camano," pp. 79–86; "Lands of the Port Blakely Mill Co., April 1, 1900," in Port Blakely Mill Co. Collection; *Book of Deeds*, 20:336–37, 394, 546, 565, 589; 21:69, 89, 134; 39:130, 307, 342, 433, PMC to Bogue and Smiley, March 7, 1902, Ames Collection, Land Letters; *Island County, Washington, A World Beater*, pp. 22, 23, 30.

22. Washington, *Logged-off Lands of Western Washington*, pp. 21–23; Washington, BSAI, *Vacant Logged-off Lands*, pp. 24–27. *Island County, Washington, A World Beater*.

23. Woodrow Rufener *et al.*, "Farming Systems in King and Snohomish Counties, Washington, 1939," WAES *Bulletin* 424:46, 71; *LLL* 2:40; U.S.D.A., *Department Bulletin 1236*, pp. 2, 8; Murphy, "Farmers on Cutover," p. 30.

24. WLLA, *Proceedings*, 5:24–31; "Washington's Logged-off Land Problems Discussed," p. 41; Austin Griffiths, "Address," *Vacant Logged-off Lands*, pp. 119–20; J. W. Brown, "Land Clearing in Washington," *LLL* 1:14.

25. "Washington's Logged-off Land Problems Discussed," p. 41; Austin Griffiths, "Address," *Vacant Logged-off Lands*, pp. 119–20; J. W. Brown, "Land Clearing in Washington," *LLL* 1:14. WLLA, *Proceedings*, 5:24–31; "Asset or Liability?", pp. 246–47; "Developing Our Land Resources," p. 172; Shoemaker, "How the State Can Clear Logged-off Lands," p. 16; H. K. Benson, "Use of State Funds in Land Clearing," *LLL* 1:12–13; Hanson, "Hanson's Plan for State Aid," *LLL* 1:16; Coulter, "Washington's Legislation for Logged-off Lands," p. 9.

26. Washington State, *House Journal*, pp. 267, 948; Washington State, Senate Journal, p. 1,102. Washington, "Murphine Law," *Session Laws*, Chap. 155; for a text of the bill with Murphine's comments, see "Washington Logged-off Land Legislation," *LLL* 1:5–7. The House and Senate passed the bill by votes of 83-5 in the House and 29-4 in the Senate.

27. Thomas Murphine, "Washington's Logged-off Land Quandary," *LLL* 2:5; "Developing Our Land Resources," p. 172; *LLL* 2:3; Washington, BSAI, *The Logged-off Lands of Western Washington*, passim; Hoover, "Rural Settlement," pp. 4, 22–27. Following the defeat of the

Murphine Bill, *Little Logged-off Lands* reasserted belief in the ability of settlement to proceed unassisted, *LLL* 2:3. Following World War I, the movement to put veterans on farms led to the passage of state aid measures, but despite the efforts of logged-off land promoters, such aid went only to people settling irrigated lands in eastern Washington. Hoover, "Rural Settlement," pp. 4, 22–27.

28. "Developing Our Land Resources," *Better Business* 1:171.

29. Kirkland, "Cost of Growing Timber," passim; U.S.D.A., *Misc. Pub. 218*, "Forest Taxation in the United States," by Fred Fairchild, gives the reform position.

30. Hoover, "Rural Settlement," pp. 29–45. Edwin Coman, Jr. and Helen M. Gibbs, *Time, Tide and Timber*, pp. 237–42.

31. Joel Shoemaker, "Wonderful Opportunities in Logged-off Lands," *Pacific Northwest Commerce* 5:16: C. W. Scharff, "Redeeming the Wooded Wilderness of Washington," *LLL* 1:19–20; "Logged-off Paradise," *LLL* 1:22; Hathaway, "Call of the Land," p. 14; Shoemaker, "Independence on Little Logged-off Farms," *LLL* 1:16; C. J. Zintheo, "This Man Says Stumps Are a Blessing not a Curse," *LLL* 1:23; C. J. Zintheo, "The Logged-off Land Problem and Its Solution," *Pacific Lumber Trade Journal* 16:55–58; "The Logged-off Land Problem," *West Coast Lumberman* 27:42; WLLA, *Proceedings*, p. 11; H. K. Benson, "Utilization of Waste Wood," *LLL* 1:12.

32. W. H. Lawrence, "A Preliminary Report on Some Experiments in Clearing Logged-off Land with a Stump Burner," WAES *Bulletin 93*, passim; H. W. Sparks, "Methods of Clearing Logged-off Lands," WAES *Bulletin 101*, passim; F. A. Huntley, "Clearing Land," WAES *Bulletin 28*, passim.

33. WAES *Bulletin 101*, p. 4; N. B. Coffman, "Settlers Agency Will Help Populate Stump Lands," *Pacific Northwest Commerce* 5:26; U.S.D.A., *Dept. Bulletin 1236*, p. 2 (the dynamite figure was computed for 1921); WAES *Bulletin 93*, passim.

34. See Table 27; WAES *Bulletin 399*, pp. 38–40; Murphy, "Farmers on Cutover Lands," p. 26. Between 1917 and 1920 the average amount of land cleared per farm per year in the county was 1.7 acres.

35. U.S.D.A., *Dept. Bulletin 1236*, p. 15; U.S.D.A., *Farmer's Bulletin 462*, pp. 10 ff; A. R. Hathaway, "Clearing Land with Cows," *LLL* 2:17; WLLA, *Proceedings*, p. 32. See Appendix B; Fifteenth Census, 1930, Agriculture, 3, Part 3, pp. 342, 348; *I. C. Times*, Dec. 2, 1921.

36. U.S.D.A., *Dept. Bulletin 1236;* Fifteenth Census, 1930, Agriculture, 3, Part 3, pp. 319–21, 341–43, 347–49. For chicken farming,

see: Sixteenth Census, 1940, Special Poultry Report, p. 646; WAES, *Bulletin 424*, pp. 21–35, 40–41, 71; Buerstatte, "Geography of Whidby," p. 119.

37. WAES *Bulletin 399*, pp. 24, 38, 48; Fifteenth Census, 1930, Agriculture, 3, Part 3, pp. 319–21; Sixteenth Census, 1940, Agriculture, 2, Part 3, 233–39; WAES *Bulletin 424*, pp. 14, 17; Murphy, "Farmers on Cutover Lands," p. 26.

38. U.S.D.A., *Dept. Bulletin 1236*, pp. 15, 18.

39. Fifteenth Census, 1930, Agriculture, 3, Part 3, pp. 319–21; Sixteenth Census, 1940, Agriculture 2, Part 3, pp. 233–39; Sixteenth Census, 1940, Agriculture, 1, Part 6, pp. 578–79; WAES *Bulletin 399*, pp. 24, 48; Sixteenth Census, 1940, Agriculture, 2, Part 3, pp. 233–39.

40. U.S.D.A., *Dept. Bulletin 1236*, pp. 15, 20–23, 33; Thomas Pressly and William Schofield, *Farm Real Estate Values in the United States by Counties, 1950–1959*, pp. 66–67.

41. "Washington's Logged-off Land Problems Discussed," p. 41; Austin Griffiths, "Address," *Vacant Logged-off Lands*, pp. 119–20; J. W. Brown, "Land Clearing in Washington," *LLL* 1:14.

42. WAES *Bulletin 399*, pp. 5, 30, 33; WAES *Bulletin 378*, p. 22; Murphy, "Farmers on Cutover Lands," pp. 36, 197; Sixteenth Census, *Agriculture*, 1, Part 6, p. 579; Washington, Department of Social Services, *Summary of Community Survey of Island County, Washington*, p. 100; WAES *Bulletin 380*, pp. 18–19; WAES *Bulletin 407*, p. 24; *CC* 9:33, 139; *I. C. Times*, Oct. 9, 1931, July 30, 1932, Feb. 8, 1934, Sept. 9, 1933, Sept. 30, 1933, Nov. 5, 1936, Nov. 10, 1938.

43. National Resources Board, *Supplementary Report of the Land Planning Committee, Part IV; Maladjustments in Land Use in the United States*, p. 31. *I. C. Times*, Sept. 14, 1934, Sept. 28, 1934.

44. Leo Isaac, "Forest Soil of the Douglas Fir Region," *Ecology* 18:265, 269, 277, 278.

45. Douglas Ingram, "Vegetative Changes and Grazing Use on Douglas Fir Cutover Land," *Journal of Agricultural Research*, 43:402–404, 411; WLLA Proceedings, p. 32; D. A. Brodie, "Adaptability of the Angora Goat Industry to Western Washington," WAES *Bulletin 78*, passim; U.S.D.A., *Dept. Bulletin 1236*, pp. 35–36; U.S.D.A., Leo Isaac *et al.*, "Plant Succession on Cutover, Burned, and Grazed Douglas Fir Areas," *Pacific Northwest Forest Research Note 26*, pp. 2–7; Washington State, *Reports of the State Fire Warden* (1905–1920), and *Reports of the Division of Forestry* (1920–1940).

46. Ingram, "Vegetative Changes," pp. 402–404; U.S.D.A., *PNW Forest Research Note 26*, pp. 2–7; Sixteenth Census, 1940, Agriculture, 3, Part 5, p. 340; U.S.D.A., *Misc. Publication 389*, p. 78; National

Resources Board, *Soil Erosion: A Critical Problem in American Agriculture, Supplementary Report of the Land Planning Committee,* Part 5, map 92; James Malin has criticized this report on the grounds that the year it took to prepare was inadequate for a survey of the entire U.S. and that the planners had no way of telling how much topsoil there was to begin with and, thus, could not tell how much had been lost. Malin, *Grasslands of North America,* pp. 142–44.

47. There are no separate statistics for Island County in 1964, but between 1932 and 1940, when the original surveys of these counties were taken, and 1962, the amount of alder in board feet increased from 11 million to 408 million, and the acreage of alder, 59,000 acres, was second only to that of Douglas fir, 274,000 acres. U.S.D.A., Forest Service, "Forest Statistics for San Juan Island and Kitsap Counties," *Forest Service Report 142,* PNW Forest and Range Experiment Station, pp. 5, 20. These areas were logged in the late nineteenth and early twentieth centuries.

48. U.S. Resettlement Administration, *Resettlement Administration Program in Oregon, Washington, and Idaho,* pp. 3–5; U.S. National Resources Board, *Supplementary Report of the Land Planning Committee to the National Resources Board,* Part 6, 9, Part 7, p. 119; WAES *Bulletin 380;* WAES *Bulletin 399;* WAES *Bulletin 407;* WAES *Bulletin 424;* Pacific Northwest Regional Planning Commission, *Migration and the Development of Economic Opportunity in the Pacific Northwest,* 38–42.

49. Rexford Tugwell, "The Resettlement Idea," *Agricultural History,* 33:160; U.S. Resettlement Administration, *Program in Oregon,* p. 3; U.S. Resettlement Administration, Region 11, "Press Release, July 16, 1937," in collected volume of Resettlement Administration Region 11, *Publications,* Pacific Northwest Collection, University of Washington.

50. Murphy, "Farmers on the Cutover Lands," pp. 60, 80, 83, 151; Resettlement Administration, Region 11, "Press Release, July 16, 1937"; Washington State Planning Council, *Second Biennial Report,* p. 70; Resettlement Administration, Region 11, *A Reconnaissance Land Classification of the Western Part of Snohomish County, Washington;* Washington State Planning Council, *Fourth Biennial Report,* p. 29. *I. C. Times,* March 23, 1939, June 3, 1937.

51. Murphy, "Farmers on the Cutover Lands," pp. 85–88, 90–94, 97, 100, 108, 145, 167–195; Sixteenth Census, 1940, Agriculture, 1, Part 6, pp. 548–51; Seventeenth Census, 1950, Agriculture, 1, Part 32, pp. 42–45; National Resources Planning Board, *Development of Resources and of Economic Opportunity in the Pacific Northwest,* pp. 25–53; *Oak Harbor Farm Bureau News,* May 31, 1951, Whidby Island Centennial Supplement, p. 7. The bases took up 5,000 acres of land, not all of it

farmland, in 1941. Washington State Department of Agriculture, *Island County Agriculture*, Washington Agricultural Data Series, p. 26.

52. U.S.D.A., *Soil Survey*, p. 42; Washington State, "To Provide for Establishing Diking Districts," *Session Laws* (1895), Chap. 117; Washington State, "Relating to Dikes and Drains," *Session Laws* (1913), Chap. 89.

53. *CC*, 7:21; "Order for the Formation of Diking District 1, March 16, 1914," Diking and Drainage District Records, Auditor's Office, Island County Courthouse. "Objection to Petition of Herbert Weedin *et al.* for the formation of a Diking District," Diking and Drainage Records, Island County; *Auditor's Annual Report*, p. 10.

54. Anthes, "Langley"; *CC*, 7:21, 67, 178, 184–85, 230; "Order Establishing Diking District 1, March 16, 1914," also orders establishing Diking District 3, Sept. 8, 1914; "Petition for District 4, n.d.," "Order Forming Drainage District 5, April 2, 1934, District 6, Feb. 2, 1940," all in Diking and Drainage District Records; Washington State, Department of Taxation and Examination, "Reports on Drainage and Diking Districts," July 31, 1932, and Washington, Department of Auditor of State Division of Municipal Corporations, "Reports on Diking and Drainage Districts," September 1938, both in Diking and Drainage District Records. Washington, *Water Supply Bulletin 14, Lakes of Washington*, by Ernest Wolcott, 1:62. Figures compiled from Diking and Drainage District Records and Sixteenth Census, *Irrigation of Agricultural Lands*, p. 442.

Chapter VII. The Urban Shadow

1. Buerstatte, "Geography," pp. 44–45; *I. C. Times*, March 18, 1927, Pamphlet File, Pacific Northwest Collection; Whidby Island Ferry Lines, "Romantic Whidby Island" (brochure, n.p., n.d.), Pacific Northwest Collection; *I. C. Times*, Sept. 5, 1913; *I. C. Farm Bureau News*, July 25, 1935.

2. Whidby Island Ferry Lines, "Romantic Whidby"; *Seattle Times*, June 1, 1930, Pamphlet File, Island County, Pacific Northwest Collection; *I. C. Times*, April 28, 1922.

3. *Island County Farm Bureau News*, July 25, 1935; *I. C. Times*, June 1, 1939.

4. Cook, *A Particular Friend*, pp. 23–24; "Island County," *The Coast* 4:68; Lester Still, "Whidby Island," *The Coast* 2:79; *P. S. Argus*, Feb. 23, 1871, April 6, 1871.

5. "The Town of San de Fuca," *West Shore* (April 5, 1890), p. 440;

1. C. Times, Nov. 16, 23, 30, 1934; *Plat Book,* Auditor's Office, Island County Courthouse, 1:17, 25, 29, 2:1, 7, 12–14, 18; Jacob Ebey to Almira Enos, March 23, 1889, Ebey Collection; *1. C. Times,* Nov. 30, 1891; E. H. Sargent, Oct. 8, 1899, Island County Historical Society.

6. *CC,* 5:330; Washington State Department of Agriculture, "Island County," Agricultural Data Series, 1956, p. 10.

7. Frank Pratt to Almira Enos, Jan 4, 1901, Ebey Collection; John Muir, *Steep Trails,* p. 221.

8. *1. C. Times,* Nov. 22, 1901; Still, "Whidby Island," p. 78; *Island County, A World Beater,* pp. 40, 44–45; *1. C. Times,* July 25, 1902.

9. *1. C. Times,* March 18, 1927, Pamphlet File, Island County, Pacific Northwest Collection; *1. C. Times,* March 24, 1922; *1. C. Times,* March 18, 1927, May 18, 1928, Pamphlet File, Island County, Pacific Northwest Collection.

10. *1. C. Times,* July 19, 1915; Washington Bureau of Industrial Studies, Institute of Transportation and Maritime Commerce, *Washington Survey: Sub-division Island County,* p. 18; *1. C. Times,* May 29, 1925, May 5, 1931; Osmundson, "Camano," p. 102.

11. *1. C. Times,* Nov. 11, 1921, March 24, 1922, April 28, 1922, June 23, 1922.

12. *1. C. Times,* May 29, 1925, April 14, 1938, May 14, 1936, Feb. 4, 1937, June 2, 1938.

13. *1. C. Times,* Dec. 9, 1921, March 3, 1922, May 29, 1925, April 8, 1932, May 20, 1932.

14. E. H. Sargent, Diary, Nov. 7, 1899, Dec. 11, 1899, Jan. 12, 1900, July 5, 1900; *1. C. Times,* June 8, 1900, Oct. 17, 1902, Oct. 31, 1902, April 1, 1902, Nov. 25, 1904, Jan. 15, 1915, Jan. 28, 1916; *CC,* 7:128, "Island County," p. 69.

15. *1. C. Times,* Oct. 29, 1915, Oct. 27, 1933, Feb. 11, 1937.

16. Puget Sound Task Force of the Pacific Northwest River Basins Commission, *Comprehensive Study of Water Related Land Resources,* 1970, Appendix 11, pp. 7–13, 7–14. *1. C. Times,* Aug. 19, 1937; Stanley Jewett *et al., Birds of Washington State,* pp. 46–47, 223, 228.

17. *CC,* 9:431; P. S. Task Force, *Comprehensive Study,* pp. 7–14; Lloyd Ingles, *Mammals of the Pacific States: California, Oregon, and Washington,* pp. 347, 365, 367, 372–73.

18. *1. C. Times,* May 14, 1939, Dec. 22, 1937.

19. Buerstatte, "Geography," pp. 56–57; *1. C. Times,* Oct. 2, 1931, July 27, 1934.

20. *1. C. Farm Bureau News,* Centennial Supplement, May 31, 1951, Sec. 3, pp. 1, 4–5; *1. C. Times,* Nov. 16, 1934; Washington, "Initiative 77," *Session Laws* (1935), Chap. 1.

21. *I. C. Times,* Feb. 17, 1938, Feb. 24, 1938; Washington, *House Journal* (1937), p. 139; Washington, *Senate Journal* (1939), p. 446; Washington, *House Journal* (1939), pp. 601, 977; Washington, "Initiative 62," *Session Laws* (1933), Chap. 3.

22. Washington, "Administrative Code," *Session Laws* (1921), Chap. 7, Sec. 110–112; P. S. Task Force, *Comprehensive Study,* pp. 7–8.

23. Nineteenth Census, 1970, Agriculture, 1, Part 46, pp. 121, 122; *Seattle Times,* April 22, 1979.

BIBLIOGRAPHY

I. Public Documents

Great Britain

Great Britain, Admiralty Records, Accountant General's Department, Log Books, Supplementary Class II, Explorations, Vancouver Expedition (microfilm).

United States

Island County, Auditor, *Annual Statement of Finances of Island County, Washington,* 1913–20, 1923–29, Pacific Northwest Collection, University of Washington Library.

Island County, Clerk, *Annual Report,* 1930–36, 1940, Pacific Northwest Collection, University of Washington Library.

Island County, County Records, Auditor's Office, Island County Courthouse, Coupeville. (A copy of the U.S. Land Office Record of Lands entered in Island County is on file here.)

Island County, Probate Records, Clerk's Office, Island County Courthouse, Coupeville.

U.S. Congress, House, *House Miscellaneous Document 38,* 33rd Congress, 1st Session, "Letters Addressed to the Commissioner of Indian Affairs" (Serial 741).

———, *House Executive Document 76,* 34th Congress, 3rd Session, "Report of Defloyd Jones" (Serial 906).

———, *House Executive Document 39,* 35th Congress, 1st Session, "Indian Affairs in the Territories of Oregon and Washington" (Serial 955).

———, *House Executive Document 114,* 35th Congress, 2nd Session, "Topographical Memoir of Captain T. J. Cram" (Serial 1014).

————, *House Executive Document 46,* 46th Congress, 2nd Session, "Report of the Public Lands Commission" (Serial 1923).

————, *House Executive Document 1,* 47th Congress, 1st Session, "Report of the Secretary of the Interior" (Serial 2017).

U.S. Congress, Senate, *Senate Executive Document 1,* 33rd Congress, 2nd Session, "Report of I. I. Stevens" (Serial 746).

————, *Senate Executive Document 56,* 36th Congress, 1st Session, "Reports of Explorations and Surveys to Ascertain the Most Practicable Route for a Railroad from the Mississippi River to the Pacific Ocean" (12 volumes).

U.S. Department of Agriculture, *Department Bulletin No. 1236,* "Farming the Logged-off Uplands in Western Washington," by E. R. Johnson and E. D. Strait (July 1924).

————, *Department Bulletin No. 1493,* "Timber Growing Practices in the Douglas Fir Region," by Thornton Munger (June 1927).

————, *Farmers Bulletin 462,* "Utilization of Logged-off Land for Pasture in Western Oregon and Western Washington," by Byron Hunter and Harry Thompson (1911).

————, Forest Service, Pacific Northwest Forest Experiment Station, *Facts Bearing upon the Instability of Forest Land Ownership in the Pacific Northwest* (September 1934).

————, Forest Service, Pacific Northwest Forest and Range Experiment Station, *Fire in the Northern Environment—A Symposium,* edited by C. W. Slaughter, Richard J. Barney, and G. M. Hansen (1971).

————, Forest Service, Pacific Northwest Forest Experiment Station, *Forest Statistics of Western Washington Counties from Inventory Phase of Forest Survey: Forest Statistics of Island County, Washington* (March 1934).

————, Forest Service, Pacific Northwest Forest and Range Experiment Station, *Forest Research Note 21,* "Highlights of Douglas Fir Natural Regeneration," by Leo Isaac (January 1937).

————, Forest Service, Pacific Northwest Forest and Range Experiment Station, *Forest Research Note 25,* "Tax Relief through Reorganization of Local Government," by Wade De'vries (1937).

————, Forest Service, Pacific Northwest Forest and Range Experiment Station, *Forest Research Note 110,* "Increment Mortality in a Virgin Douglas Fir Forest," by Robert Steele and Norman Worthington (April 1953).

————, Forest Service, Pacific Northwest Forest and Range Experiment Station, *Forest Research Note 26,* "Plant Succession on a Cutover, Burned, and Grazed Douglas Fir Area," by Elmer Reid, Leo Isaac, and G. D. Pickford (March 1938).

————, Forest Service, Pacific Northwest Forest and Range Experiment Station, *Forest Research Note 102*, "Effects of Slash Burning on Soil pH," by Robert Tarrant (July 1954).

————, Forest Service, Pacific Northwest Forest and Range Experiment Station, *Forest Research Note 172*, "Effects of Cattle and Big Game Grazing on Ponderosa Pine Plantations," by Paul Edgerton (December 1971).

————, Forest Service, Pacific Northwest Forest and Range Experiment Station, *General Technical Report PNW-8, The Natural Vegetation of Oregon and Washington*, by Jerry Franklin and C. T. Dyrness (1973).

————, Forest Service, Pacific Northwest Forest and Range Experiment Station, *General Technical Report PNW-10, An Annotated Bibliography of the Effects of Logging on Fish of the Western United States and Canada*, by Dave R. Gibbons and Ernest R. Salo (1973).

————, Forest Service, Pacific Northwest Forest and Range Experiment Station, *General Technical Report PNW-24, Environmental Effects of Forest Residues Management in the Pacific Northwest* (1974).

————, Forest Service, Pacific Northwest Forest and Range Experiment Station, *Forest Survey Report 142*, "Forest Statistics for San Juan, Island and Kitsap Counties" (May 1962).

————, Forest Service, Section of Education and Information, *Forest Facts and Statistics for the North Pacific Region* (Portland, 1936).

————, Forest Service, Southeastern Forest Experiment Station, *Fire: A Summary of Literature in the United States from the Mid-1920s to 1966*, by Charles Cushwa (January 1968).

————, *Miscellaneous Publication 218, Forest Taxation in the United States*, by Fred Fairchild and Associates (1935).

————, *Miscellaneous Publication 389*, "Forest Resources of the Douglas Fir Region," by H. J. Andrews and R. W. Cowlin (December 1940).

————, *Miscellaneous Special Report 7, Tide Marshes of the United States*, by D. M. Nesbit (1885).

————, Soil Conservation Service, *Soil Survey: Island County, Washington*, Series 1949, no. 6 (1958).

————, Soil Conservation Service, *Erosion History Data File, State of Washington*, compiled 1936–44 (microfilm, University of Washington).

————, Soils Bureau, *Field Operations of the Bureau of Soils, 1910: Soil Survey, Western Puget Sound*, Washington (1910).

————, Soils Bureau, *Soil Survey of Island County, Washington*, by E. P. Carr and A. W. Mangum (1905).

————, Soils Bureau, *Reconnaissance Soil Survey of the Eastern Part of Puget Sound*, by A. W. Mangum and party (1911).

————, *Technical Bulletin 201*, "The Yield of Douglas Fir in the Pacific Northwest," by Richard McCardle (October 1930).

————, *Technical Bulletin 286*, "Decay and Other Losses in Douglas Fir in Western Oregon and Washington," by J. S. Boyce (April 1932).

————, *Technical Bulletin 706*, "Wild Animal Damage to Seeds and Seedlings on Cutover Douglas Fir Lands of Oregon and Washington," by A. W. Moor (June 1940).

————, *Yearbook of Agriculture*, 1938 (Washington, D.C., 1938).

————, *Yearbook of Agriculture*, 1957 (Washington, D.C., 1957).

U.S. Department of Commerce, Bureau of the Census, *Eighth Census of the United States, 1860*.

————, Bureau of the Census, *Eighth Census, 1860*, Manuscript Census, Island County, Washington.

————, Bureau of the Census, *Ninth Census of the United States, 1870*.

————, Bureau of the Census, *Ninth Census, 1870*, Manuscript Census, Island County, Washington.

————, Bureau of the Census, *Tenth Census of the United States, 1880*.

————, Bureau of the Census, *Tenth Census, 1880*, Manuscript Census, Island County, Washington.

————, Bureau of the Census, *Eleventh Census of the United States, 1890*.

————, Bureau of the Census, *Twelfth Census of the United States, 1900*.

————, Bureau of the Census, *Thirteenth Census of the United States, 1910*.

————, Bureau of the Census, *Fourteenth Census of the United States, 1920*.

————, Bureau of the Census, *Fifteenth Census of the United States, 1930*.

————, Bureau of the Census, *Sixteenth Census of the United States, 1940*.

U.S. Department of the Interior, Bureau of Land Management, Portland, Oregon, Abstract of Land Office Receipts and Patents, Seattle.

————, Field Notes of the United States Surveyor.

————, Bureau of Indian Affairs, *Annual Report of the Commissioner of Indian Affairs*, 1851–70.

————, Federal Water Pollution Control Administration, *Transcript of Proceedings of the Conference on the Matter of Pollution of the Navigable Waters of Puget Sound, the Straits of Juan de Fuca and Their Tributaries and Estuaries* (Seattle, September 6–7, October 6, 1967).

————, Geological Survey, *The Forests of the United States*, by Henry Gannet, Extracts from the *19th Annual Report of the Geological Survey*, 1897–98 (Washington, D.C., 1899).

————, Geological Survey, Professional Paper 5, Series H. Forestry 2, *The Forests of Washington: A Revision of Estimates,* by Henry Gannet (Washington, D.C., 1902).

U.S. Indian Claims Commission, Colin Tweddell, "A Historical and Ethnological Study of the Snohomish Indian People," Expert Testimony, Docket 125.

U.S. National Archives, Records of the United States Exploring Expedition under the Command of Lt. Charles Wilkes, 1838–42, Letters Received by the Navy Department Relating to Expedition (microfilm).

————, Record Group 75, Records of the Bureau of Indian Affairs, Washington Superintendency (microfilm).

U.S. National Resources Board, *State of Planning: A Review of Activities and Progress* (Washington, D.C., 1935).

————, *Supplementary Report of the Land Planning Committee to the National Resources Board,* Parts 1–11 (Washington, D.C., 1935–38).

U.S. National Resources Committee, Pacific Northwest Regional Planning Commission, *Forest Resources of the Pacific Northwest* (Washington, D.C., 1938).

U.S. National Resources Planning Board, *Puget Sound Region: War and Post War Development* (Washington, D.C. 1943).

U.S. Resettlement Administration Region 11, *Miscellaneous Publications 1935–38* (collected in Pacific Northwest Collection, University of Washington).

U.S. Works Progress Administration, *Projects in Operation in Counties of Washington State (1936)* (Pacific Northwest Collection, University of Washington Library).

————, *Told by the Pioneers Tales of Frontier Life as Told by Those Who Remember the Days of Territory and Early Statehood of Washington* (3 volumes, Olympia, 1937).

————, *Trees and Men,* by Herbert Resner (Seattle, 1938).

————, Washington Pioneer Projects Records, Island County, Washington State Department of Public Welfare Files, Washington State Library, Olympia, Washington.

Washington State Agricultural Experiment Station, *Bulletin 28,* "Clearing Land," by F. A. Huntley (Pullman, Washington, 1897).

————, *Bulletin 78,* "Adaptability of the Angora Goat Industry to Western Washington," by D. A. Brodie (Pullman, 1906).

————, *Bulletin 93,* "Some Experiments in Clearing Logged-off Land with a Stump Burner," by W. H. Lawrence (Pullman, 1910).

————, *Bulletin 101,* "Methods of Clearing Logged-off Lands," by H. W. Sparks (Pullman, 1911).

————, *Bulletin 216*, "An Economic Study of Poultry Farming in Western Washington," by George Severance (Pullman, 1927).

————, *Bulletin 288*, "Present Land Uses—Washington: Types of Farming Series, Part I," by Rex E. Willard and Neil W. Johnson (Pullman, 1933).

————, *Bulletin 378*, "The Drought Farmer Adjusts to the West," by Richard Wakefield and Paul Landis (Pullman, 1939).

————, *Bulletin 380*, "Social Characteristics of Parttime Farmers in Washington," by Carl F. Reuss (Pullman, 1939).

————, *Bulletin 399*, "Settlement Experience and Opportunities on the Cutover Lands of Western Washington," by Carl P. Heisig (Pullman, 1941).

————, *Bulletin 407*, "After Three Years: A Restudy of the Social and Economic Adjustment of a Group of Drought Migrants" (Pullman, 1941).

————, *Bulletin 424*, "Farming Systems in King and Snohomish Counties, Washington, 1939" (Pullman, 1942).

————, *Bulletin 426*, "Back to the Country—the Rurban Trend in Washington Population" by Carl F. Reuss (Pullman, 1942).

Washington State, Auditor, *Biennial Reports to the State Legislature,* 1892–1918.

Washington State, Board of Equalization, *Minutes and Official Proceedings,* 1894–1942.

Washington State, Board of Horticulture, *Biennial Reports,* 1891–96.

Washington State, Board of Tax Commissioners, *Biennial Reports,* 1906–16.

Washington State, Bureau of Statistics, Agriculture, and Immigration, *Biennial Reports: A Review of the Resources and Industries of Washington,* 1895–1909.

————, *The Logged-off Lands of Western Washington* (Olympia, 1911; revised edition, 1915).

————, *Washington: Descriptive and Statistical Information for the Traveller, Homebuilder and Investor* (Olympia, 1922).

Washington State, *Code of Washington,* 1896.

Washington State, Commission on Forest Legislation, *Report,* 1910 (typewritten copy in Pacific Northwestern Collection, University of Washington).

Washington State, Commission of Horticulture, *Report,* 1901, 1907, 1908.

Washington State, Commissioner of Public Lands, *Biennial Reports,* 1890–1936.

————, *Vacant Logged-off Lands of the State of Washington* (Olympia, 1917).

————, Department of Agriculture, *Island County Agriculture*, Washington County Agricultural Data Series (Olympia, 1956).

Washington State, Department of Conservation, *Water Supply Bulletin 14, The Lakes of Washington*, by Ernest Wolcott (2 volumes, Olympia, 1961).

Washington State, Department of Conservation and Development, *Biennial Reports of the State Fire Warden and State Forester to the State Board of Forest Commissioners*, 1905–20.

————, *Reports of the Forestry Division*, 1920–44.

Washington State, Department of Game, *Biological Bulletin 7*, "Plant Food Resources for Waterfowl in the Pacific Northwest," by Theodore Scheffer and Neil Hotchkiss (Olympia, 1945).

————, *Biological Bulletin 13*, "The Blacktailed Deer of Western Washington," by Ellsworth Brown (Olympia, 1961).

Washington State, Department of Taxation and Examination, Division of Taxation, *First Biennial Report*, 1924.

Washington State, Department of Water Resources, *Water Supply Bulletin 25*, "Pleistocene Stratigraphy of Island County," by D. J. Easterbrook (1968).

Washington State, Division of Forestry, *Forest Resources of Washington* (Olympia, 1940).

Washington State, Forest Advisory Committee, *A Long Range Forest Program for the State of Washington* (Olympia, 1942).

Washington State, Forest Board, *First Report*, 1924.

Washington State, Forestry Department, *Forest Protection Laws*, 1905, 1913–17.

Washington State, Geological Survey, *Bulletin B, Glaciation of the Puget Sound Region*, by J. Harlen Bretz (Olympia, 1913).

————, Geological Survey, *Bulletin 12, Bibliography of Washington Geology and Geography*, by Gretchen O'Donnel (Olympia, 1913).

Washington State, *House Journals*, 1890–1940.

Washington State Planning Council, *Biennial Reports*, 1934–40.

Washington State, Puget Sound Task Force of the Pacific Northwest River Basin Commission, *Comprehensive Study of Water-Related Land Resources of the Puget Sound Area and Adjacent Waters* (17 volumes, 1970).

Washington State, Secretary of State, *The Lumbering Industry in Washington* (Olympia, 1941).

————, *The State of Washington: An Official Report of the Resources of the State up to and Including January 1, 1894* (Olympia, 1894).

————, *Washington: Products, Peoples and Resources, All Counties* (Olympia, 1934).
Washington State, *Senate Journals*, 1890–1940.
Washington State, *Session Laws*, 1890–1940.
Washington State, Tax Commission, *Biennial Reports*, 1916–1922.
Washington State, Tax Commission, *Biennial Reports*, 1928–1940.
Washington Territory, Immigration Board, *Washington Territory: Its Soil, Climate, Productions and General Resources*, by A. H. Stuart (Olympia, 1875).
Washington Territory, *Laws of Washington Territory*, 1869–71, 1885–88.

II. COURT CASES

U.S. Court of Claims, Seattle, *Duwamish et al. vs. U.S.*, Docket No. 275., Consolidated Petition, August 1932 (trial briefs in Pacific Northwest Collection, University of Washington Library).

III. NEWSPAPERS AND JOURNALS

Island County

Island County Times, 1891, 1900–18, 1921–22, 1928–40.
Oak Harbor Farm-Bureau News, July 25, 1935; Centennial Edition, May 31, 1951.
Whidby Islander, 1963.
Whidby News, 1973.
Whidby Record, 1969.

Port Townsend

Democratic Press, 1877–81.
Northwest, 1860–62.
Puget Sound Argus, 1870–89.
Register, 1860–61.
Weekly Message, 1867–71.

Olympia

Pioneer & Democrat, 1852–61.
Washington Standard, 1860–80.

Seattle

Seattle Times, 1979.

Little Logged-off Lands and *Little Logged-off Farms* have been used so extensively that I have cited the journals themselves as well as specific articles. Likewise extensive background material has been taken from *Tall Timbers Fire Ecology Conference Proceedings,* volumes 1–13.

IV. MANUSCRIPTS

Ames, Edwin. Papers, University of Washington Library.

Anthes, Jacob. Mss, History of Langley; Washington, Pacific Northwest Collection, University of Washington Library.

Bagley, Clarence. Collection, University of Washington Library.

Bagley, Daniel. Collection, University of Washington Library.

Beckman, Victor. MSS, Survey of the Lumber Industry of Western Washington, Pacific Northwest Collection, University of Washington Library.

Broughton, W. R. Mss, Log Book of the Chatham Tender, British Museum, Add. Ms. 17543 (microfilm, University of Washington Library).

Crockett, Walter, to Dr. Harvey Black, October 15, 1853, Washington State Library, copy in University of Washington Library.

Dunbar Scrapbooks, Pacific Northwest Collection, University of Washington Library.

Ebey Collection, University of Washington Library.

Fay, Robert. Collection, Washington State Library, Olympia.

Griffiths, Austin. Mss, "Great Faith: Autobiography of an English Immigrant Boy in America," Pacific Northwest Collection, University of Washington Library.

Haller, Granville. Papers, University of Washington Library.

Island County Historical Collection, Coupeville.

Kellog, Albert. Mss., "Personal Reminiscences of Whidby Island," University of Washington Library.

Meany Pioneer File, Pacific Northwest Collection, University of Washington Library.

Pamphlet File, Island County, Pacific Northwest Collection, University of Washington.

Pope and Talbot Collection, University of Washington Library.

Port Blakely Mill Company Collection, University of Washington Library.

Puget, Peter. Mss., "Fragment of Journal," British Museum, B.M. 17546 (microfilm, University of Washington Library).

Swan, James G. Mss., "Correspondence with the Smithsonian Institution" (microfilm, University of Washington Library).

————, Mss., "Letters: Photocopy of Letters to Washington Newspapers," Pacific Northwest Collection, University of Washington Library.

————, Papers, University of Washington Library.

Swift, H. A. Mss., "Notes on Whidby Island, Letters from the *Island County Times*," Pacific Northwest Collection, University of Washington Library.

Swift, Louise. Papers, University of Washington Library.

Tolmie, William. Mss., "History of Puget Sound and the Northwest Coast of America," Bancroft Collection, University of California, Berkeley (microfilm, University of Washington Library).

Washington Mill Company Collection, University of Washington Library.

Wilson, George, O. Mss., "Diary," Pacific Northwest Collection, University of Washington Library.

V. Books

Ackerknecht, Erwin. *The History and Geography of the Most Important Diseases* (New York, Hafner Publishing Company, 1965).

Allen, E. T. *Practical Forestry in the Pacific Northwest* (Portland, Western Forestry and Conservation Association, 1911).

Alley, B. F. *Washington Territory: Descriptive and Historical* (Olympia, Cavanaugh, 1886).

Andrews, Ralph. *This Was Logging* (Seattle, Superior Publishing Company, 1954).

Bailey, Liberty Hyde. *The Country Life Movement* (New York, The Macmillan Company, 1913).

————, *Cyclopedia of American Agriculture,* 4 volumes (New York, Macmillan & Co., 1907–11).

Baker, O. E., Ralph Borsodi, and M. L. Wilson. *Agriculture in Modern Life* (New York, Harper and Brothers, 1939).

Bancroft, Hubert Howe. *History of Washington, Idaho and Montana, 1845–89,* volume 31 of *Works* (San Francisco, The History Company, 1890).

————, *Chronicles of the Builders,* 7 volumes (San Francisco, The History Company, 1892).

Bates, Marston. *The Forest and the Sea: A Look at the Economy of Nature and the Ecology of Man* (New York, Random House, 1960).

Bidwell, Percy and John Falconer. *The History of Agriculture in the Northern United States, 1620–1860* (Washington, Carnegie Institution of Washington, 1925).

Blanchet, F. N. *Historical Notes and Reminiscences of Early Times in Oregon* (Portland, 1883).

————, *Historical Sketches of the Catholic Church in Oregon During the Past Forty Years* (Portland, 1878).

Bogue, Alan. *From Prairie to Corn Belt: Farming on the Illinois and Iowa Prairies in the Nineteenth Century* (Chicago, University of Chicago Press, 1963).

Borsodi, Ralph. *Flight from the City* (Suffern, New York, School of Living, 1947).

————, *This Ugly Civilization* (New York, Simon and Schuster, 1929).

Bryan, Alan Lyle. *An Archaeological Survey of North Puget Sound*, Occasional Papers of the Idaho State College Museum, Number 11 (Pocatello, Idaho State College Museum, 1963).

Buchanan, R. H., Emrys Jones and Desmond McCourt (eds.). *Man and His Habitat: Essays Presented to Emry Estyn Evans* (London, Routledge and K. Paul, 1971).

Butler, B. Robert. *The Old Cordilleran Culture in the Pacific Northwest.* Occasional Papers of the Idaho State College Museum, Number 5 (Pocatello, Idaho State College Museum, 1961).

Carstensen, Vernon. *Farms or Forests: Evolution of a State Land Policy for Northern Wisconsin, 1850–1932* (Madison, University of Wisconsin, College of Agriculture, 1958).

Clark, Andrew H. *The Invasion of New Zealand by People, Plants and Animals: The South Island*, Rutgers University Studies in Geography, No. 1 (New Brunswick, New Jersey, Rutgers University Press, 1949).

Clark, Andrew H. *Three Centuries and the Island: A Historical Geography of Settlement and Agriculture in Prince Edward Island, Canada* (Toronto, University of Toronto Press, 1959).

Clark, Ella C. *Indian Legends of the Pacific Northwest* (Berkeley, University of California Press, 1960).

Clark, John G. *The Frontier Challenge: Responses to the Trans-Mississippi West* (Lawrence, Kansas, University Press of Kansas, 1971).

Collins, June. *Valley of the Spirits: The Upper Skagit Indians of Western Washington* (Seattle, University of Washington Press, 1974).

Coman, Edwin T. and Helen M. Gibbs. *Time, Tide, and Timber, A Cen-*

tury of Pope and Talbot (Stanford, California, Stanford University Press, 1949).

Cook, Jimmie Jean. *A Particular Friend, Penn's Cove: A History of the Settlers, Claims and Buildings of Central Whidbey Island* (Coupeville, 1972).

Cox, Thomas. *Mills and Markets: A History of the Pacific Coast Lumber Industry to 1900* (Seattle, University of Washington Press, 1974).

Craven, Avery. *Soil Exhaustion As a Factor in the Agricultural History of Virginia and Maryland, 1605–1860,* University of Illinois Studies in the Social Sciences, No. 1 (Urbana, University of Illinois Press, 1925).

Crosby, Alfred. *The Columbian Exchange* (Westport, Connecticut, Greenwood Publishing Company, 1972).

Curti, Merle, *The Making of an American Community: A Case Study of Democracy in a Frontier County* (Stanford, Stanford University Press, 1959).

Darling, Frank Fraser. *West Highland Survey: An Essay in Human Ecology* (Oxford, Oxford University Press, 1955).

———, *Wilderness and Plenty,* The Reith Lectures, 1969 (Boston, Houghton Mifflin, 1970).

Daubenmire, Rexford. *Plant Communities* (New York, Harper and Row, 1968).

Detling, Larry. *Historical Background of the Flora of the Pacific Northwest,* University of Oregon Museum of Natural History Bulletin 13 (Eugene, University of Oregon Museum, 1968).

Drucker, Philip. *Indians of the Northwest Coast* (Garden City, New York, Natural History Press, 1963).

Dugan, James. *The Great Iron Ship* (New York, Harper, 1953).

Dupont, Inc. *Developing Logged-off Lands of the Northwest with Dupont Explosives* (Wilmington, Delaware, Dupont de Nemours Powder Company, 1916).

Ekrich, Arthur. *Man and Nature in America* (New York, Columbia University Press, 1963).

Elton, Charles. *The Ecology of Invasions by Animals and Plants* (London, Methuen, 1958).

Evans, Elwood and Edmond Meany. *The State of Washington: A Brief History of the Discovery and Settlement and Origins of Washington* (Tacoma, Washington, Tacoma Daily News, 1893).

Fosberg, F. R. (Ed.). *Man's Place in the Island Ecosystem* (Honolulu, Bishop Museum Press, 1963).

Gates, Charles. *The First Century at the University of Washington* (Seattle, University of Washington Press, 1961).

Gates, Paul. *History of Public Land Law Development* (Washington, U.S. Government Printing Office, 1968).

Gibbs, George. *On the Indians of Western Washington and Northwestern Oregon,* bound with W. H. Dall's *Tribes of the Extreme Northwest* (Washington, U.S. Government Printing Office, 1877).

Gilkey, Helen M. *Weeds of the Pacific Northwest* (Corvallis, Oregon State College, 1957).

Gilkey, Helen M., and La Rea, J. Dennis. *Handbook of Northwestern Plants* (Corvallis, Oregon, Oregon State University, 1967).

Goodrich, Carter, *et al. Migration and Economic Opportunity: The Report of the Study of Population Redistribution* University of Pennsylvania, Wharton School of Finance and Commerce (Philadelphia, University of Pennsylvania Press, 1936).

――――, *Migration and Planes of Living, 1920–1934.* (London, Oxford University Press, 1935).

Gunther, Erna. *Ethnobotany of Western Washington* (rev. ed., Seattle, University of Washington Press, 1973).

Gunther, Erna. *Ethnobotany of Western Washington* (rev. ed., Seattle, University of Washington Press, 1973).

――――, *Indian Life on the Northwest Coast of North America as Seen by the Early Explorers and Fur Traders During the Last Decades of the Eighteenth Century* (Chicago, University of Chicago Press, 1972).

Guthrie-Smith, H. *Tutira: The Story of a New Zealand Sheep Station* (Edinburgh, W. Blackwood, 1921).

Haeberlin, Hermann, and Erna Gunther. *The Indians of Puget Sound,* University of Washington Publications in Anthropology, Volume 4, Number 1 (Seattle, University of Washington Press, 1930).

Hansen, Henry Paul. *Post Glacial Forest Succession, Climate and Chronology in the Pacific Northwest,* American Philosophical Society Transactions, New Series, Volume 37 (Philadelphia, American Philosophical Society, 1947).

Harstad Associates. *The General Plan for Island County, Washington* (n.p., 1964).

Hays, Samuel. *Conservation and the Gospel of Efficiency* (Cambridge, Massachusetts, Harvard University Press, 1959).

Helgeson, Arlan. *Farms in the Cutover* (Madison, State Historical Society of Wisconsin, 1962).

Hibbard, Benjamin. *A History of Public Land Policies* (New York, The Macmillan Company, 1924).

Hidy, Ralph W., Frank Ernest Hill, and Allan Nevins. *Timber and Men: The Weyerhaeuser Story* (New York, Macmillan, 1963).

Hines, H. K. *An Illustrated History of the State of Oregon* (Chicago, Lewis Publishing Company, 1893).

———, *An Illustrated History of the State of Washington* (Chicago, Lewis Publishing Company, 1893).

Hitchcock, C. Leo, *et al*. *Vascular Plants of the Pacific Northwest*, 5 volumes (Seattle, University of Washington Press, 1969).

Hofstadter, Richard, *Age of Reform* (New York, Knopf, 1959).

Holbrook, Stewart. *The American Lumberjack* (New York, Collier Books, 1962). (Originally published as *Holy Old Mackinaw*.)

———, *Green Commonwealth* (Seattle, Dogwood Press, 1945).

Horsfall, J. G., and A. E. Dimond. *Plant Pathology*, 2 volumes (New York, Academic Press, 1960).

Hudson, Lois Phillips. *Reapers of the Dust: A Prairie Chronicle* (Boston, Little Brown, 1964).

Hulbert, Archer. *Soil: Its Influence on American History* (New Haven, Connecticut, Yale University Press, 1930).

Hunt, Herbert and Floyd Kaylor. *Washington West of the Cascades* (Chicago, The S. J. Clarke Publishing Company, 1917).

Huntington, Ellsworth. *The Red Man's Continent* (New Haven, Connecticut, Yale University Press, 1921).

Huth, Hans. *Nature and the American* (Berkeley, University of California Press, 1957).

Immigration Aid Society of North-western Washington. *Northwestern Washington: Its Soil, Climate, and General Resources* (Port Townsend, Washington, Puget Sound Argus, 1880).

Ingles, Lloyd G. *Mammals of the Pacific States: California, Oregon, and Washington* (Stanford, California, Stanford University Press, 1965).

Ise, John. *The United States Forest Policy* (New Haven, Connecticut, Yale University Press, 1920).

Island County, Washington, A World Beater (n.p., n.d.).

Jewett, Stanley, *et al*. *Birds of Washington State* (Seattle, University of Washington Press, 1953).

Jones, George Neville. *A Botanical Survey of the Olympic Peninsula, Washington*, University of Washington Publications in Biology, Volume 5 (Seattle, University of Washington, 1936).

Kane, Paul. *Wanderings of An Artist Among the Indians of North America* (Toronto, The Radisson Society of Canada, 1925).

Kellog, George Albert. *A History of Whidbey's Island* (Oak Harbor, Washington, 1934).

Kirkendall, Richard. *Social Scientists and Farm Politics in the Age of Roosevelt* (Columbia, University of Missouri Press, 1966).

Kirkland, Burt. *The Cost of Growing Timber in the Pacific Northwest as Related to the Interest Rates Available to Various Forest Owners* (Seattle, 1915).

Kjekshus, Helge. *Ecology Control and Economic Development in East African History: The Case of Tanganyika* (London, Heinemann, 1977).

Kroeber, A. L. *Cultural and Natural Areas of Native North America,* University of California Publications in American Archaeology and Ethnology, Volume 38 (Berkeley, University of California Press, 1935).

Larson, Agnes. *The White Pine Industry in Minnesota* (Minneapolis, University of Minnesota Press, 1949).

Larson, Henrietta. *Jay Cooke: Private Banker* (Cambridge, Massachusetts, Harvard University Press, 1936).

Leopold, Aldo. *A Sand County Almanac with Other Essays on Conservation from Round River* (New York, Oxford University Press, 1966).

Lillard, Richard. *The Great Forest* (New York, A. A. Knopf, 1947).

Lord, Russell. *The Care of the Earth: A History of Husbandry* (New York, Nelson, 1962).

Lyle, J. T. S. *State Taxation and the Lumber Industry* (n.p., 1921).

Lyon, T. Lyttleton, Harry Buckman and Nyle Brady. *Nature and Properties of Soil* (New York, Macmillan, 1952).

Magrini, Louis. *Meet the Governors* (Seattle, L. A. Magrini, 1946).

Malin, James. *The Grasslands of North America—Prolegomena to Its History* (Lawrence, Kansas, privately printed, 1947).

———, *Winter Wheat in the Golden Belt of Kansas* (Lawrence, Kansas, University of Kansas Press, 1944).

Marsh, George Perkins. *Man and Nature* (Cambridge, Massachusetts, Harvard University Press, 1965).

Martin, Alexander, Herbert S. Zim, and Arnold Nelson. *American Wildlife and Plants* (New York, McGraw-Hill, 1951).

Martin, Calvin. *Keepers of the Game* (Berkeley, University of California Press, 1978).

Meany, Edmond. *History of the State of Washington* (New York, The Macmillan Company, 1924).

Meeker, Ezra. *Pioneer Reminiscences of Puget Sound* (Seattle, Lowman & Hanford, 1905).

Murie, Olaus. *The Elk of North America* (Harrisburg, Pennsylvania, The Stackpole Company, and Washington, Wildlife Management Institute, 1957).

Nash, Roderick. *Wilderness and the American Mind* (New Haven, Connecticut, Yale University Press, 1976).

Newcombe, C. F. (ed.). *Menzies Journal of Vancouver's Voyage, April to October, 1792,* Archives of British Columbia Memoir, No. 5 (Victoria, British Columbia, W. H. Callin, 1923).

Northwest Regional Council. *Forestry Depletion in Outline* (Portland, Northwest Regional Council, 1940).

Northwest Scientific Association. *Biology of Alder,* Proceedings of a Symposium Held at Pullman, Washington, April 14–15, 1967 (Portland, Pacific Northwest Forest and Range Experiment Station, 1968).

————, *Research on Coniferous Forest Ecosystems: First Year Progress in the Coniferous Forest Biome,* Proceedings of a Symposium Held at Bellingham, Washington, March 23–24, 1972 (Portland, Pacific Northwest Forest and Range Experiment Station, 1972).

Oliphant, J. Orin. *On the Cattle Ranges of the Oregon Country* (Seattle, University of Washington Press, 1968).

Pressly, Thomas J., and William Schofield. *Farm Real Estate Values in the United States by Counties, 1850–1959* (Seattle, University of Washington Press, 1965).

Rappaport, Roy. *Pigs for the Ancestors: Ritual in the Ecology of a New Guinea People* (New Haven, Connecticut, Yale University Press, 1967).

Richardson, Elmo. *The Politics of Conservation: Crusades and Controversies, 1897–1913* (Berkeley, University of California Press, 1962).

Robbins, Roy. *Our Landed Heritage* (Lincoln, University of Nebraska Press, 1942).

Rosenman, Samuel (ed.). *The Public Papers and Addresses of Franklin D. Roosevelt,* 13 volumes (New York, Random House, 1938–1950).

Sauer, Carl. *Land and Life* (Berkeley, University of California Press, 1963).

————, *Agricultural Origins and Dispersals* (New York, American Geographical Society, 1952).

Schmitt, Peter. *Back to Nature: The Arcadian Myth in Urban America* (New York, Oxford University Press, 1969).

Sears, Paul. *Deserts on the March* (Norman, University of Oklahoma Press, 1947).

Semple, Ellen. *American History and Its Geographic Conditions* (Boston and New York, Houghton and Mifflin Company, 1903).

Shelford, Victor. *The Ecology of North America* (Urbana, University of Illinois Press, 1963).

Shepard, Paul. *Man in the Landscape* (New York, Random House, 1967).
————, and Daniel McKinley. *The Subversive Science: Essays Toward an Ecology of Man* (New York, Houghton Mifflin, 1969).
Slaughter, C. W., Richard Burney, and G. M. Hansen. *Fire in the Northern Environment: A Symposium* (Portland, Pacific Northwest Fire and Range Experiment Station, 1971).
Smith, Henry Nash. *Virgin Land* (Cambridge, Massachusetts, Harvard University Press, 1950).
Smith, Marian (ed.). *Indians of the Urban Northwest* Columbia University Contributions to Anthropology, Number 36 (New York, Columbia University Press, 1949).
————. *The Puyallup-Nisqually,* Columbia University Contributions to Anthropology, Number 32 (New York, Columbia University Press, 1940).
Smith, Robert Leo (ed.). *The Ecology of Man: An Ecosystem Approach* (New York, Harper & Row, 1972).
Snowden, Clinton. *The History of Washington: The Rise and Progress of an American State,* 5 volumes (New York, The Century History Company, 1911).
Swan, James. *The Northwest Coast, or Three Years Residence in Washington Territory* (reprint, Seattle, University of Washington Press, 1957).
Thomas, William L. (ed.). *Man's Role in Changing the Face of the Earth,* 2 volumes (Chicago, University of Chicago Press, 1970).
Thornwaite, C. Warren. *Internal Migration in the United States,* Bulletin Number One, The Study of Population Redistribution, University of Pennsylvania, Wharton School of Finance and Commerce (Philadelphia, University of Pennsylvania, 1934).
Vancouver, George. *A Voyage of Discovery to the North Pacific Ocean and Round the World,* 6 volumes (London, J. Stockdale, 1801).
Van Wagenen, Jared. *The Golden Age of Homespun* (Ithaca, New York, Cornell University Press, 1954).
A Volume of Memoirs and Genealogy of Representative Citizens of the City of Seattle and County of King, Washington (New York, 1903).
Washington Logged-Off Land Association. *Proceedings of the Washington Logged-off Land Association* (Seattle, 1909).
Webb, Walker Prescott. *The Great Plains* (Boston, Ginn and Company, 1931).
Wilkes, Charles. *Narrative of the United States Exploring Expedition During the Years 1838, 1839, 1840, 1841, 1842,* 5 volumes (Philadelphia, Lea and Blanchard, 1850).
Wilkeson, Samuel. *Wilkeson's Notes on Puget Sound* (n.p., n.d.).

VI. ARTICLES

Albrecht, William. "Physical, Chemical, and Biological Changes in the Soil Community," in *Man's Role in Changing the Face of the Earth*, edited by William L. Thomas, 2:648–73 (Chicago, University of Chicago Press, 1970).

Anderson, Edgar. "Man as a Maker of New Plants and Plant Communities," in *Man's Role in Changing the Face of the Earth*, edited by William L. Thomas, 2:763–77 (Chicago, University of Chicago Press, 1970).

"Asset or Liability: The Problem of Logged-off Lands," *Better Business*, 1:246–48.

Austin, R. C. and D. H. Baisinger. "Some Effects of Burning on Forest Soils of Western Oregon and Washington," *Journal of Forestry* 53:275–80, (April 1955).

Bagley, Clarence (ed.). "Journal of Occurrences at Nisqually House," *Washington Historical Quarterly* 6:179–97, 264–78 (July, October 1915); 7:59–75, 144–68 (January, April, 1916).

Bates, Marston. "Man as an Agent in the Spread of Organisms," in *Man's Role in Changing the Face of the Earth*, edited by William L. Thomas 2:788–804 (Chicago, University of Chicago Press, 1970).

Benson, H. K. "Use of State Funds in Land Clearing," *Little Logged-off Lands* 1:12–13 (Aug. 1912).

Berner, Richard C. "The Port Blakely Mill Company, 1876–1889," *Pacific Northwest Quarterly* 57:158–71 (October 1966).

Boyd, Robert. "Another Look at the 'Fever and Ague' of Western Oregon," *Ethnohistory* 22:135–54 (Spring 1975).

Brown, J. W. "Land Clearing in Washington," *Little Logged-off Lands* 1:14 (January 1913).

Buchanan, Iva L. "Lumbering and Logging in the Puget Sound Region in Territorial Days," *Pacific Northwest Quarterly* 27:34–53 (January 1936).

Carlson, Roy. "Chronology and Culture Change in the San Juan Islands," *American Antiquity* 25:562–87 (April 1960).

Coffman, N. B., "Settlers' Agency Will Help Populate Stump Lands," *Pacific Northwest Commerce* 5:26 (December 1911).

Cary, Austin. "The Cary Report on Douglas Fir Lumber Production," *West Coast Lumberman* 42:50–63 (May 1, 1922).

Collins, June. "John Fornsby: The Personal Document of a Coast Salish Indian," in *Indians of the Urban Northwest*, edited by Marian Smith (New York, Columbia University Press, 1949) pp. 287–341.

————. "The Growth of Class Distinctions and Political Authority Among the Skagit Indians During the Contact Period," *American Anthropologist* 52:331–42 (July–September 1950).

————. "The Mythological Basis for Attitudes Toward Animals," *Journal of American Folklore* 65:353–58 (October to December 1952).

Coulter, Arthur. "Washington Legislation for Logged-off Lands," *Little Logged-off Lands* 1:9 (March 1913).

Curtis, John T. "Modification of Mid-latitude Grassland and Forest by Man," in *Man's Role in Changing the Face of the Earth,* edited by William L. Thomas 2:721–36 (Chicago, University of Chicago Press, 1970).

Darling, Frank Fraser. "The Ecological Approach to the Social Sciences," in *The Subversive Science: Essays Toward an Ecology of Man,* edited by Paul Shepard and Daniel McKinley (Boston, Houghton Mifflin, 1969) pp. 316–27.

Darling, Frank Fraser, and Raymond F. Dasmann. "The Ecosystem View of Human Society," in *The Ecology of Man: An Ecosystem Approach,* edited by Robert L. Smith (New York, Harper & Row, 1972) pp. 40–45.

"Deterioration of Fire Killed Douglas Fir," *Timberman* 37:13–17 (December 1935).

"Developing Our Land Resources," *Better Business* 1:171–73 (August 1916).

Easterbrook, D. J. "Late Pleistocene Glaciation of Whidbey Island, Washington," Geological Society of America, Special Papers 76, *Abstracts for 1963,* p. 198.

Farrar, Victor (ed.). "The Nisqually Journal," *Washington Historical Quarterly* 10–15 (July 1919 through July 1924), printed serially.

————. "The Diary of Colonel and Mrs. I. N. Ebey," *Washington Historical Quarterly* 7:239–46, 307–21 (July, October 1916); 8:40–62, 124–53 (January 1917, April, 1917).

Franklin, Jerry. "Comparison of Vegetation in Adjacent Alder, Conifer, and Mixed Alder-Conifer Communities," in Northwest Scientific Association, *Biology of Alder,* Proceedings of a Symposium held at Pullman, 1967 (Portland, Pacific Northwest Forest and Range Experiment Station, 1968).

Gunther, Erna. "Analysis of the First Salmon Ceremony," *American Anthropologist* 28:605–17 (July to December, 1924).

Haeberlin, Hermann. "Mythology of Puget Sound," *Journal of American Folklore* 37:371–438 (July to December 1924).

Hanson, Howard. "Hanson's Plan for State Aid," *Little Logged-off Lands* 1:16 (November 1912).

————. "State Aid in Clearing Logged-off Land," *Little Logged-off Lands* 1:7 (May 1912).

Hart, John Fraser and Eugene Cotton Mather. "The American Fence," *Landscape* 6:4–9 (Spring 1957).

Hathaway, A. R. "Call of the Land," *Little Logged-off Lands* 1:14 (May 1913).

————. "Clearing Land with Cows," *Little Logged-off Lands* 2:17 (July 1913).

Hodgson, Allen. "Logging Waste in the Douglas Fir Region," Joint Publication of *Pacific Pulp and Paper Industry and West Coast Lumberman* (January 1930).

Hoffman, J. V. "The Establishment of a Douglas Fir Forest," *Ecology* 1:49–54 (January 1920).

————. "Natural Reproduction from Seed Stored in the Forest Floor," *Journal of Agricultural Research* 1:7–26 (October 1917).

Hrdlička, Aleš. "Tuberculosis Among Certain Indian Tribes of the United States, Smithsonian Institution, Bureau of American Ethnology, *Bulletin 42* (Washington, 1909).

Ingram, Douglas. "Vegetative Changes and Grazing Use on Douglas Fir Cutover Land," *Journal of Agricultural Research* 43:387–417 (September 1, 1932).

Isaac, Leo. "Fire: A Tool Not a Blanket Rule in Douglas Fir Ecology," *Tall Timbers Fire Ecology Conference* 2:8–9 (March 1963).

Isaac, Leo and H. G. Hopkins. "The Forest Soil of the Douglas Fir Region, and Changes Wrought Upon It by Logging and Slash Burning," *Ecology* 18:264–79 (April 1937).

"Island County, Washington," *The Coast* 4:68–72 (September 1902).

Izett, John. "Whidby Island History," *Washington Historian* 1:199–200 (July 1900).

Kautz, Francis. "Extracts from the Diary of A. V. Kautz," *Washington Historian* 1:115–19 (April 1900); 181–86 (July 1900).

King, Arden. "Archaeology of the San Juan Islands, A Preliminary Report on the Cattle Point Site," in *Indians of the Urban Northwest*, edited by Marian Smith (New York, Columbia University Press, 1949).

Kingston, C. S. "The Introduction of Cattle into the Pacific Northwest," *Washington Historical Quarterly* 14:163–185 (July 1923).

Kuchler, A. W. "The Broadleaf Deciduous Forests of the Pacific Northwest," *Annals of the Association of American Geographers* 36:122–47 (June 1946).

Lively, D. O. "Cattle Raising Successfully Carried Forward on Cutover Timber Lands," *Timberman* 11:20 (May 1910).

Long, George S. "Address on Utilization of Arable Logged-off Lands," *Timberman* 14:26–27 (June 1911).

———. "Comprehensive Plans for Colonizing Logged-off Lands in Washington," *Timberman* 14:34–35 (September 1911).

Martin, Calvin. "The European Impact on the Culture of a Northeastern Algonquian Tribe: An Ecological Interpretation," *William and Mary Quarterly* 31:3–26 (January 1974).

Miller, Loye. "Some Indians Midden Birds from the Puget Sound Area," *Wilson Bulletin* 72:392–97 (December 1960).

Munger, Thorton. "The Cycle from Douglas Fir to Hemlock," *Ecology* 21:451–59 (October 1940).

Murphine, Thomas. "Washington's Logged-off Land Quandary," *Little Logged-off Lands* 2:5 (December 1913).

Newton, Michael, *et al.* "Role of Red Alder in Western Oregon Forest Succession," in Northwest Scientific Association, *Biology of Alder,* Proceedings of a Symposium held at Pullman, Washington, 1967 (Portland, Pacific Northwest Forest and Range Experiment Station, 1968).

Odum, Eugene. "The Strategy of Ecosystem Development," in *The Ecology of Man: An Ecosystem Approach* edited by Robert L. Smith (New York, Harper & Row, 1972), pp. 28–39.

Oliphant, J. Orin. "The Cattle Trade on Puget Sound," *Agricultural History* 7:129–49 (July 1953).

Pennick, James. "Three Themes from the First Conservation Movement," in *The Progressive Era,* edited by Lewis Gould (Syracuse, Syracuse University Press, 1974) pp. 115–32.

Roeser, J. R. "A Study of Douglas Fir Reproduction under Various Cutting Methods," *Journal of Agricultural Research* 28:1233 (June 1924).

Rutledge, Peter and Richard Tooker. "Steam Power for Loggers: Two Views of the Dolbeer Donkey," *Forest History* 14:20–24 (April 1970).

Scharff, C. W. "Redeeming the Wooded Wilderness of Western Washington," *Little Logged-off Lands* 1:19–20 (September 1912).

Shoemaker, Joel. "Wonderful Opportunities in Logged-off Lands," *Pacific Northwest Commerce* 5:16 (December 1911).

———. "Independence on Little Logged-off Farms," *Little Logged-off Lands* 1:16 (March 1913).

———. "Let the State Clear the Logged-off Lands," *Little Logged-off Lands* 1:33–34 (June 1912).

Smith, Marian. "The Cultural Development of the Northwest Coast," *Southwestern Journal of Anthropology* 12:272–94 (Autumn 1956).

Still, Lester. "Whidby Island," *The Coast* 12:78–80 (September 1902).

Suttles, Wayne. "The Early Diffusion of the Potato among the Coast Salish," *Southwestern Journal of Anthropology* 7:272–88 (Autumn 1951).

Taylor, Herbert. "Aboriginal Populations of the Lower Northwest Coast," *Pacific Northwest Quarterly* 54:158–65 (October 1963).

Taylor, Herbert C. and Lester Hoaglin. "The 'Intermittent Fever' Epidemic of the 1830s on the Lower Columbia River," *Ethnohistory* 9:160–78 (Spring 1962).

"The Town of San de Fuca," *Westshore* (April 5, 1890), p. 440.

Thompson, Harry. "Logged-off Land," *West Coast Lumberman* 28:33 (May 1915).

Tugwell, Rexford. "The Resettlement Idea," *Agricultural History* 33:159–63 (October 1959).

Twight, Peter. "Ecological Forestry for the Douglas Fir Region," *National Parks and Conservation Magazine* 47:8–9 (August 1973).

Vassault, F. I. "Lumbering in Washington," *Overland Monthly* 20:23–32 2nd Series (July 1892).

"Washington's Logged-off Land Problem Discussed," *Pacific Lumber Trade Journal* 17:41–43 (June 1911).

Williamson, Richard. "Productivity of Red Alder in Western Oregon and Washington," in Northwest Scientific Association, *Biology of Alder,* Proceedings of a Symposium held at Pullman, 1967 (Portland, Pacific Northwest Forest and Range Experiment Station, 1968).

Yonce, Frederick. "Lumbering and the Public Timberlands in Washington: The Era of Disposal," *Journal of Forest History* 22:4–17 (January 1978).

Zintheo, C. J. "The Logged-off Land Problem and Its Solution," *Pacific Lumber Trade Journal* 16:55–61 (January 1911).

————. "This Man Says Stumps Are a Blessing Not a Curse," *Little Logged-off Lands* 1:23 (June 1962).

VII. Theses and Dissertations

Anderson, Burton. "Scandinavian and Dutch Rural Settlements in the Stillaguamish and Nooksack Valleys of Western Washington." Ph.D Dissertation, University of Washington, 1957.

Buerstatte, Frederick. "The Geography of Whidby Island." M.A. Thesis, University of Washington, 1948.

Gerlach, Arch Clive. "Precipitation in Western Washington." Ph.D. Dissertation, University of Washington, 1943.

Hansen, Henry Paul. "Postglacial Forest Succession and Climate in the Puget Sound Region." Ph.D. Dissertation, University of Washington, 1937.

Hoover, Glenn. "Rural Settlement in Western Washington." M.A. Thesis, University of Washington, 1922.

Mapes, Carl Herbert. "A Map Interpretation of Population Growth and Distribution in the Puget Sound Region." Ph.D. Dissertation, University of Washington, 1943.

Mattson, John Lyle. "A Contribution to Skagit Prehistory," M.A. Thesis, Washington State University, 1971.

Meany, Edmond S., Jr. "History of the Lumber Industry in the Pacific Northwest." Ph.D. Dissertation, Harvard University, 1935.

Murphy, Campbell Garret. "Farmers on Cutover Timber Lands in Western Washington State." M.A. Thesis, University of Washington, 1970.

Osmundson, John Skinner. "Man and His Natural Environment on Camano Island, Washington." M.A. Thesis, Washington State University, 1964.

Rakestraw, Lawrence. "A History of Forest Conservation in the Pacific Northwest, 1891–1913." Ph.D. Dissertation, University of Washington, 1955.

Schoen, John. "Mammals of the San Juan Archipelago: Distribution and Colonization of Native Land Mammals and Insularity in Three Populations of *Peromyscus Maniculatus*." M.A. Thesis, University of Puget Sound, 1972.

White, Richard. "The Treaty of Medicine Creek: Indian-White Relations on Upper Puget Sound, 1830–1880." M.A. Thesis, University of Washington, 1972.

Yonce, Frederick. "Public Land Disposal in Washington." Ph.D. Dissertation, University of Washington, 1969.

INDEX

Acer sp. *See* Maple
Agriculture: Salish, 15, 32-33, 48; and ecological change, 35-36, 52-53, 74-75; land clearing, 40, 42-43, 63, 107, 127-28; prairie farms, 40-53, 57-58, 63-66; farm technology, 40-42, 127-28, 138-39; plowing and loss of water retention, 43; crops, 43-47, 50, 61-65, 67-68, 128-30; hay production, 50; land in farms, 54-58, 63, 118; land values, 55, 59, 61, 132; on forested lands, 55-65, 79, 113-37; number of farms, 56, 154; tenancy, 57-58, 65, 70; markets and production, 61-63, 67-68, 129-30; subsistence farming, 61, 130-31; fertilizer, 70; chicken farming, 122, 129-30; dairying, 128. *See also* Livestock; Logged-off lands; Oats; Potatoes; Wheat
Alder: in native forest, 11; increase of, 109, 135
Alderwood Manor: settlement of, 126-27
Archaeology: sites near Island County, 11-13
Attridge, Robert, 84

Back-to-the-land movement, 114, 116-17

Bald eagle: eliminated from county, 151
Beaver: trapping of, 30
Boeing Corporation, 154
Bracken fern: as food, 18, 21; and fires, 21-22, 135; as obstacle to plowing, 42-43; as weed, 69; as part of forest understory, 78; poor animal feed, 135

Cattle: and destruction of Salish crops, 48; early production of, 49; grazing and native vegetation, 49-50, 51
Chinese: settlement and eviction, 64-67; mentioned, 75
Clallam Indians: territory, 15
Climate, 3, 5, 9
Clover Valley, 121, 122, 123
Code, Nicholas, 85
Conifer forest: origins, 9-11; Salish burning of, 24-25; ecology of, 77-79; logging of, 85-93, 106-12
Conservation: local versus national, 92-93; opposition to logging, 92, 111; and development of tourism, 148-49; protective legislation, 148-49, 151-53
Coronet Bay, 12
Coupeville: as rumored railroad terminus, 58, 144; and eviction of